T0208371

At Least One Balcony

Learning to Live in Granada

Boyce Quinn

iUniverse, Inc.
New York Bloomington

At Least One Balcony
Learning to Live in Granada

iUniverse books may be ordered through booksellers or by contacting:

iUniverse
1663 Liberty Drive
Bloomington, IN 47403
www.iuniverse.com
1-800-Authors (1-800-288-4677)

Because of the dynamic nature of the Internet, any Web addresses or links contained in this book may have changed since publication and may no longer be valid.

ISBN: 978-1-4502-2448-2 (sc)
ISBN: 978-1-4502-2447-5 (dj)
ISBN: 978-1-4502-2446-8 (ebk)

Library of Congress Control Number: 2010904981

Printed in the United States of America

iUniverse rev. date: 5/7/2010

For Kay
My partner in life and Spanish adventure

With thanks to

My daughter Flannery
For her love and support in getting us started

And my friend Anne Beirne
Whose initial encouragement, editorial guidance, and ongoing cheerleading were invaluable

Contents

Introduction xi

Dawn of a New Life 1
Our First Hours in Granada

Balcony Dreams 5
Imagining Ourselves Abroad. But Where? And When?

The Spanish Inquisition—Part 1 16
Establishing Our Worth, Innocence, and Sanity

Upon Waking in Granada 22
Finding Casa Fantastica!

The Spanish Inquisition—Part 2 31
The Road to Legitimacy Is a Marathon, Not a Sprint

Making la Casa Our Home 35
Our World Grows, Block by Block

The Streets of Granada 1: Tapas 47
Exploring a World of Unidentified Frying Objects

Moroccan Adventures 54
Pummeling a Robber, Bartering Berber Style

Thanksgiving 64
It's Not Just about the Turkey

The Spanish Inquisition–Part 3 67
The Marathon Continues

The Streets of Granada 2: Café Afternoons 70
Of Air Kisses and Strolling Minstrels

No Place Like Home for the Holidays 79
Especially When You Aren't There

The Spanish Inquisition—Part 4 87
Ever Hopeful, We Press On

Drowning in a Sea of Spanish Verbs 89
When a doe is not a deer, when a breast is not a breast

Learning to Live with Elvira 97
To Sleep or Not to Sleep, that Was the Challenge

The Streets of Granada 3: Walking the City 105
Clasp Hands Behind Back, Remain Alert

The Roar of March 112
New Friends, First Visitors, and Terror in Madrid

The Rain in Spain 122
Praise the Lord and Pass the Wine and *Tapas*

The Streets of Granada 4: Pollo Asado .132
Take Out It Was, Fast Food It Wasn't

At Long Last Spring 136
Mountains, Weddings, and a Pilgrimage

Our First Visit Home 145
Along a Surprisingly Bumpy Road

Now Living High in the Albaicín 153
We Move from Bourbon Street to Casa Tranquility

August on the Hill 160
Surviving the Heat, Listening to the Street

The Streets of Granada 5: Beauty but No Beasts 170
Of Gorgeous Women and Civilized Men

Madrid via the Scenic Route 173
A Tale of Best-Laid Plans Gone Awry

A Village in the City 179
Learning the Neighborhood, Meeting New Friends

The Streets of Granada 6: Fund Solicitations 187
Service Rendered, Wanted or Not, With a Smile

Adventures in Cookie Diplomacy 192
Becoming Goodwill Ambassadors to Spain

Letting the Holiday Happen 198
Santa Comes to the Albaicín

Señora Albaicinera y Señor Albaicinero .205
At Home in the Heart of Granada

Epilogue 212

Acknowledgments 215

Introduction

In the fall of 2003, my wife Kay and I moved from Mill Valley, California, where we'd lived for twenty-five years, to Granada, Spain. To live in a foreign country had been a longtime dream. We love to travel and had always found it to be rejuvenating; the challenge of actually living in another culture would be, we hoped, like drinking daily from the fountain of youth. There was also a practical consideration: living in Spain, or anywhere less expensive than Mill Valley—roughly 99 percent of the known world—would allow us to retire early.

Although we hadn't planned to be permanent expatriates, we didn't know how long we'd stay away. Our goal was to live well and enjoy every day; it was not to rehabilitate a villa or test our survival skills by, for instance, raising goats in a mountain village.

It was, we felt, a reasonable goal, something that anyone willing to live with uncertainty could do. We had a modest pension to live on and a bit of savings to get started. Kay, a retired flight attendant, would continue to receive travel benefits, so we'd be able to visit our family and friends without breaking the bank. Flannery, our twenty-six-year-old Spanish-speaking daughter, had offered to help us settle in. We also had enough experience to know that within every grand adventure lurks more than a little misadventure.

On the other hand—for there's always that other hand—neither Kay nor I spoke Spanish. We knew no one in Granada; we'd never even been there. In fact, we didn't know one person living in Spain. And we had no place to live once we got there. None of that deterred us. We were optimistic and excited to begin our new life in Granada.

We hadn't the slightest idea what we were getting ourselves into. Finding out, and learning what to do about it, is what this book is about.

Dawn of a New Life

Our First Hours in Granada

Kay and I arrived at the Estación de Autobuses in Granada at four-thirty in the morning, October 10, 2003. Our daughter Flannery was waiting at the gate, a wide, sleepy smile on her face. After a quick round of hugs, we counted, for what seemed the twentieth time that day, our seven bags, then made our way through the station, up the ramp, and outside into a surprisingly balmy predawn. It was very quiet. Still a bit groggy from the long trip, we waited at the taxi stand, trying to give our daughter far more information about our journey than she, who'd had little enough sleep herself, was prepared to absorb. After a ten-minute wait, a taxi arrived and we loaded our bags. "Plaza Nueva," Flannery instructed the driver, and off we raced through the dark, empty city streets. We'd been up for a day and a half and were exhausted, so I have only shadowy memories of our first views of Granada. *We made it,* I remember thinking. *When can I lie down?*

Fifteen minutes later we piled out of the cab, counted our bags again, paid the driver, and looked around. Dominated by a large, noisy fountain in its center, Plaza Nueva was lined with dark, shuttered cafés and shops. Scattered here and there were stacks of chairs and tables chained together. Across the plaza a circle of young people stood laughing and talking and drinking beer, the tips of their cigarettes glowing in the dark. Flannery led us across the plaza and along a narrow cobblestone street toward our hotel. The walk was short, no more than a hundred yards, but we must have passed at least another half-dozen café-bars, all closed. Along the street young people strolled or stood leaning against the walls, drinking beer and shouting to each other. No one seemed to be drunk, but then no one seemed to be completely sober either.

"This is where the young people come to party," Flannery said. "Two hours ago it was hard to make your way through the crowds."

Although the name suggested otherwise, the Hostal Antares was not a youth hostel, though according to Flannery, who'd been staying there for a week, most of its occupants were young travelers on limited budgets. A *hostal*, as best I could gather, is a hotel which offers few if any services.

Flannery had informed us that she'd upgraded to a room for three. What she hadn't told us was that our upgraded room was *up* a steep *grade* of four flights of stairs, two flights and a landing per floor. Among the many services that the Hostal Antares did not provide was an elevator. Seven bags divided by three people equaled one extra trip down and back up for me. The room had three single beds, two small bedside tables, and a wardrobe. Our seven bags, along with Flannery's two, took up more than half the available floor space, leaving just enough room to move around. The room was lit by a lamp and one dim lightbulb hanging from the ceiling. The bathroom, whose thin plywood walls suggested that it had been a recent addition, contained within its five-by-five-foot space a toilet, shower stall, sink, and bidet. But our bathroom was—and this is not to be dismissed—not down the hall, not on the landing, not on another floor. It was within the confines of our own room, *"en suite,"* as they say in Europe. Knowing that I would not find myself in a dark hallway without any idea of how to get back to our room was comforting.

These were modest lodgings indeed. But with any luck we wouldn't be needing the hostal's limited comforts for very long, so it was, at least for the time being, sufficient. At that moment, five-thirty in the morning, many, many hours after leaving San Francisco, any reasonably soft, horizontal surface was welcome.

We hung up our coats, dug through our bags for our toiletries, brushed our teeth, and fell on our beds. Through the window I heard what I hoped were the last of the revelers shouting to each other in the narrow street. I was so tired I couldn't get to sleep right away, and my thoughts drifted back to the beginning of the day. It seemed days ago since we'd boarded the airporter bus at its Mill Valley stop. It was a ride we'd taken many times before, especially Kay, who'd made the twenty-five-mile commute to San Francisco International Airport a couple of thousand times.

It had not been an easy trip. From San Francisco, we'd flown on United to Frankfurt, Germany, from where we'd planned to fly on standby tickets to Malaga, on the Spanish coast, and then bus up to Granada. But every flight to Malaga was full, as was every hotel in Frankfurt, due to the international book fair. Fortunately, our standby tickets could be used to fly to Madrid. After waiting almost seven hours for an open flight, we'd flown to Madrid and taxied to the bus station, only to find we'd missed the nine o'clock bus by minutes. There were no night trains. We'd called Flannery with the second revised plan of the day, then waited for the eleven thirty bus. Five hours later we arrived in Granada.

So how long had the trip taken? We'd left Marin County Thursday morning, and it was now Friday morning in Granada; Spain was nine hours east of California. Did I add nine hours to Friday or take it away from Thursday? Was it still yesterday in California? Or tomorrow?

Failing to complete the calculation—sleep deprivation does take its toll—my thoughts moved to the next day, which, I suddenly realized, had already begun. First, we needed to find an apartment. Although the *hostal* was only €60 a night, staying there and eating three times a day in restaurants would get expensive quickly. I'd done some research on the Web and had an idea of what a furnished apartment should cost, but I had no idea of availability. Actually, what I'd learned was how much apartments cost per square meter. I'd done the conversion, but of course I couldn't remember the formula. How lucky we were that Flannery was returning to the States at the same time we were moving to Granada. She'd been teaching English in Munich for the past two and a half years and had decided to return to California to attend graduate school. She'd lived abroad for four of the past five years, and Kay and I were extremely happy at the prospect of spending an extended time with our daughter before switching continents again. Flannery had not only offered to help us settle in, but was willing to stay through Christmas, by which time, we hoped, we'd be getting around town, speaking at least a little Spanish, and hanging out with new friends.

The second item on my list was to check in with the authorities as soon as possible in order to get our resident visa process going. Supposedly we'd completed the difficult part of the process in San Francisco, so it should go easier now that we were here. I reminded myself that we'd expected that ordeal to be much simpler than it had proved to be; perhaps it would be better to just take it a day at a time.

I heard another burst of shouting and laughter from the street below. If this was how Thursday night ended, what would the weekend be like? I listened for the sounds of sleep from Kay and Flannery. I wondered if it would be difficult to meet people. I knew that tens of thousands, if not hundreds of thousands, of English lived in Spain. Most lived on the coast, but surely some lived in Granada. Gin and tonics. Tea and crumpets. I'd never pictured myself hanging out in a tea room, but if that's what it took, well, I was ready for anything. But first a place to live. There was so much to do. Our clock's alarm was set for nine thirty. *Go to sleep,* I told myself. *Go to sleep.*

I remembered the day when Kay and I had looked each other in the eye and said, "Let's do it." We'd reached across the table and shook hands on it, which we only did when making momentous decisions. The image was surprisingly clear. From a small table in a small diner to this small bed in the small room in Granada. Unbelievable.

Go to sleep, I told myself. *Stop thinking.* I heard the rasping whine of a motor scooter. More laughter. The ticking of the clock. Then I lost consciousness.

Balcony Dreams

Imagining Ourselves Abroad. But Where?
And When?

Our journey to Granada had begun almost exactly five years earlier, in the fall of 1998, when Kay and I attended a union-sponsored retirement seminar. There we learned that Kay, who had been a United Airlines flight attendant since 1964, would be fully vested in her retirement pension at the age of sixty. I was working as a freelance writer and was as vested as I would ever be, which is to say that my pension was a bank account with my name on it. I had no qualms about giving myself the rest of my life off.

After the seminar, we stopped at a small diner for a glass of wine to discuss just what this new information might mean. We'd dreamed of living abroad for as long as we'd been together, almost thirty years, and we hoped to do it while still healthy and fit. Until that very day, our dream had hovered in the distant realm of "maybe someday." As we sat there talking and sipping our wine, we realized that we could make "someday" sooner than later.

As for the present, we were living a most enjoyable life on the outskirts of Mill Valley, in Marin County, California. Our house was three miles from the Pacific Ocean and five from the Golden Gate Bridge and San Francisco. Both kids were doing well. My son Baxter, who also lived in Marin, had recently met Renée, a fabulous woman we were crazy about, and we had high hopes for their future together. Our daughter Flannery had just begun her senior year at the University of California at San Diego. We were rich in friends, in good health, and had enough discretionary income to finance our annual, sometimes semiannual, trips. So why leave? Why give up such a full, rich life for an adventure that could prove to be a nightmare?

The question we actually asked ourselves was: *Why not?* We'd read about people in their fifties, our age, who'd made life-altering decisions to follow their dream—to live on a boat, open a restaurant, raise organic vegetables, become potters—so why shouldn't we? Our dream, to live abroad, had been born in travel, and that's the dream we needed to follow. We'd been traveling together since before getting married; fortunately Kay's job made getting there and back, wherever there and back might be, affordable. We had shelves of slide boxes (that certainly dates us) documenting our journeys. In addition to at least a dozen trips to Mexico, we'd trained over much of Europe, ridden the dirt tracks of Kenya and Tanzania on photo safari, shivered in snow-covered temples in Japan, stayed on a cattle station in Australia, and bused across Iran back in the Shah's day. We'd learned that we thrived in foreign places, that we didn't get homesick, and that we reveled in the unfamiliar. We'd also learned that we traveled well together, and that we didn't hit the crisis button when plans went awry, as plans often do. These were not insignificant lessons. Traveling has its stressful moments, moments that can turn even the jolliest of Jekylls into Mr. or Ms. Hyde.

A love of the foreign wasn't the only reason we wanted to live abroad. Putting in the garden for the twenty-fifth time, painting the dining room for the sixth time, and going to the same supermarket for the two thousand five hundredth time was absolutely not the way we wanted to spend the next couple of decades. We were ready for something, as Monty Python said, completely different. Something dramatic. Something far more exciting than living on automatic pilot.

Our first decision, that we were going to do it, was made that day before we'd finished our wine. We clinked glasses, shook hands on it, and somehow suppressed a powerful impulse to stand on our chairs and announce our plan to the entire place. The second decision, when to go, was made that evening at home. The target date: July 2004, when Kay would turn sixty. Deciding where we were going to live and how long we'd live there could come later. Making a six-year plan had already stretched the time boundaries of our imaginations.

As time went on, we began to discuss destination. Where did we want to live? That discussion, we discovered, led to the place where fantasy and reality collided, where visions of a Paris walkup or a Tuscan farmhouse crashed into the number of digits between the dollar sign and the decimal. So the discussion turned to where could we afford to live? That list was short. There was Mexico, which we knew we could afford. We like Mexico, we really do. We'd spent time in the Yucatan, Puerto Vallarta, Matzatlan, San Miguel de Allende, and Oaxaca, and we had visited Mexico City a number of times, particularly while Flannery was studying at the university there. The problem with Mexico was that Mexico was all you got—traveling north put you back in the States; traveling south was a variation on a Latin American theme. Whereas in Europe, you board a train and in a few hours, or even less, you're in another country, seeing a different culture, hearing another language, and eating different food.

European Day Dreams

Europe had something else going for it: we could imagine ourselves living there. This is not to be underestimated. You've heard the phrase, "I can't even imagine myself eating dog or living in North Dakota or having the map of Tasmania tattooed on my back, or _____;" you fill in the blank. If you can't imagine it, how can you do it?

Kay and I had definitely imagined ourselves living in Europe. Not a country house, mind you. Negotiating the cost of digging a new well, to say nothing of negotiating the narrow, winding road to the village, was someone else's dream. What we imagined was living in a nineteenth-century European building on a narrow, cobblestone street, a building we'd enter through a massive door with a large brass knob in the center, then climb the circular staircase to our apartment, an apartment with ten-foot ceilings and parquet floors, a claw-foot tub so long we'd have to toss the soap back and forth, a gigantic wardrobe instead of a closet, and, most important of all, a balcony. There had to be at least one balcony, a balcony with double wooden shutters that you flung open, scaring the pigeons from the ledge; a balcony that looked out over a café or, better yet, a small plaza filled with old men reading newspapers on ancient benches, mothers pushing strollers, and lovely, beret-topped young girls riding bicycles. On warm days, through the open shutters, we'd be able to hear the tinkle of the bicycles bells, along with the gong of nearby church bells. We saw ourselves standing on the sawdust-covered floor of the central market, rows of chickens and rabbit carcasses hanging just above our heads, as white-aproned butchers hawked just slaughtered lamb and black-kerchiefed ladies loudly declared the freshness of their produce. We imagined ourselves greeting the owner of our local café by name as he served us our "usual." In the evening we'd sit on our balcony, a glass of wine in hand, and watch the sun slowly slide behind the bell tower. That our fantasies were formed by movies made them no less enjoyable.

Europe it would be. Exactly where in Europe could be decided later. As to the question of how long we'd live in Europe, this, too, could be decided later. We'd always talked about living a year in another country. Why not two? Or three? We didn't want to commit ourselves. One year seemed too short, and the idea of becoming permanent ex-pats seemed a bit extreme. Two or three years seemed right; we decided to let our experience there—wherever there turned out to be—guide us.

The next consideration was how to make it happen. We needed to make a plan. We began accumulating information. We filled folders. I even created a timeline—a little compulsive, but it proved highly useful.

Our plan was fairly simple. We needed to rid ourselves of debt and build a Getaway Slush Fund. We didn't own our home, so we wouldn't have to deal with becoming landlords or selling it and taking a capital gains tax hit. On the other hand, we had no equity, no nest egg. And in Marin County, California, that's a mighty big egg. When we'd moved to the outskirts of Mill Valley in 1978, we couldn't afford to buy the house we rented. We couldn't afford to buy any house in Mill Valley, for that matter. And that was before property values exploded. But we loved living there. We'd made many wonderful friends, none of whom we planned to lose (we hoped they'd visit us wherever we moved). We'd been deeply involved in the school system, which had served our family well, and I had worked on campaign committees for everything from the election of city council members to passing a school-financing parcel tax. As the years went by, we loved Mill Valley more and more.

As the years went by, houses became more and more unaffordable. We have no regrets. Owning a house might have given us more options; it might have made leaving more difficult. More important than owning a home or not owning a home was that we'd enjoyed a wonderful life there. That's what really counted.

The Slush Fund grew slowly but steadily. We made a savings plan. No charging. As accounts were paid off, money that once paid those bills went into the Fund. No new cars. We could live with the ones we owned. Within a couple of years, we had no car payments, low insurance premiums, and even lower prestige—driving an eleven-year-old Geo Tracker and a seven-year-old Ford pickup puts you pretty near the bottom of the Marin County automotive food chain.

We made it a point to buy only clothing and equipment that were really necessary and that we could use in our next life. Amazing how paying cash rather than using a credit card changes discretionary spending. We'd refrained from buying camping gear or kitchen equipment and kept the purchase of CDs and books to a minimum. We didn't replace the ailing toaster oven or the rusting gas grill. No new sport coat, no new blouses. If it wasn't going with us, why buy it? We could carry only so many suitcases. If we bought it and couldn't take it, it would go into storage. Money that would have otherwise enriched the local economy was directed to the Fund. We were debt free well before our projected departure.

We knew we'd lose dental coverage when Kay retired, so we worked out a program with our dentist to prioritize our dental needs and to max out our coverage through the first half of 2004. We felt that by the time we left, teeth-wise we would be in pretty good shape. Of course our dentist didn't agree with this assessment, but his standards were pretty high, as were his fees, which he wasn't paying.

All this saving up and paying off didn't mean we stopped traveling. One can take the concept of delayed rewards only so far. Six years, which had been the timeframe when we'd begun planning, is a long time to live without taking a trip. There were no guarantees that the plan would come to fruition. Who knew what the coming years might bring. Serious illness? Death? I hate to be morbid, but you have to consider the possibilities. Now was now, and the future would be what it would.

Other than a bus trip across South America from Buenos Aires to Santiago, Chile, to celebrate the new millennium with Flannery, who was teaching English there, our trips over the next few years were to Europe. We spent two weeks in a friend's cottage in Yorkshire. We stayed on Lake Como in Italy, and then hiked in Switzerland on the way to visit Flannery, who had moved to Munich. We drove through Portugal with one set of friends and shared a house in the south of France with another. All this could fall under the category of research, though we weren't able to write it off.

We Crunch the Numbers

Even as we narrowed down our possessions, we narrowed down the list of European countries where we could afford to live. For the first two years, until Kay's Social Security kicked in, we needed to live on roughly $25,000 a year. We decided that I would wait until sixty-five to take Social Security; it would be our inflation fighter. Our Getaway Slush Fund would cover emergencies, so we weren't vulnerable there. Where could one live reasonably well on $25,000?

London—in fact all of Great Britain—was far too expensive. Paris was also out of the question. Although there were areas in the southwest of France we might have afforded, we didn't see ourselves living in a small town. Ireland's new-found prosperity had made it as expensive as Britain; I wasn't sure we could even afford to visit. The remainder of northern Europe lacked the charm of the south and was far too cold and too expensive. Eastern Europe was affordable, but presented significant language challenges, and seemed a bit too underdeveloped. We wanted every day to be an adventure, not a struggle.

That left the Mediterranean countries. There was Greece. I'd never been to Greece. Kay had, but it had been years before. We'd seen *Zorba the Greek*, eaten Greek food, drunk *retsina* and danced, along with other *retsina* drinkers, through a Greek restaurant and out onto the sidewalk. I decided that grape leaves and *retsina* were tastes that would take more than a few years to acquire. We had no desire to learn Greek and living on an island held no appeal. We eliminated Greece. Other countries just up the coast, like Albania, Serbia, and Croatia, eliminated themselves.

Italy was high on the list, but the most desirable areas, Tuscany, Umbria, the west coast, even the northern lake country, had been discovered and rediscovered. Italy was expensive and becoming more so every day.

We'd enjoyed the three weeks we spent in Portugal in the spring of 2002. The food was good. It was affordable. The language was somewhat difficult and of no use anywhere else but Brazil. We tried to imagine ourselves living in Portugal. Lisbon had its charms, as did Porto, but neither was particularly exciting. What comes to mind when you think about Portugal? Besides port? How much port could we drink?

Spain emerged as the leading candidate. We'd spent two weeks in Madrid and Barcelona years before, and we'd liked it. Kay wanted to learn to speak Spanish and to cook Spanish cuisine. I was drawn by its very foreignness: Flamenco music, the mystique of the bullfight, its Roman and Moorish history. There were exciting cities; great museums; an abundance of castles, palaces and fortresses; plus lots of coastline. Learning to speak Spanish, as opposed to Portuguese or Greek, to say nothing of Hungarian or Czech, would be extremely useful, not only in Latin America and California, but in my home state of North Carolina. Although not that far from France and Italy, the land south of the Pyrenees seemed like another world. Picturing ourselves living there made us smile with pleasure and anticipation.

Spain it would be. But where in Spain? Flannery helped us make the decision when she sent us an e-mail from Spain, where she'd been traveling with friends.

"I've found your home in Spain," she'd declared. "Granada is absolutely, definitely the place for you." It was, she informed us, not too big and yet big enough. It was old, picturesque, filled with history, affordable, and, unlike the coast, very, very Spanish.

We had no reason to doubt her. We'd been dragging her around with us since she was a toddler, and she knew our taste and style very well. Flannery had inherited our love of travel and even our dream of living abroad. In fact, she'd beaten us to it, having lived a year in Mexico City, a year in Santiago, Chile, and more than two years in Munich. Over the years she'd recommended towns, hotels, and restaurants, and she'd never steered us wrong. Flannery chose Granada, and we chose to follow her recommendation, sight unseen. It was a decision we've never regretted.

It did seem appropriate that we know at least a little something about our future home, so we did a bit of research. For two hundred and sixty years, Granada had been the capital of the last Islamic state on the Iberian Peninsula. There the Moors built the Alhambra, the combination palace, fortress, and royal city that overlooks the rest of Granada from high on its hill. It's considered one of the finest examples of Islamic architecture in the western world. In 1492 the Alhambra was surrendered to Isabel and Fernando, the Catholic monarchs, ending almost eight hundred years of Moorish presence in what was to become Spain. That time-consuming, treasury-draining task out of the way, Isabel now saw her way clear to underwrite Columbus, who had been hanging around the court for several years in hopes of having his voyage west financed.

We'd picked the country and Flannery had picked the city; now all we had to do was to stay on course. But September 11, 2001, changed our timetable. The airlines went into a tailspin, and on December of 2002, United Airlines filed for bankruptcy. Flying, which Kay had once enjoyed, had become a job with reduced service and staffing and a less than congenial atmosphere. There seemed no reason to think that things were going to get better. July 2004 was too far away. Kay was ready to go.

As we'd been planning our great escape for several years, we hoped that moving the departure date up wouldn't present any significant problems. I ran the numbers. Although early retirement would reduce Kay's pension by a few percentage points, remaining on the payroll for another few months, or even to her sixtieth birthday, was not going to make a huge difference. Our savings would grow, but that gain was balanced by the possibility that some unexpected event, like a major automobile breakdown, could wipe that growth out. We weighed, again and again, all the known factors, plus and minus. We discussed the situation to the point of near exhaustion, and we came to two conclusions. First, there was no way that we could master every detail and tie up every loose string; there were too many factors beyond our control, and attempting to identify, understand, and make a decision on each one was a task we'd never complete. And second, there was no "right" moment to make the move. May, July, September—one month was as good as another. We'd done our homework; our financial goals had been achieved; it was time to go, and to go as soon as possible. Kay submitted her retirement paperwork in January. Effective date: March 31, 2003. I notified our landlord that we'd be leaving our house at the end of June, giving us three months to organize and put our stuff in storage. The die was cast.

Baxter and Renée, now parents of two-year-old Gray, had invited us to live with them during July and August, which would enable us to spend lots of time together, imprint ourselves on Gray, enjoy retirement and farewell parties, and say good-bye to friends who wouldn't believe that we were moving to Spain until we left the house.

We Burn Our Bridges

My last day writing marketing copy was the final Friday in March. Kay's last flight arrived in San Francisco the next day. Baxter, Renée, Gray, and I met the airport bus at the commuter parking lot a mile from our home. We'd outfitted the bed of our pickup truck with a rug, director chairs, a table, a portable CD player, hors d'oeuvres, champagne, even a step ladder to get up and down. Our parking-lot party was a retirement celebration unlike any other.

The spring was spent taking care of details like mailing change of address forms (we would be using Baxter's address), closing bank and charge accounts, terminating auto insurance, and canceling subscriptions. Our biggest task was pruning, packing, and transporting our goods to storage. We didn't know how long we'd be gone, although we assumed that we'd eventually return, and we wanted those possessions that were really important to us to be waiting—those and only those. We created three lists. The A list consisted of those items we absolutely wanted to keep: books, music, photos, kitchen equipment, artwork, electronics equipment, some clothing, and a few pieces of furniture. The C list contained those items which we could live without, didn't need, or wanted to replace, like the couches, easy chairs, dining room table and chairs, desk, lamps, and boxes of housewares. These we sold either over the Internet or at our yard sale. The B list was the stuff in between A and C, things we'd keep if there were room in storage. If there wasn't, good-bye. We spent the month of June driving our loaded pickup the eighteen miles to our storage unit. As it turned out, almost everything on the B list fit.

With the exception of one rather trying day, moving our stuff to storage went well. That day's comedy of errors began with my decision not to secure the chest of drawers. The drawers all stuck, so why bother? Compounding my lack of foresight, I put the chest in with its back against the cab and the drawers facing the rear of the truck. We were driving up a long hill on the freeway when a passing car—I was in the slow lane—honked and pointed to the bed of the truck. In the side view mirror I could see clothes flapping in the wind.

"One of the drawers is open," Kay shouted, "and clothes are coming out!"

"Your drawer or mine?" I asked.

"Yours," she answered. I glanced in the driver's side mirror and saw my favorite blue broadcloth shirt go airborne.

I immediately slowed, put on the turn signal, and headed for the next exit. Would I have any shirts left? Once off the freeway, I pulled into the closest parking lot. We inspected the damage. Kay's drawer was partially open but nothing seemed to be missing. My drawer was a mess. I'd never know for sure the extent of my losses, except for my favorite blue broadcloth shirt.

Fortunately, there was rope in the cab to secure the drawers. We began. The chest was packed in too tightly against the cab to get the rope behind it, so we needed to run the rope from corner to corner, from front right leg over the top to rear left, and so forth. I tied the rope to the front leg and tossed it across the bed to Kay, where she was to tie it to rear leg and toss it back. She caught the rope and tossed it back. I tossed it back to her. She tossed it back to me. We were experiencing a failure to communicate. I, in my frustration, uttered an unkind word. Kay answered that she'd not been given proper instruction. I responded by insinuating that no amount of instruction would have likely been sufficient. She expressed extreme disappointment in my attitude. Harsh words were spoken and ... well, let's leave it at that. I was not behaving well. By now Kay was in tears and I was feeling very angry and very stupid. Suddenly the absurdity of it hit us both. We were standing in the parking lot of the La-Z-Boy chair store, tossing a rope back and forth over a truck bed and calling each other names. How ridiculous. By the time we met at the end of the truck bed, we were weak with laughter, tears rolling down our faces. We hugged and kissed and apologized and I promised to be more patient. We swore it wouldn't happen again. And it didn't.

For the rest of the month, on every trip up that hill, I looked for my blue shirt. What could have happened to it?

We left our home of twenty-five years on June 30. Dismantling the material part of our lives wasn't as difficult as we'd anticipated. I think doing so day by day over the course of a month softened the blow. Being excited about what was to come, as opposed to dwelling on what had been, also helped. We hadn't put in a garden or replaced plants, the rooms were empty, the kids long gone. By the day of our departure, the house was already beginning to fade into the past, joining other apartments and flats we'd lived in.

We held a reasonably successful yard sale and in August and sold the pickup. We gave the Geo Tracker to my son with the understanding that we would use it during visits, saving us the expense of renting a car. We also gave him our pop-up camping trailer, which would make a fine guesthouse for our visits. Flannery, who was living in Munich, had no use for either. Our plan was to visit my family in North Carolina in early September, return to California for our bags, and then continue on to Granada to meet Flannery on the first of October.

There was one more important piece of business to take care of. In order to live in Spain beyond the ninety days allowed tourists, and to go and come as we wished, we needed Spanish residency visas. We knew that many people ignored this requirement and lived for years in Europe without a problem. However, our life-in-Spain plan included a trip home to see the family every nine months or so, and we didn't want this to be a problem. We began the process in early July, assuming it would take a month, perhaps two at the most. We didn't know that we would become victims of the "Spanish Inquisition."

The Spanish Inquisition–Part 1

Establishing Our Worth, Innocence, and Sanity

I'm aware that the term "Spanish Inquisition" may seem like hyperbole. We weren't, after all, put to the rack, nor were we hung by our thumbs. Perhaps the Spanish Inquiry would have been more accurate, for that's what the process of obtaining the visa was, an inquiry concerning our financial, physical, and legal status. But the Spanish Inquiry sounds so bureaucratic, and it lacks drama. Spanish Inquisition—now that captures how we felt.

Why then, did we persist in our quest to procure a resident visa? Kay and I had had endless discussions about how we wanted to live, and we'd decided that a primary theme for the rest of our lives would be less stress. Less-Stress would be our anthem, our motto, our mantra. Not stress free, which, as best I can tell, entails being dead, but *less* stress. When faced with the choice between "more trouble but less stress" and "taking a chance and hoping for the best," we would, we decided, always choose the former.

The Less-Stress Test is particularly important to apply when traveling. Traveling holds the potential for more stressful moments than almost any other activity, though I'm informed that having a kitchen remodeled could also claim that distinction. A number of factors are used to make travel decisions: cost, convenience, location, personal inclination, time, power (who's running this trip, anyway?), and possibly children. To that list we've added the stress evaluator. Many people would consider it too much trouble to go to the train station to buy tickets days before departure. For us, it's stressful to go to the train station an hour before departure not knowing whether the train is sold out. The path to Less-Stress is buying tickets days in advance. If the ten o'clock bus to Malaga is delayed by traffic, we could miss our one thirty check-in at the airport. This is very stressful. So we take the nine o'clock, and, if we're early, we reward ourselves with a relaxing beer while we wait. Renting a car, following a road map through a countryside lacking road signs, and then navigating through the medieval quarter of a European city is, to us, among the most stressful activities known to man. Watching the countryside flow by from our train compartment, a glass of wine in one hand, a piece of cheese in the other, is surely one of life's ultimate stress free pleasures.

So for us, just the thought of not being allowed to reenter Spain after a visit home because we'd overstayed the ninety days allowed was stressful. This was a risk we were not willing to take, and we were determined to do whatever it took to get the proper documents.

Fortunately for us, the Spanish Consulate, which handles all visa requests for the entire northwestern United States, including Hawaii and Alaska, was located in San Francisco. Otherwise we would have had to go through the entire process by mail. Our first visit to the Spanish Consulate took place the first week of July. We drove into San Francisco in the morning, located the very unassuming consulate offices, searched for and found a parking place, walked back to the office, were buzzed in, signed in, and sat, waiting, with another dozen people. What we wanted, and what we understood (for reasons I can no longer remember) we would receive, was a resident visa valid for three years, which was roughly the length of time we thought we'd be living in Spain. We assumed that we would be required to provide proof of income and medical insurance, and we had with us what we thought were the appropriate bank statements and proof of insurance forms.

After what seemed a reasonable time, our names were called, and we passed through a metal detector. The lady at the window was very pleasant, very helpful. She couldn't have been nicer. Simply supplying bank and insurance forms was not sufficient, she told us. There were forms to complete. She gave us the forms along with a sheet of instructions. I thanked her and told her we'd see her soon. She laughed and shook her head.

"I don't think so," she said, and laughed again.

Now what did that mean?

When we looked over the application form during lunch, we discovered what she had known that we didn't. In addition to providing proof of income and medical coverage, applicants must provide documents stating that they are healthy, mentally sound, carry no infectious diseases, and are neither alcoholics nor drug addicts. A document affirming that the applicant is not a criminal or a menace to society is required. If claiming to be married, an additional document averring the validity of the marriage certificate is mandatory. Passports must be valid for at least one year. The instructions were very clear: if your application was incorrect or incomplete in any way, you had to reapply. The application fee was a nonrefundable $100 per person.

We made a list of requirements and the agencies we needed to contact. A little legwork, a few phone calls, we thought, no big deal. I needed to renew my passport, but otherwise, it shouldn't be that difficult. After all, we were a drug-free, law-abiding, medically insured, income receiving, disease-free, relatively sane, passport-possessing, legally married couple.

We were required to produce a document stating the amount of Kay's monthly pension check (they weren't interested in how much money we had in the bank). This was simple enough, requiring a written request to United Airlines. The same was true for obtaining a document certifying that we were, in fact, covered by a company-underwritten health insurance.

Certifying that we were not addicts, alcoholics, insane, or diseased required a checkup and a letter from our doctors. Our HMO was very cooperative and we were able to schedule appointments the following week. By the end of July, we'd received letters testifying to our good health, both physical and mental.

Because proof of our future income was based on Kay's pension, we had to establish beyond a shadow of doubt that we were in fact married, in order to obtain my visa. A marriage certificate, even one with an embossed stamp, would not suffice. We would have to produce a document certifying that our marriage certificate was valid. I'd not been aware that counterfeit marriage certificates were floating around. Were there bogus marriage chapels in Las Vegas performing fraudulent services so that gold diggers could claim a piece of Sugar Daddy's estate? Were counterfeit certificates used by illegal immigrants to obtain green cards? If you walked through the seedier area of town, would a man step from the shadows to ask: Ecstasy? Grass? Marriage certificate?

Obtaining this document required a trip to San Francisco City Hall. Luckily we'd been married in San Francisco and not in Vermont or Florida, which would have made our quest even more of an ordeal. Once at City Hall, we had to find the proper document-dispensing office, have them trace and locate their copy of our marriage certificate, and certify it, all for only thirteen bucks.

We then took this new document to the office of the Secretary of State of the State of California—fortunately just a few blocks away— where we procured still another document stating that all other previous documents were in fact valid. The charge for this was another $26.

When we'd mentioned to friends that we were required to prove that we were not and had never been criminals, we were told that our local police department would be the place to go. That, we found out, was not the way it works. This was how it works. You must request a criminal record check from the Department of Justice from the state in which you reside. Once you've received the form, you must submit it, along with a set of digital fingerprints, to the Department of Justice. Yes, digital. Gone are the days of inky fingers, it's all in the computer now. There were two places in Marin County where digital prints were done: the sheriff's department in the northern part of the county, near where we lived, and where the wait for an appointment was two weeks, and the sheriff's department in the southern part of the county, where the wait was one week. And what difference would one week make? A lot, for we'd learned that the Department of Justice could take sixty days or more from the day a request was received to process it. Apparently, assisting citizens fleeing the country was not the department's highest priority.

A week later, we had our fingerprints digitally scanned. The diligent and very friendly deputy was able to check the results immediately. This was important, for taking digital fingerprints is not an easy task, even with "good" fingerprints. It can be extremely difficult if your fingerprints are not in good condition. This has nothing to do with having filed down your prints or having dipped your fingers in acid, like in the movies. Age and occupation are major factors.

"Typing," the deputy said, "wears down the prints. I've run into people who didn't have enough prints to establish their identity. Took 'em months to get a clearance."

I tried to remember if I'd worn gloves when I laid the brick patio. I wondered if people who climbed rocks or walked on their hands had any prints at all.

Playing the Waiting Game

The prospects of meeting Flannery in Granada the first of October were growing dimmer. We regretted that we hadn't begun this process in April, immediately after Kay had retired. Or even May. Why had we waited till July? What we'd thought would take three weeks was taking forever. But we pressed on, and by the first of September, almost seven weeks after beginning the process, we had all the required documents except the one from the Justice Department. We were in limbo with nothing to do but wonder why we hadn't known about this. Everything had gone so smoothly until now, and stress was beginning to show its nasty head. Our farewell trip to North Carolina to visit my family, which we'd planned for early September so that we could return and finish packing, had been delayed. We couldn't leave. What if our fingerprints hadn't been accepted and we weren't here to repeat the process? On the other hand, we had to do something. The powerlessness of waiting was killing us. We decided to take all the documents we had to the consulate to be sure that everything we had so far was correct and acceptable.

Once again, living so near San Francisco was to our advantage, and off to the city we went with our papers. The young woman with whom we'd dealt before looked over our documents. Everything was fine, she informed us. We told her that we were still waiting for our Justice Department clearance.

"You're not criminals, are you?" she asked.

"Absolutely not!" we declared, innocent smiles plastered across our faces.

"Well, I'll take your papers and begin processing them, and you can bring me the Justice Department document when you come to pick up your visas. Just be sure to bring it."

So in mid-September, off we went to North Carolina. I called Baxter and Renée every few days to see if the document had arrived. Nothing. Finally, in the first days of October, after two weeks of waiting, I called the Department of Justice's voice mail system and explained our situation. A very nice gentleman returned my call the next morning to explain the delay. It seems that comparing new digital prints to ancient ink prints took longer. *Fossil prints,* I thought. Good thing we weren't dealing with handprints in the cement. He apologized for the delay and promised to mail the documents himself that day.

Two days later Renée called to tell us that we had mail from both the Justice Department and the Spanish Consulate. With our urging, she opened them. We had our good citizenship award and a letter notifying us that our visa application had been approved. We flew back to San Francisco the next day, and the following morning we were waiting by the door of the consulate when it opened. We gave the kind lady our Justice Department documents, and she returned our passports and copies of all our documents.

We were elated—until we examined our passports. To our dismay, we discovered that glued inside our passports were not the three-year resident visas we thought we'd be receiving, but special *visados*, or visas. Attached to each was a small green piece of paper with the following instructions:

"In your passport a visa for Spain has been authorized. The Foreign Ministry wishes you a happy trip and a nice stay. Don't forget the following rules: 1. Make sure your passport is stamped by the police services upon entering Spain. This first entrance must take place within ninety days. 2. In order to receive your residency permit, contact the civil government of your province as soon as possible. Thank you very much for your cooperation."

"Be sure to take all your documents," the lady smiled. "You'll need them to apply for your permits."

The Inquisition had not yet run its course.

The next day, dragging seven carry-on bags and clutching a thick folder of documents, we left for Spain.

Upon Waking in Granada

Finding Casa Fantastica!

Minutes after I'd gone to sleep, or what seemed like only minutes, the buzz of the alarm pierced my sleep, a shrill buzz that threatened never to end. Apparently, Kay was having difficulty finding the clock. Suddenly the buzzing stopped and was replaced by moaning. Kay's.

"I can't," Kay moaned.

"Do we have to?" I asked.

"We have to," Flannery replied. *She is young,* I thought to myself, *and has only lost a little sleep, no more than going to a party. We, on the other hand, are old, and are suffering sleep deprivation, jet lag, excessive time-zone dislocation, and baggage handler's syndrome.*

"Mercy," I cried.

"We have two apartments to see by eleven."

With any luck, she told us, we might be able to move in that day. And if we checked out by noon, we wouldn't have to pay for another night at the *hostal*. We quickly showered and headed down the street for breakfast. Over our first Spanish breakfast, Flannery, who'd been in Granada for almost a week, told us that she'd already rejected a handful of apartments as either too remote, too dorm like, too dingy, or too modern. She'd not even considered the five- and six-story modern apartment buildings that ring Granada, going on and on, block after block, uninterrupted by parks or even churches, with nothing to recommend them but low rent.

The first place she showed us was halfway up the hillside in the Albaicín (although the older, Arabic-based spelling, Albayzin, is also used, I'm going to stick with Albaicín), the historic, once-Moslem quarter. The narrow, three-story house, room stacked upon room, was located across an eight-foot-wide pedestrian street from a small two-level plaza. There was a large fountain on the lower level of the plaza and trees and benches on the top. The apartment's chief recommendation, in addition to its excellent location, was a rooftop terrace, which had, Flannery said, a spectacular view of the Alhambra. There were two major drawbacks: the kitchen, which Flannery described as tiny, with a mini fridge and a two-burner electric stove; and the rent, €700 a month.

No matter how fabulous the view, €700, about $800 at that time, was far more than we'd budgeted. We'd been in Granada only a few hours and hadn't bought so much as a potato, so we had no idea of what our cost of living would be, but I'd done enough research on the Internet to know we could do better. Saying no to this house turned out to be a good decision, as shortly after our arrival the dollar began to fall, a development we hadn't factored into our calculations. When we arrived in Granada, the exchange rate was 1.14, meaning that it cost one dollar and fourteen cents to buy one euro. A year later the cost of a euro had risen to $1.37, before easing down. At $1.37, the monthly cost of this Alhambra view would have risen from $800 per month to $960, a difference of more than $1,900 a year. Living in an apartment with a champagne view, but without sufficient funds to buy champagne, didn't make sense.

The second place was on Calle Elvira, just up the street from the Hostal Antares where we were staying. We walked back down the hill and over to Elvira around eleven or so in the morning. The day was bright and sunny and the narrow street was quiet. All the buildings were old and very European, mostly three stories, with shops and cafés on the first floor and two stories of apartments above. Everything seemed a bit rundown and shabby.

We stood across the narrow street and looked the place over. The building sat on a corner, with a narrow lane running along side that headed straight up the hill, becoming little more than narrow steps within twenty-five yards. There was a café-bar on the ground floor, which was closed, and two apartments above. The available apartment, or flat, occupied the entire second floor (that's first floor to Europeans), immediately above the café. The apartment had not one, not two, but three—yes, three—balconies. It was easily the nicest building on the "block." The rent, Flannery had told us, was only €400. So far, so good.

Flannery called the realtor and an agent arrived about twenty minutes later. He unlocked the heavy steel entry door, and then led us up the stairs, through the apartment door and into the foyer. To the right of the foyer through double glass doors, there was a large living room with two balconies, each with French doors (I wondered if the Spanish called them French doors), thick shutters on the inside, and heavy, roll-down blinds on the outside. Off the living room was a bedroom with its own balcony. On the left side of the foyer opposite the living room another set of glass doors opened to a light well.

A short hallway ran from the foyer toward the back of the apartment. There was a small broom closet, then an efficient kitchen with full-size fridge, four-burner gas stove, and marble countertop. Next came the bathroom, with a small shower, bidet, sink, and toilet. Both the kitchen and the bathroom had large windows with double shutters. At the end of the hall there was a second, larger bedroom with two more double-shuttered windows, one, like the windows in the kitchen and bathroom, overlooking the lane, the other looking into the light well. Both bedrooms had large built-in closets with drawers and double beds with new mattresses.

Located on a corner, with three balconies and four double windows, the apartment was very bright. It was midday, and sunlight streamed into every room. The walls were white and clean. The floors were tile. The rent included water. It was, the agent declared, "*Fantastico!*"

We held a brief conference. We didn't need to step into the next room because the agent didn't speak a word of English. Flannery, who'd seen a number of apartments over the course of the past week, said she hadn't seen anything nearly as nice. It was nicely furnished: The living room held a small sofa, coffee table, end table, small bookcase, and a dining table with four chairs. There were pots and pans; plates and utensils in the kitchen; and brooms, mop, and mop bucket in the closet. We commented again on the clean white walls and how the sunlight flooded the living room; we re-inspected the fridge, stove, and the new mattresses. *All this,* I thought, *and three balconies.* We decided to take it, and followed the agent back to the office. The owner, Manuel, was called and joined us there a half an hour later. The contract was explained to Flannery, who explained it to us, and we signed. The lease, as is the custom in Spain, was for eleven months. Anything longer, we were told, made getting rid of tenants difficult, if not impossible. The usual move-in fees in Spain are one month's rent in advance, a security deposit equal to two month's rent for a furnished apartment, and a realtor's fee of one month's rent. That adds up to four month's rent—in our case, €1600. We'd been in Granada for less than eight hours, and that was far more than we had on hand. Raising the full amount would require daily trips to the ATM.

"*No problema,*" both Manuel and the realtor declared. They said we could pay them next week and allowed us to move in immediately.

As Manuel led us back to the apartment, he told us that the building had been renovated and modernized in 1989, which was why the apartment was in such good shape. Once we got there, he was going to explain how things worked. This was good, because a European apartment works in a very non-American way. Here was the key, which must be turned three times, each turn locking a different lock. Here was the telephone to answer the downstairs door and the button that unlocked that door; here was the master electrical switch; here's how to roll up the heavy outside blinds that covered each window. Here, in the kitchen under the counter, was the butane gas cylinder, called a *bombona,* that fueled the hot water heater that hung on the wall just above the sink. The hot-water-on-demand system was energy efficient and very economical, he told us. The flame was electrically ignited when you turned the hot water faucet; there was no pilot flame and no hot water tank. The water was as hot as you wanted it to be and the supply was unlimited, as long as you had gas. The *bombona,* which also supplied gas to the stovetop, was good for two to four weeks.

The apartment, like most rentals in Granada, had no oven. There was a small washing machine under the kitchen counter, a pretty typical arrangement, and a clothesline on the covered roof, which we shared with our upstairs neighbors, Enrique, a thirty-something teaching assistant at the university, and his girlfriend.

The apartment had three heat sources—a large, gas heater, also fueled by a *bombona*, which could be rolled from room to room; a small, electric oil-filled radiator, also on wheels; and a heating and air conditioning unit installed high in the wall in the living room.

There was a backup *bombona* under the sink. The gas truck came by every few days, Manuel told us, but he didn't know the schedule. "Just listen for the sound of the tanks," he told Flannery. All instruction was in Spanish, and Flannery translated for us.

Manuel then commenced to demonstrate the gas system. He turned the dial to the on position, set the flame setting and the hot water to cold water mix, flipped a switch on top of the *bombona* to open the line, and turned on the hot water. Nothing. The *bombona* was empty. "Good," he exclaimed, "I can show you how to change the *bombona*." He pulled the backup from beneath the sink and hooked it up. Empty. He rolled the heater from the closet, removed the tank, and switched it on. Empty. It was Friday afternoon. No hot water. No cooking. Not good.

"I'll be right back," Manuel told Flannery, and went upstairs to see if Enrique was home and if he could borrow his backup until next week.

"You get all that?" Flannery asked. She looked into our dazed, sleep-deprived eyes, and shook her head. "I'll go over everything again tomorrow," she promised.

Manuel soon returned with a tank, which he hooked up. When he turned on the hot water, neat rows of flame suddenly appeared, and within seconds, hot water was flowing from the tap. He turned the water off and the flame immediately disappeared. We applauded. Well, Kay and I did.

Before he left, he explained that he would come by around the first of each month and slip the amount of the electric bill, which was in his name, under the door. He would phone later to arrange a time to drop by and collect the rent and electric bill. Water was included in the rent. The arrangement was perfect: Our bills were to be paid in cash, so opening a bank account wouldn't be necessary. Kay's pension was automatically deposited into our account in the States, so we would finance ourselves with the assistance of an ATM. We were also fortunate in that Manuel was a very nice man, eager to help and seemingly delighted with what we were doing, that we'd chosen Granada, and that Flannery, who spoke Spanish so well, was here with us to help. His daughter, who worked with him in the family business, was about the same age.

After Manuel left, we went down the street to Hostal Antares, paid for another night (checkout was at noon and it was well after one), grabbed our bags, and walked back up the street and up the stairs to deposit them in the bedroom of our European apartment, then sat on the couch in our Spanish salon. For the first time in two days, there was nothing that had to be done, no planes or buses to catch, no bags to haul around, no apartments to see, no leases to sign. Suddenly I realized that getting off the couch was going to be a challenge. We desperately needed more sleep. But the apartment, although reasonably well equipped, was not supplied with linens, and pulling ourselves together for a shopping trip was out of the question. We were exhausted. We threw bedspreads over the beds, then collapsed into our first Spanish siesta.

We awoke late in the afternoon, gathered ourselves, and headed out into the city, where we bought the bare necessities—sheets, an extra pillow and pillowcases, towels, enough food for dinner, wine, soap, plus any incidentals we could think of. We returned to the apartment, where Kay put together a simple meal.

If there were ever a time to pinch yourself, this was it. Here we sat, roughly sixteen hours after arriving, forty-eight hours (the nap had restored my ability to calculate) after leaving Marin County, and we were eating dinner in our own apartment. We were so excited that having neither a claw-foot tub nor a view of a small park didn't matter. After all, we had three balconies, all with double glass doors and shutters. We lived on a street that had been a major thoroughfare before America was discovered. Even after awakening from an afternoon nap, I felt as if I were still dreaming.

Both Kay and I are fully aware of the invaluable role that our twenty-six-year-old daughter played in the beginnings of our new life in Granada. Now, it isn't necessary to have a daughter or son who speaks the language to find a place to live. Nor is it necessary to have their guidance through the thicket of required documents, like lease agreements, visa applications, and such. There are, after all, English-speaking rental agents and the Internet. If you speak the language, you won't need much help. Millions of Americans have moved to foreign countries and very, very few of them were met and assisted by a daughter, son, or even friend. Our moving to Granada was not contingent upon having Flannery there to help us.

However, if you want to be met at the station, escorted to your hotel, have a rental agent waiting for your call, and move into an apartment the same day you arrive, it is absolutely necessary to have a "Flannery." We were very, very fortunate.

Flannery told us she had a surprise for us, so after dinner we left the apartment and walked down Elvira, then up Calle Calderería, a narrow street lined with Moroccan tea houses and bazaars, then up from there, up and up the winding lanes and steps of the Albaicín toward the Mirador San Nicolás, the most famous lookout point in Granada. Following Flannery's instructions, we climbed the last steps up to the *mirador* without looking toward the viewpoint. At her cue we turned. There it was, the Alhambra, dramatically illuminated and dominating the hill across the narrow valley, the last bastion, fortress, and palace of the Moors. It was awesome.

We took a deep breath. Standing there in the October night gazing at what could have been a mirage seemed almost surreal. Down the hill, our clothes were hanging in our closets, our towels by the shower, our toiletries neatly arranged on shelves in the bathroom of our apartment. We'd shopped and cooked our first meal. We were overwhelmed and suddenly very, very tired. Our journey was over. We had arrived. We were here. And now it was time to go to bed, this time for a full night's sleep.

Christmas in October

Our second Granada awakening was not nearly as painful as the first, at least not physically. Waking up that first morning in our new apartment required a few moments for reality to establish itself. For one thing, the room was dark. The shutters were solid wood, not louvered, and the only light in the room came from the light well where we'd left the shutters partly open. I remember lying there and letting my eyes adjust to the dim light. The ceiling was white and seemed far too high. The floor was tiled, and at the far end of the room by the light well, the wall was lined with closet doors, four of them. The wall at the end of the bed was white and blank. To my left, above the bed, I could make out daylight through tiny cracks in the shutters. The last time I'd opened my eyes after a full night's sleep had been in California, and that seemed a long time ago.

I looked at Kay and found her brown eyes staring at me.

"We did it, didn't we? We're really living in Granada," she whispered.

After reassuring each other that we were indeed living in Granada, we hugged in delight, and then leapt from the bed like two kids on Christmas morning. This was the first morning of our new lives and there was so much to buy, so much to do. We needed to do an inventory and make a list. But first we needed breakfast. Flannery, who was already on European time, was up and waiting, and out we went.

While eating breakfast, Flannery advised us to stock up. It was Saturday, she reminded us. On weekdays, stores closed for siesta at two and reopened at five thirty. On Saturday stores stayed open a bit longer, perhaps until three, but they did not reopen until Monday. And next Monday was a holiday. Nothing would be open from that afternoon till Tuesday morning.

"Tuesday?"

"Tuesday," she repeated.

"Nothing open at all?"

"Nothing," she repeated again. "Well, maybe a *panadería*." A bakery.

It seems that the Spanish, who celebrate a number of national, regional, and city holidays, amazingly treat a holiday as a holiday, not as a commercial opportunity. Trains run, cafés serve, pharmacists dispense, and bakers bake. But the vast majority of the population takes the day off. What a strange and marvelous concept.

Following Flannery's advice, we'd bought everything we could find. We returned to the apartment in mid-afternoon with as many bags as we could carry. We had everything necessary to survive till Tuesday. We thought. That afternoon, while I was taking a shower, the water suddenly turned cold. We were out of gas.

It seems that the *bombona* Manuel had borrowed from Enrique had been almost empty. Now it was completely empty, which meant no hot water for showers or washing dishes, and, just as important, no gas for cooking, not until … we had no idea. When were deliveries made? This was a desperate situation. Neither Kay nor I had any idea what to do. But our quick-thinking, Spanish-speaking daughter did.

"Grab a tank, Popi," she said. "Maybe someone in the neighborhood has a full one they'll sell us."

Down the stairs and out onto the street we went, a street so empty of life that my first reaction was that some terrible disaster had taken place. It was five o'clock on a Saturday afternoon and there was not a person, not a car, not an open business in sight. It felt like a ghost town. This was what it was like, I was to discover, during siesta on a Saturday afternoon in Granada. I put the *bombona* down in the middle of the street and looked one way and then the other. It was eerie.

"Wait here," Flannery said. "I'll see if I can find something."

She walked down to the corner, then turned, smiled, and waved me on. We were lucky. El Circulo, the café-bar on the corner, had just reopened. There weren't any customers, but there was a young man behind the bar.

Manuel had told us that a *bombona* cost €8,80. "Let's offer them €10," I said.

That's what we did. Flannery described our plight to the young man, who took our empty tank and money in exchange for a full, lifesaving, shower-providing, stove-fueling tank of gas. The Welcome Wagon couldn't have provided a warmer reception to the neighborhood.

By Tuesday, having survived the first of many three-day Spanish holidays, we'd completed a careful inventory and were ready to do some serious shopping. Some things we'd need to get right away, others in the weeks ahead. Our shopping spree actually lasted a few months. There was always something we hadn't thought of, some essential piece of equipment that we hadn't known was essential till the moment we needed it.

So far, our new home at 40 Calle Elvira was living up to our fantasies very nicely.

The Spanish Inquisition—Part 2

The Road to Legitimacy Is a Marathon, Not a Sprint

Our new life in Granada wasn't simply a merry-go-round of shopping and exploring. There was business to take care of, namely, transforming our ninety-day *visados*, or visas, into real, honest-to-goodness resident permits, which we'd been erroneously calling residency visas. It couldn't be that difficult. Kay and I had survived and learned from the San Francisco version of the Spanish Inquisition. And, we now had Flannery with us, who'd run the visa gauntlet in three countries.

Our First Visit to the Police Station

Our first Tuesday morning, the fourteenth day of October, we went, as instructed, to the civil government, which turned out to be the Police Department, to get our passports stamped and to begin the process. We found ourselves in a large three-story courtyard. Glass-enclosed offices lined two opposing walls, each with three service windows. The floor was made of paving stones and there were benches in the center. It was raining lightly, but although the courtyard had a translucent fabric roof, a few drops made their way through, inevitably to wherever I happened to be standing.

On one side of the courtyard there was a short line leading to the window labeled information, and another window for registering change of address (all residents are required to provide the police a current address). On the other side, two long lines zigzagged across the courtyard as standees attempted to avoid the drips. We began with information.

Even though the line was short, it took about twenty minutes to reach the window. Flannery told the man that we needed our passports stamped. The man looked at our passports.

"Over there," he said and pointed to the shorter of the two long lines across the courtyard.

"That line?" Flannery asked.

He pointed again.

We got in line and slowly inched our way toward the window. At the head of the line a tiny nun stood. She was apparently waiting for someone, because each time it became her turn, she waved the next person forward. Behind us in line, a family of *Gitanos* (Spanish for Gypsy, as Romany people are called in Spain) talked and smoked.

Just as we reached the head of the line, the waiting nun was joined by two more tiny nuns. Not one of the three was five feet tall. Arriving at the window at the same time was a tall, very black African man and his wife. She was enshrouded in a flowing, colorful, traditional African dress. The *Gitano* man behind us began to berate them all for breaking in line. The nuns ignored him and began whatever business they had at the window. The African man defended himself vigorously. He said he'd been told to come to the front of the line with whatever document he'd been missing the first time, Flannery told us. The *Gitano* continued to harangue them, his voice loud and harsh.

"He's only following instructions," Flannery said to the man in Spanish. He ignored her.

The nuns completed their business, then the Africans, and finally, after standing in line for forty-five minutes, we reached the window. "This is the wrong line," the woman said. "Go to that line." She pointed at an even longer line that led to the other window.

"But we were told to stand in this line," Flannery said.

"Next," she called out.

We looked at the long line. I muttered foul comments about the Spanish bureaucracy. I questioned the heritage of the man at the information window. A raindrop hit the back of my neck and ran under my collar. We decided to come back the next day.

Our Second Visit to the Police Station

The next morning we arrived at 9:20. The police station opened at nine, and the line was long. We waited. The closer we came to the window, the more people returned to the window with missing documents or copies. Finally, forty minutes later, we arrived at the window. "We need our passports stamped," we said.

"No," we were informed, "you need to fill out these forms and return with two photos each and with multiple copies of all the documents stamped by the consulate in San Francisco."

I took a deep breath. I reminded myself that we were retired and had sufficient time to complete the task at hand. No matter how frustrating it was. We would, I instructed myself, fill out the applications, have photos made, and enjoy the day.

Our Third Visit to the Police Station

We set the clock for an even earlier rising and arrived at the police station Thursday morning at 8:40. A short line, no more than seven or eight people, stood waiting at the door. At nine, the doors were opened, and we found ourselves tenth in line. Where the extra people came from I don't know. But with two windows open, we didn't anticipate a long wait. We saw familiar faces from our previous visits.

At one of the windows, a very stubborn woman who obviously didn't like the answers she was getting refused to comply with whatever it was that the clerk was asking her to do, or to leave the window. The women at both windows, along with what appeared to be a supervisor, spent fifteen minutes arguing with her. All work stopped; the line didn't move. Eventually a man was summoned. After a brief discussion, he led her from the window and escorted her upstairs. I listened for screams but heard nothing.

Around nine thirty, we reached the window. A very pleasant woman began to go through our papers. We needed more copies of our applications. Fortunately Flannery had made note of a nearby copy service and rushed out and made copies while the woman looked through our papers. Upon her return, Flannery identified each document: proof of insurance, proof of non-criminality, proof of income, proof of sanity, etc.

The clerk at the adjoining window listened closely as Flannery described each document. She shook her sour face and said something to our clerk. I looked to Flannery for a translation. "She said that our papers should be in Spanish, that she won't accept any documents she can't read."

"That's ridiculous! Isn't that why the documents were processed in San Francisco? That's why they stamp each document, to show that it …" I felt Flannery's eyes burning my face even as Kay's fingers dug into my arm. Perhaps I was getting a little excited.

"What if we had ended up at her window?" I whispered.

"But we didn't," they whispered back.

Maybe the fact that we hadn't ended up at Señora Sourpuss's window signaled a change in luck, I thought, trying to find a positive note. Surely this was a sign. Our sweet, kind lady gave her coworker a curt smile as she glued our photos to our applications, put the document in order, and stapled the stack together. In about thirty days, she told us, we would receive a letter instructing us to come in for our permits.

We left the police station and headed for the nearest café for a celebratory breakfast.

Making la Casa Our Home

Our World Grows, Block by Block

Over the next few days we explored our neighborhood. Our street, Calle Elvira, is just over a half mile long and can be walked from end to end in less than fifteen minutes. It begins at Puerta de Elvira, the largest and certainly most imposing of the surviving Moorish gates. It was through this four-story arch and down Calle Elvira that the Catholic monarchs Isabel and Fernando entered Granada on January 2, 1492, to accept the surrender of the Alhambra. Some three hundred and fifty years later Napoleon's French troops poured into the city through Puerta de Elvira. Before they left they knocked down the inner gate and fortress for easy access, leaving only the massive arch.

At the other end of the street is Plaza Nueva, the point of our arrival in Granada and only five minutes from our apartment. Dominated by the Royal Chancellery of Granada and the fountain, Plaza Nueva is lined with cafés and shops. Cuesta Gomerez, the road up to the Alhambra, begins at the plaza.

Calle Elvira marks the lower boundary of the Albaicín, Spain's best-preserved Arab quarter and the only part of the Muslim city to have survived the *Reconquista*, or Catholic reconquest, reasonably intact. From Calle Elvira, a maze of twisting cobblestone alleys and passageways, narrow steps, and steep, rubble-strewn paths zigzag steeply uphill between stucco Moorish houses stacked like blocks. On top, in the upper Albaicín, there are café-filled plazas, churches, monasteries, and restaurants. The views of the city and the Alhambra are as fabulous as they are famous.

Except during the early morning and late afternoon when the city seemed to sleep, Calle Elvira was a busy street, filled with both vehicle and foot traffic. Although the streets leading down to the broad Grande Via de Colón are wide enough for traffic, not one street on the uphill side was. Surfaced with paving stones with a shallow drainage trench in the center, our street was just wide enough for a car or small truck. The sidewalk, when there was one, was lined with short, decorative metal posts, whose purpose, I guessed, was to protect pedestrians from whining motor scooters (despised, we were told, by every *Granadino* who didn't own one) and honking cars. To the Spanish driver, pushing through narrow, crowded streets presents a not-to-be-missed opportunity to blow the horn. They gleefully mash the center of the steering wheel until the blare of the horn begins to waver as if it were about to expire. It is then briefly released, no longer than necessary to recover, then crushed again. Enrique, our upstairs neighbor, told me that the Spanish definition of a car is, "the thing you carry your horn in." Apparently the Spanish have grown immune, as they seemed oblivious to horns being blown only inches away. There was not a pause in the conversation or a glance back as they very leisurely moved to the side of the street. It was an immunity that Kay and I never acquired, and the blast of a horn just behind us never failed to send us reeling to the sidewalk behind the protective posts.

Three- and four-story buildings lined the street, almost all with a small business downstairs and two or three floors of apartments above. There were, when we moved there, two modest hotels, ten café-bars, seven bars, four restaurants, and three *schaurma* shops. Grocery shopping was easy as there were two *carnicerias* (meat markets), two *panaderías* (bakeries), a *fruteria*, two tiny "convenience" stores, and a *supermercado*, which wasn't very super at all, just a small, neighborhood market that sold everything from paper towels to fresh meat. And there was Granada Ten, a movie theater in the evening, an extremely popular disco after midnight.

Just down the street between our apartment and Plaza Nueva, Calle Caldereria began its steep cobblestone climb up the hill. Barely four people wide and filled with the sound of Arabic, the street was lined with Moroccan teahouses and small shops selling *ceramica artesana*, tea, tea glasses, shawls, drums, and other North African merchandise. Tiny tables occupied by tea drinkers, merchandise displays, and throngs of browsing tourists made the passageway even narrower, and movement often came to a standstill. It was not a street that one could easily hurry through.

El Espejo (The Mirror), the café-bar downstairs, was not the only attraction of our little intersection, a miniature Times Square. To the left of us was Café-bar La Tortuga, to the right, Café-bar El Circulo. In addition to the three cafés, people were drawn to the *schaurma* shop directly across the street. There were several *schaurma* shops along our end of Elvira and the one across the street was one of the most popular, often staying open till five in the morning. A *schaurma* (also spelled *chaurma*, or *schwarma*, sometimes two spellings on the same sign) is a Middle Eastern wrap, and, although there are variations, the basic *schaurma* contained strips of rotisseried chicken sliced from a huge skewer of filleted breasts, tomato, cabbage, lettuce, yogurt, and sauce rolled up in thin pita bread. The result is a large, inexpensive, hand-held meal, the perfect fuel to keep people going, which is to say drinking, till dawn.

Striking Gold

Our explorations, of course, extended beyond our street and immediate neighborhood. There are few if any better ways to learn a new city than shopping, and our apartment was in an ideal location. As we shopped, we discovered that the Mercado San Agustín, the city's central market, as well as the cathedral and Plaza Bib-Rambla, Granada's largest and busiest square, were only a five-minute walk away. The pedestrian shopping area lay immediately beyond Plaza Bib-Rambla. We could walk to the Alhambra in fifteen minutes, or be sitting in a café on the river just beneath its soaring towers in ten. There was even a modern and reasonably priced Internet facility nearby.

Gran Via de Colón, the city's main boulevard and bus artery, ran parallel to Elvira, which allowed us to live the ultimate hassle-free life: one without an automobile. The bus system made getting around town easy, though we didn't use it very often as most destinations in the city were within easy walking distance.

Although our kitchen did have the basics—a couple of pots and pans, some glasses, clear glass dinnerware, and a set of playhouse utensils, the kinds of items that sell for fifty cents at a yard sale at five o'clock in the afternoon—it was not equipped for serious cooking. Our shopping list was long: baking pans and frying pans, funnels, rolling pin, garlic press, dish drainer, kitchen scissors, tongs, and proper cutlery. We also needed household items like bedding, toiletries, wastebaskets, candlesticks, clothes hangers, a wall clock, extension cords, and pliers. The list went on and on. There was no oven, so we needed a microwave and a toaster oven. Other than the short, unusually firm sofa and a black canvas director's chair, there was nowhere to sit, so we needed a comfortable chair or another short couch.

There were, thankfully, no one-stop shopping malls in central Granada—no Walgreen's, no Sears, and no K-Mart—and only one department store, the famous El Corte Inglés, an excellent, Spanish-owned, English-style emporium. Months later we discovered two large "box stores" and one somewhat seedy mall, all on the outskirts of town, but I'm glad we didn't know about them at the time. Walking the streets day after day, shopping list in hand, required dozens of stops. Finding everything in one store on one afternoon would have spoiled the fun. Doing it the slow way filled our days and left us knowing the downtown area very well.

We quickly discovered that the best places to buy almost everything were the 100 *peseta tiendas*, although some stores used the Euro equivalent, €,60 *tiendas*, about 75¢. Similar to dollar stores in the states, there were *tiendas* everywhere, sometimes two or three on a block. Although the general price range was €,60 to €2, you could buy a light bulb for €,25, a platter for €1, a grocery cart for €12, a blender for €25 a mini-sound system for €50, or a coffee table for €60.

During the course of our first year in Granada, we bought roughly two hundred items (I kept a list) and the majority of them were purchased at our favorite *tienda*. Located only three blocks from our apartment just across the lane from the central market, it was a gold mine of inexpensive, necessary equipment. It was so inexpensive that items that hadn't been necessary became so. How can you not buy a magnifying glass when it cost only €,60? A small price for being able to read the fine print on a city map. This small *tienda* was such a gold mine that we named it Tienda de Oro.

Tienda de Oro, like most of these small stores, was family owned and operated. The parents ran the store and their teenage kids helped out on weekends and after school. The parents were both around forty. He was tall, heavyset, and a bit gruff. She was very short, no more than five foot tall, squat, with a round face and wide smile. As we were in the store at least twice a week during those first few months, she soon came to recognize us. She and Flannery chatted away and she got to know the basics of our life: that we were retired, had moved from California, and were setting up house on Calle Elvira.

Our visits to the Tienda de Oro got a little sticky after Flannery's departure. If you speak a few words of Spanish (or any other language), people often think you know more. This sweet woman was absolutely determined to talk with us. Not *at* us, *with* us. Every time we came in, she asked about Flannery, where she was and what she was doing. We, mainly Kay, would answer as best she could. Then, if there wasn't a line forming behind us, for the store was very popular, our friendly proprietress would ask a few more questions. We hadn't a clue what she was saying. Eventually it would wind down to "*no entiendo.*" She would smile and shrug, her husband would roll his eyes and look at the ceiling, and we would pile a *hasta luego* on top of an *adios* on top of a *muchas gracias* and flee into the street. This pretend conversation would be repeated at the conclusion of each shopping visit, though as time went on we were able to understand a bit more.

Shopping could present challenges. Hardware stores, for instance, were expensive and were not self-service. Try describing to a bewildered clerk an eyehook, which we found no Spanish word for in our dictionary.

Buying medicine presented similar difficulties. In the United States, it's not necessary to go to a pharmacy, as almost everything you need to relieve a headache, backache, stomach ache, or toothache can be found at the supermarket. You can buy eye drops, nose drops, and cough drops, plus hundreds if not thousands of health-related items in an array of brands, sizes, and strengths, all organized along wide aisles for your shopping convenience. You can even have your prescription filled while you sort through the tomatoes. Not in Granada.

In Granada you go to the *farmacia*. There's one every few blocks. There was one intersection from where I could see five *farmacias*, each easily identified by its green, blinking neon cross. They were all small and fully staffed; a *farmacia* no larger than an American living room might have three or four white-coated clerks behind the counter. And behind the counter was where ninety-nine percent of everything was located. Like hardware stores, these were not—I want to make this perfectly clear—self-service stores. One does not browse the aisles in search of the best deal in aspirin. If you needed aspirin, you waited in line for your turn, and then asked the person behind the counter for *aspirina*. It pays to take your dictionary along.

We'd been told that there was nowhere in Granada to buy English language books, so one of my projects the summer before our departure had been to prowl the used bookstores, yard sales, and Goodwill stores for books. The books had to be inexpensive, the cheaper the better, as we assumed we'd be discarding them. They had to be paperbacks, or, preferably, trade paperbacks, as we were going to be carrying them, or dragging them, half way around the world. A third requirement was that they had to offer the maximum in time consuming reading pleasure. So-called summer beach books did not qualify, as they could be read in a day or two. Time was what we now had plenty of, all the time to read all those books we'd intended to read someday but hadn't because we hadn't had the time or, perhaps as likely, the inclination.

Included in our literary baggage—we'd stuffed six or seven books into each of our seven bags—was *The Count of Monte Cristo*, by Alexandre Dumas, more than five hundred pages of post-Napoleonic era intrigue; Henry Fielding's *Tom Jones*, seven hundred pages of small type and ribald adventure; John Barth's *Giles Goat-Boy*, seven hundred sixty pages of, according to the jacket "theology, sociology, and sex;" and *The Pickwick Papers*, by Charles Dickens, a novel of eight hundred pages with no discernible plot. And, of course, we packed a copy of *Don Quixote*. Our Penguin Classic edition of *Don Quixote* had compressed this monumental novel (actually it's two novels) to a mere nine hundred forty pages by using the same diabolically small print used to describe medical side effects and warranty violations.

If you think that sounds like heavy reading, you should try lugging them from airport bus to airport check-in, from baggage claim to taxi stand to bus station and onto the bus, where you have to load and later retrieve them from the underneath baggage area yourself.

As it turned out, we were misinformed. It was possible to buy English language books in Granada, though new books were rather expensive. During our tramps around the city, we discovered three bookstores with small sections of used English language books. We were also able to buy inexpensive paperback editions of English classics at the November book fair, so we were able to supplement our small library.

There were evenings, especially after a day climbing the hills of Granada, when we were simply too tired to read. We'd brought a small, book-size radio/clock/CD player with us, along with a few dozen CDs, but it didn't take long to go through our entire collection. As for going out on the town to hear music, the club scene began far too late for us, rarely before eleven, more often midnight; and movies, unfortunately, were always dubbed. Only a few theaters in the largest cities showed original version movies and Granada is not a larger city.

We Contribute to the Spanish Economy

Although furnished apartments in Granada were often equipped with a television, ours wasn't. So we bought a TV and a DVD player. We didn't have a satellite dish, so we didn't get English language stations. As for Spanish television, it was truly horrible. We had to turn our brains up in order to understand the language, and down to ignore the content. Among the more popular shows were dubbed reruns of *Family Matters* and *I Dream of Jeannie*. There were game shows and interview shows. The phrase used to describe local news shows in America—"If it bleeds it leads"—applies in spades to Spanish news shows. In Spain, the blood flowed throughout the show, through murders, car wrecks, and house fires, interrupted only by soccer coverage, particularly footage of practice sessions followed by interviews with the coach and the owner. The news ended with another murder. It's not necessary to speak the language to enjoy watching sporting events, and I learned to enjoy ping pong, team handball, and even badminton, all of which were shown in the afternoon. Soccer and basketball were shown in the evening.

The DVD player saved the day, and soon we were snuggling in for the evening with an American or English movie (Spanish and other foreign language films did not have English subtitles) and popcorn popped in our new microwave. There was a Blockbuster located about twenty minutes away, and we opened an account. No credit card was necessary, just proof of address. We showed them our lease and our passports. If you don't return the video, I guess they send the police to your house.

Flannery also introduced us to the video club machines. These ATM-like machines dispensed DVDs like candy bars. We purchased a card inside during business hours, then used the card to rent and to return movies twenty-four hours a day. There were hundreds of movies available; the problem was that all titles were in Spanish. If you thought you recognized a title, you clicked on its title and the screen displayed the box cover and cast. I'm sure there were dozens of good films we never saw because of the title translation. The screen also displayed the credit left on your card; when it was low, you simply came by during open hours and bought more credit. It was very convenient and cheaper than Blockbuster.

By the end of November, our apartment was reasonably well equipped. In addition to the TV, DVD player, and microwave, we'd bought a very comfortable short sofa, another end table, reading light, coffee maker, toaster oven, hot pot for heating water for tea, a printer for the laptop computer, throws and pillows for the couch, and enough plates and glasses to have a small party. Putting aside an adequate slush fund had turned out to be more important than we'd thought.

One item we didn't have to buy was a telephone. Flannery had purchased a cell phone for us and had loaded it with minutes. When our minutes got low, we simply walked down the street to the neighborhood phone center, where you could buy a phone card, top up your own cell phone, or make an international call in one of three tiny plywood phone booths. We soon discovered that using our cell phone to call home was much more expensive than calling from the phone center. Fortunately, it cost nothing to receive a call. We were in touch; we sent our cell phone number to family and friends, and we called them from the phone center.

Within weeks our new lives had taken on a rhythm and pattern. Once a week we took our weekly allowance from a nearby ATM, where we had a choice of eight languages in which to transact our business. We bought the *International Herald Tribune* three times a week from the kiosk down the street. We checked our e-mail at Navegaweb, the internet center, three or four times a week.

A division of labor slowly evolved. Kay had always been our family's primary chef. I cooked when she was flying and just enough when she was home to give her a break. The kitchen was just large enough for two cooks but impossible for three, so Flannery now became associate chef and I the chief bottle washer. Flannery had cooked for us from time to time over the years, but this was the first time that she and her mother had shared a kitchen together on a regular basis, and not as teacher and student. This was not a situation that guaranteed success. But it worked. They enjoyed it and I ate like a king. Kay particularly loved doing the marketing and figuring out how to use the local products. She bought meat at the city market, where her chicken butcher and her pork butcher soon recognized her and greeted her with a smile, and our produce from a very friendly lady whose stand was located on a narrow lane just outside the market.

As the weeks and months went past, the kitchen became Kay's laboratory, and she was constantly experimenting. She had two Spanish cookbooks, one given to us by Flannery as a housewarming gift, plus *The Joy of Cooking* and *The Memphis Cookbook*, both belonging to Flannery. Kay discovered Spanish products, like *tomate frito*, a tomato sauce made of fried tomatoes, and *nata*, a cooking cream that she'd never used before. Although she added a few Spanish dishes to her personal cookbook, for the most part she cooked the dishes she always cooked, but using Spanish ingredients. She didn't try to duplicate the original dish; she made an incredibly delicious Spanish version.

The Gas Man Cometh

My primary chore, in addition to keeping up with e-mail and taking care of online business like banking and bill paying, was keeping us supplied with gas. It was possible to call for delivery, which we once did, only to find ourselves sitting at home for two days waiting. What worked better was to listen for the delivery truck. The sound of the tanks being dropped to the street and empties being thrown on the truck was unmistakable. And hearing it was important, as the truck was often wedged into some alley or side street out of view. Once the spare was empty, our ears were tuned. If there was a delivery schedule, we never figured it out. Having an empty spare for more than a few days tended to put us on edge. The thought of a cold shower in January was not inviting.

I always had an ear cocked for the clang of the *bombona* hitting the cobblestone street. If I didn't hear it first, I would hear Kay's call.

"Boyce! Gas man's here!"

Out I would scramble from wherever I was, searching for shoes, a sweater, and money, exact change if possible. Then I wrestled the empty *bombona* from beneath the sink and headed down the stairs. If the truck was in view, I leaned against the door, crossed my arms against the cold, and waited for him to see me. If I couldn't see the truck, I walked down the street to find it. Sometimes I found the truck, but the man was missing. When that happened, I carried my empty to the truck and waited for him there. I didn't want to take a chance on him driving by and not seeing me.

This wiry little guy, he couldn't have weighed more than a hundred and forty pounds, threw a tank on his shoulder and lugged it up the steps and winding lanes to houses high on the hillside. Sometimes I waited fifteen minutes for him to return with the empty. How far had he gone? This was one tough guy, but he was not, judging by his demeanor, a real social guy.

"*Señor*," I would shout as he approached his truck. "*Una bombona, por favor.*"

He would nod, take my empty and throw it on the truck, then pull off a full one and put it on the ground. I paid him the €8,80.

"*Muchas gracias.*"

"*Nada*," he mumbled. I had the feeling that to him that was a sentence. It was the only word I ever heard him speak.

Taking out the garbage was everyone's job. There were no individual garbage cans in Granada. Whether they existed in other Spanish cities, I don't know. but the system in Granada made sense, as there was no room on the narrow street to put a can. It was quite efficient. Collection centers were installed throughout the neighborhood wherever there was room. There was a small dumpster on our corner where people deposited their garbage, tied in plastic bags. An amazing array of discards appeared almost daily by the dumpster, everything from broken furniture and mattresses to appliances. The dumpster was emptied every day, even holidays, at dawn.

Recycling was handled in a similar manner, with recycling stations installed wherever there was room. Each station consisted of a hinged metal trapdoor topped with three or four short, shiny, roll-top cans. Each can was designated for either glass, paper and cardboard, plastic items, or garbage. Every day or two, the trapdoor was opened by a hydraulic lift, and each underground, elevator-size container was lifted on a hook, emptied over a specially equipped truck, then lowered back in. At some locations, the underground containers were simply plastic dumpsters that were raised, rolled out, and emptied.

Spreading American Cheer

By early December, we'd been seeing the faces on our segment of Calle Elvira for almost two months. And they'd been seeing ours, though there were no signs that they recognized us. Actually, there weren't that many faces to see. The building across the lane was vacant, as were two other buildings along the street. The neighbors directly across the street kept their shutters closed and we rarely saw them. The owner of the *schaurma* shop often stood in the street people watching. The antique shopkeepers went back and forth from shop to shop, where they stood chatting, arms crossed, outside one shop while keeping an eye on their own. They had few customers and only went inside when there was business.

"It doesn't seem right walking by the same people day after day without saying hello," Kay said. "I don't care if that's what the Spanish do or not."

Manuel had told us that people from Granada were not very friendly. *Granadinos,* he'd said, were often rude and were not very helpful.

"They seem nice to us," we'd said.

"Then they probably weren't *Granadinos,*" he'd replied. It's worthy of mention that Manuel is not a native of Granada.

Our impression of the Spaniards we'd encountered—we didn't know whether they were *Granadinos* or not—was that they were helpful enough, and reasonably friendly, but not warm and welcoming, at least not to outsiders. If we wanted to bring them into our circle of American cheer, it was up to us. So every day as we passed up and down our street, we said hello. *"Buenos dias." "Hola."*

At first they seemed surprised, if not a little bewildered, and even looked around as if to see who we were talking to. When they realized that we were talking to them, they nodded and muttered *"Bon," "Buenos,"* or occasionally *"Bon dia." Granadinos* do not say *buenos dias.*

At the market, we always said hello, asked them how they were doing, made some superficial observation about the weather or whatever, and made it a point to say thank you and good-bye. Pretty soon they were chattering away at us, and we were smiling and nodding as if we had any idea what they were saying. But everyone was smiling and that's what counted.

Everyday held some challenge, but we were making progress and feeling more at home. Granada was proving, at least so far, to be all that Flannery said it was: the perfect place for us to live.

The Streets of Granada 1: Tapas

Exploring a World of Unidentified Frying Objects

When Kay and I were in Madrid thirty-plus years ago, *tapas,* the snacks that accompany each drink ordered at a café-bar or restaurant, were free. At the cafés, we stood at the bar, the crunch of peanut shells beneath our feet, and ordered a glass of wine. Beneath the glass bar were rows of small dishes filled with peanuts or olives, various small fish or calamari, miniature croquettes, pickled vegetables, all sorts of things. When we ordered a drink, we simply pointed to the dish we wanted and it was handed over the bar. We loved it. We were young and traveling on a shoestring, and it was the closest thing to a free lunch we'd experienced.

Much to our dismay, we'd heard that *tapas* were no longer free, at least not everywhere. So we were happy to discover that there was one important exception: the province of Granada. Although one might receive a handful of potato chips or olives with a drink elsewhere in Spain, Granada was the only place where the *tapas* were both substantial and always free.

Tapas are served with alcoholic drinks, soft drinks, and juice but not with coffee. Unless there are more than three or four people, the *tapa* is usually served on one plate, with a fork, if a fork is needed, for each person. Some cafés serve *tapas* from the time they open till the time they close. Others stop around four and begin again around seven. *Tapas* vary greatly from café to café and from day to day. They also vary from first drink to second to third and so on. Most cafés in Granada delivered their *tapas* in a specific order; with your first drink you get this, with your second, that. "*Dos primeras,*" the waiter calls out, two first *tapas*. Or, "*Una segunda,*" one second *tapa*. At some cafés the *tapas* change almost daily. You never know what you're going to get.

Tapas became an integral part of our daily routine. After a morning filled with projects—writing letters, potting plants, washing, mending, reading the paper—we usually left the house around noon, a list of errands in hand, a slight grumbling in the stomach. At least mine. I'm easily filled but often hungry.

Our first stop was usually Navegaweb, the computer and Web center near Plaza Nueva. By the time we answered our e-mails and checked on our bank account, or whatever business needed doing, it was one o'clock. Time for *tapas*.

Deciding where we'd enjoy a refreshing, relaxing malt beverage and *tapas* required answering a number of questions. Did we have another errand, and if so, in what direction? Which café offered the best view or people watching? If the day was hot, which café had shade trees and umbrellas? If it was cool, where could we take our *tapas* in the sun? The time was a consideration, as some cafés were so packed by two that it was impossible to find a seat or even get to the counter. Then there was the *tapa* itself. Was there a particular *tapa* that we hungered for? Where hadn't we been lately? What were we having for dinner? We didn't want to go to a café that specialized in fish if we were having fish that night. How hungry were we? Amounts varied. Last but not least, there was the issue of mood. Did we want to stick with the known *tapas* world? The tried and true? Or were we primed for culinary adventure? Were we ready to consume unidentified frying objects?

Sometimes the permutations were so complex that we couldn't decide where to go. When that happened, the only solution was to adjourn to the nearest café to decide over a beer and *tapas* where to go for a beer and *tapa*. Retirement was not, as we had assumed it would be, free of important decision-making.

Fortunately, there were several excellent, nearby choices. Bodegas Castañeda, very popular and very traditional (wine casks lined the walls while dozens of serrano hams hung from the ceiling) had interesting *tapas,* like boiled shrimp and stews, but you had to stand at the bar, as tables were reserved for diners. Bodegas La Antigualla, just around the corner, was a student hangout that offered a slice of serrano ham in a small, soft bagel-like roll with lettuce, aioli, and French fries. Finding a seat there was always difficult unless you arrived early. There were two *cervecerias* that we frequented. (I love the term *cerveceria.* Beer joint. No beating around the bush there.) Cerveceria La Riviera was one of the few cafés where you chose your *tapa;* we usually ordered *albóndigas,* or meatballs. Another favorite was Cerveceria Minotauro, which served a *lomo* (pork loin) sandwich along with olives and potato chips. At each of these places, the price of a beer or glass of wine, along with *tapa,* was €1,50 or so, less that $2.

We often headed for the esplanade by the Rio Darro, where we had a choice of five or six cafés. Our favorite served a slice of bread with a thick piece of Manchego cheese and cold cuts on top, dripping in olive oil, with a handful of olives. In the opposite direction, well beyond the cathedral, there was a small café off Plaza Gracia where the first *tapa* was often a delicious pork stew, four or five chunks of meat for each of us, along with *patatas pobre,* a traditional dish of sliced potatoes, green peppers, and garlic simmered in olive oil until soft, plus bread. There was a bodega in still another direction whose *tapas* consisted of slices of roast ham on bread with French fries that was absolutely fantastic. Once again, the price of a beer or glass of wine was around €1,50.

But there's more to *tapas* than eating free food. It's the experience. For the Spanish, *ir de tapas,* to go out for *tapas,* is about meeting friends and having a conversation over a drink and a snack. It's rare to see a Spaniard having a beer and *tapas* alone. For Kay and me, the socializing was limited mostly to each other, except when we had guests. But we enjoyed the people watching, waiter watching, discussing the day and making plans, or simply resting after a long walk, all enhanced by the pleasure of a delicious, or at least interesting, afternoon snack.

There are several theories concerning the history of the *tapa.* According to one legend, the practice of serving food with every drink began with Alfonso, the king of Castile, who, after recovering from an illness by taking wine and small snacks between meals, ordered taverns to serve food along with wine. A more widely accepted theory is that the *tapas* originated with the custom of covering (*tapa* means "lid" or "cover" in Spanish) a glass of wine with a slice of bread or a small saucer to keep the flies out, a custom said to have begun in Andalucía. Eventually, the story goes, some enterprising bodega keeper put a bit of food on the cover, perhaps a slice of ham, maybe a few olives. And thus began the tradition of serving a *tapa,* or a small saucer of food, with each drink.

According to Enrique, our upstairs neighbor, the *tapa* originated in Granada during the siege of the city by Isabel and Fernando. The siege lasted several years, leaving the army little to do but hang around and drink. Drunkenness was rampant. A displeased Isabel commanded that henceforth, drink could not be served without food, for even then it was well known that drinking on an empty stomach is a sure path to inebriation. This theory may not explain the origins of the *tapa*—I suspect that Enrique was repeating a local bit of color—but it does shed light on why both Spain and Italy, which have high rates of wine and beer consumption, have low rates of alcoholism, at least compared to northern European countries. Spaniards almost always eat when they drink.

Rolling the Culinary Dice

But enough history. There were those days when, being in a more adventuresome mood, we decided to roll the culinary dice, to cast our digestive fates to the wind. In other words, to let fall on our plates what may.

Of course, that's just what we'd done during our beginning days in Granada, when every *tapa* brought with it the possibility of being, shall we say, a gustatory challenge. We discovered that most of the *tapas* we were served would be considered palatable by all but the pickiest eater. This was particularly true in the downtown area where there were more tourists. Eating *tapas* in the neighborhoods was a bit chancier.

It was possible to check a place out. Sometimes we detoured through a café to see what they were serving. Potato chips? We shook our heads in dismay. Sometime we were too quick to judge. Once we tried a café and had potato chips and olives delivered to our table. Disappointed, we sipped our beers, bemoaned our fate, and swore never to return. Soon, before we'd finished, we saw paella being served. We'd come before they'd had time to prepare their *tapas*. We made a note: return, but never before one.

We'd become terrible *tapas* snobs.

But back to adventures in eating, to those occasions when we did not attempt to avoid culinary surprises. The good thing about taking your chances was that we were exposed to foods that we would never have otherwise tried. The down side is that we were exposed to foods that we would never have otherwise tried. Smorgasbord or minefield, you never knew.

Our first such experience was a *tapa* consisting of three sausages: chorizo, one that looked and tasted very much like salami, and something very black. Two small pieces of each sausage, along with bread, were served on one plate.

"What's that one?" Kay asked suspiciously.

"I'm pretty sure it's *morcilla*," I said. I'd read about *morcilla* and assumed that eventually I'd get a chance to try it out.

"Which is?" she asked, poking it as if to see if it were still alive.

"Blood sausage. Also called black pudding."

Kay pushed both pieces of *morcilla* to my side of the plate, wiped the tines of her fork on her napkin, then tucked the napkin under her plate.

I tried it. It had a tough, almost unchewable skin—maybe you weren't supposed to eat the skin—and a strong, dark, earthy taste, with a somewhat grainy texture. It was okay. Not my favorite, but enjoyable, though a little bit went a long way. *Morcilla* came my way a few times, and I always ate it, but I never ordered it.

Stew was a commonly served *tapa*. It made sense. The café could cook up tubs of stew in the morning, then simply dish out small servings for the rest of the day. It got better as the day progressed. The stew was almost always pork, usually with chunks of potato and perhaps some beans.

Something from Inside of Something

There was a café in the heart of the city we enjoyed so much we dubbed it our winter headquarters, the place we'd go on cold, wet winter days. The ambiance was pleasant, the waiters friendly, and the first *tapa* was often a delicious pork stew. One day, on what might have been our tenth visit to winter headquarters, we were served, as usual, a small, ceramic dish of stew. Except it didn't look like the usual pork stew. There were small chunks of meat-like things floating around with white beans in a thin broth.

Kay leaned over and peered into the dish. "It looks like something from inside of something," she said.

I took a bite and agreed. There were things, like organ meats, from inside of another thing, probably a pig.

"Do you think there's anything in there I can eat?" she asked.

"The beans?"

She shook her head, pushed the dish to my side of the table, and asked if she could have the largest piece of bread.

Like *morcilla*, it was a dish I took some pleasure in but wouldn't order.

The thought of what a food *is* has never been a problem for me. If it tastes good, it tastes good. I find both tongue and *rabo de toro*, or bull's tail, to be delicious.

And I don't have a problem with textures, as Kay does. She deserves a lot of credit, for she was willing to try some pretty strange foods, and a few, to her own surprise, she liked. Like *boquerones*, fresh, bite-sized anchovies that are headed, breaded, deep-fried, and served in a pile with lemon. She doesn't love them, but she usually takes a few from my platter. She also developed a liking for *pulpo*, deep-fried octopus tentacles, which, when properly prepared, are crunchy and quite delicious. When not properly prepared, they can be a bit rubbery.

One dish that sounded particularly enticing to me was *anchoas marinadas*, anchovies marinated in vinegar and herbs. The heads and tails are removed from these finger-sized fishes, then they're filleted, butterflied, and marinated overnight, where they "cook" in the vinegar. I ate them in Malaga, on the coast, and they are amazingly delectable. Kay tried one and enjoyed it.

There was a café in the Albaicín called Los Caracoles. The first time we went—we were with Kay's brother Mason and his friend Monte— we didn't notice the name of the café, which wouldn't have mattered anyway as we didn't know the word then. The *tapa* was a large bowl (it was intended for four) of *caracoles,* or snails, in a thick, spicy, garlicky brown sauce. Well, Monte and I were pleasantly surprised. Kay and

Mason were appalled. While Monte and I ate our shares and theirs, Kay and Mason bided their time until our next stop.

Kay has shown lots of pluck during our adventures in eating. As for me, the world of *tapas* is a briar patch and I'm Br'er Rabbit. Just throw me in!

Moroccan Adventures

Pummeling a Robber, Bartering Berber Style

By mid-November, having sufficiently settled in, we decided to give ourselves a break from shopping, equipping, and exploring. A trip, we decided, would be just the thing. My birthday was coming up and we decided to celebrate it in Marrakech, Morocco. We knew that we would be there in the middle of Ramadan, the holy month, and we assumed that some of the activities we normally enjoyed, like having a glass of beer or wine with lunch, might be curtailed. On the other hand, visiting a Moslem country during Ramadan could be a unique cultural experience. Little did we know how unique it would be.

We traveled by bus from Granada to the coast and then west along the Mediterranean to the port city of Algeciras. From there we took the ferry to Morocco. There were only a couple of dozen passengers on the ship. From the lounge, which we had almost to ourselves, we could see Spain, Africa, and the Rock of Gibraltar. The trip across took only an hour and a half.

We docked at Tangier at 2:00 p.m. As we disembarked, we were met by a group of men dressed in *jellebas*, a hooded, robe-like garment. Each presented his tourist office credentials and kindly offered to take us to "an excellent hotel" or guide us around the city. Having already selected a hotel in our guide book, and knowing that it was nearby, we declined. One of the gentlemen insisted on walking along with us. He spoke, as do many Moroccans, very good English. He informed us that because it was both Friday and Ramadan, everything (as in *everything*) closed at five o'clock and that everyone (as in *everyone*) would be heading straight home to break his or her day-long fast. He knew the way to our hotel, which was located behind the wall in the Medina, or old city, and since we didn't even know where the gate was, his guidance proved very helpful. Once at the hotel, we rewarded him accordingly.

We'd chosen the Continental Hotel, which overlooked the port and much of the Medina, because of the description in the Michelin guide. "Writers, artists, and famous men have stayed here and the salons and patios have figured in films." I pictured mysterious men wearing dark glasses and white suits sitting in the lounge beneath slowly turning fans. Regardless of its fame, it was almost empty, more than a bit threadbare, and did not accept Visa. There was no lounge. We checked in, took two rooms, and headed off into the town in search of an ATM, train tickets to Marrakech, and supplies for the room.

Suffice it to say that Tangier's port was not particularly attractive. The waterfront was lined with warehouses, cranes, parking lots, a long dock, and a stone seawall. We discovered a travel office nearby that sold train tickets but accepted cash only. Finding an ATM machine was now a must. From the boulevard that ran along the waterfront, the streets climbed up into the medina. What little we'd seen of the medina was a maze and we didn't have much time, so we walked down the boulevard for a few blocks, but finding no ATM, turned uphill toward the new town. After a few blocks of climbing, we hadn't even found a commercial district. It was after four and time was growing short. We stopped on a corner and looked around. I'm sure we all had the same expression on our faces, the one that plainly says, "I haven't the slightest idea where I am." We were approached by a friendly man who spoke excellent English; he asked if he could help, then walked us two blocks and pointed out an ATM. We now had a pocket full of *dirhams*. We found a small store and bought enough supplies—water, cookies, juice and crackers—to fill a large, plastic shopping bag.

The straightest line between where we were and the hotel was through a large, bustling square and surrounding *souk*, a maze of narrow streets lined with street merchants and shops. It was now nearing five and the traffic—people, cars, bicycles, and motor bikes—grew increasingly crowded. It was becoming more and more difficult to make my way through the throng with a large shopping bag dangling from my hand. Kay and Flannery were close by, though staying together was not easy. It was so crowded that I couldn't see where I was putting my feet. At one point Kay looked down to see what was so slippery beneath her feet, to discover she was walking on fish heads.

Eventually we found a street that headed downhill, and we could see the harbor and the boulevard at the bottom. The street was only one lane wide and the sidewalks were narrow. We were definitely swimming against the current. Cars were pushing uphill through the crowd, which filled the street from building to building.

As I made my way down along the sidewalk, a man stepped away from the wall where he'd been leaning and lowered his shoulder into my chest. As he did this I felt myself being touched from behind. Fortunately, I carry my wallet in one front pocket, my money in the other. I twisted away and pushed through the crowd out into the street, stopping only inches from the cars, where I waited for Kay and Flannery.

"You okay?" asked Flannery, who had seen what had happened. I checked my pockets. "They didn't get anything," I told her.

"Let's stay closer together."

We continued down the hill. I realized that I could protect only one pocket because the other hand was weighed down with the bag. A couple of minutes later, I again felt a shoulder against my chest and fingers against my hip. Before I could react, the man suddenly broke away. Behind me I heard Flannery's shout—it was an unrepeatable oath—and as I turned I saw her whack the would-be pickpocket across his shoulders with her open hand. Ducking his head, he disappeared into the crowd.

We flew together as if magnetized.

"He had his fingers at the edge of your pocket," Flannery said. She was shaking. We were extremely nervous. It seemed that every man on the street was staring at us (there were almost no women), and we still had a couple of blocks to work our way through. From that point on we made sure not to get separated, staying in physical contact as we made our way down to the boulevard.

The crowd thinned as we reached the bottom of the hill, and suddenly we found ourselves standing almost alone on the street. We checked our possessions again. Nothing was missing. Walking back toward the hotel, we came across another travel agent who advised us to go to the train station for our tickets. "Take a petite taxi," he told us, "the greens ones, they're less expensive." It was now after five and the streets were almost deserted. We walked back to the hotel, where we left Kay, along with our supplies and valuables. Flannery and I left for the train station with just enough money for the taxi and train tickets. There were few pedestrians and little automotive traffic along the boulevard, and the few petite taxis we saw were occupied. Things were not looking good. The station was not far away, at least according to the map, so walking seemed our only alternative.

Running the Gauntlet, Twice

Then a larger taxi slowed and the driver nodded at us. We waved and he stopped. It wasn't a petite taxi but at this point, it didn't matter. Train station? Yes. And off we went.

Our driver was an English-speaking, jolly sort of fellow. He told us that during Ramadan Moslems could not eat, smoke, drink anything, including water, or have "relations." He laughed when he said this.

"By the end of the day," he said, "everyone is very irritable. They are thirsty. They are wanting a cigarette. They are wanting to be home. Especially they are wanting to eat. Soon the streets will be deserted because everyone, even the police, have gone home to break their fast. The only people out will be bad people."

As he talked, we passed through what seemed a ghost town. The sidewalks were empty. We saw only two or three cars.

"You are lucky I saw you," he said. "It would be very foolish to be walking to the station. All around the train station it is very dangerous."

Soon he turned off the seaside boulevard. After a few blocks, we approached a large roundabout. Two men were standing in the street blocking entrance into the roundabout. They had stopped one car, which was parked at the edge of the street, and they waved at our approaching taxi to stop. Our driver held down the horn and blasted through, sending both men scrambling.

"I am telling you, it is very, very bad here," he said, "very dangerous. Those men would want money from you. I will wait for you at the station and take you back to your hotel."

"Yes!" we cried.

The train station was new and very attractive. Finding the proper window was easy, as only one was open. Flannery and I took our place behind three other ticket buyers. There were two people behind the window, five standing in line, and one man sweeping. Otherwise, the station was deserted. I bought three one-way tickets for Marrakech—we weren't sure how long we'd be staying—then we rushed back outside, hoping our driver would still be there. He was. On the way back we encountered the same ruffians at the same roundabout. They stepped out into the street, but he drove through, shouting out the window at them. They shouted back. Our driver slammed on the brakes, put the car in reverse, and began to back up. Flannery and I looked at each other. This did not seem like a good idea to us. In fact, it seemed like a very, very bad idea. Suddenly the driver stopped, flung a few more insults through the window, and then drove on. The thought that Flannery and I had planned to walk to the station made my heart pound.

Our driver drove us as close to the hotel as possible—the narrow alley leading to the hotel had been dug up and was impassable—and said he would pick us up at eight in the morning for our nine o'clock train.

We had dinner in the hotel, along with two other guests. Our frazzled nerves called out for a relaxing drink. But there is no (as in *no*) alcohol in the medina, not even in our hotel's restaurant. Back in our room, we looked out the window at a very quiet, very dark city, then went to bed.

The train trip from Tangier to Marrakech took nine and a half hours, including the hour spent on the platform in Casablanca. During the first hours we passed through a rugged landscape populated with flocks of sheep and goats, each tended by a shepherd or two; donkeys pulling carts or being ridden; villages of windowless mud huts; and the most litter-strewn ground I'd ever seen. Mile after mile, millions of plastic shopping bags and drink bottles covered the ground, snagged on the stubble of whatever grew there.

As we neared Casablanca, we looked out the window at well-tended cultivated fields, followed by the industrial and suburban sprawl that rings most cities. Present day Casablanca, we'd read, has nothing to do with the movie of the same name. It is Morocco's economic capital and the fourth largest city in Africa, but, according to the guidebook, with little of interest to the traveler. But no matter the reality, standing on the train platform under a large sign announcing Casablanca put a grin on our faces. We took a photo.

As the train moved east across Morocco toward Marrakech, the rolling land became increasingly barren but still quite beautiful. The landscape was smooth and round, as if each hill had been drawn with a protractor. We arrived at six thirty, took a taxi to our hotel in the new town (we'd learned our lesson about staying in the medina), where we took a small apartment with a bedroom, small kitchen, an enormous bathroom, and a living room with two daybeds, a u-shaped sitting area, and a TV.

The French influence on the new town was unmistakable, with broad boulevards lined with shops, restaurants, and sidewalk cafés and huge roundabouts with fountains in the center. The walk from our hotel to the medina along the main boulevard, Avenue Mohammed V, took thirty minutes. Unfortunately, our first walk was made in a driving rain. As in Tangier, we noticed that the cafés were filled with men sitting at empty tables. Even the Ramadan fast couldn't keep them from their favorite café, even if they weren't allowed to consume anything.

It had stopped raining by the time we reached Place Jemaa El Fna, "The Square," where we encountered, once again, the *jelleba*-clad tourist office-approved guides. There was absolutely no way, they told us, that we could find our way around the *souks* without a guide. The price was only 150 *dirhams*, a bit over $15, for two to three hours. We agreed. Our guide, Mubarek, spoke decent English and was quite charming.

There were, he told us, over four thousand shops in the *souks*. Each trade—potters, coppersmiths, cotton dyers, carpet makers, carpenters, leather craftsmen, spice merchants—has its own district. With few exceptions, the products for sale were made in the shop as you watched. At night the *souks* are closed behind multiple gates and doors; no one lived there. Mubarek was right; without him we would still be wandering aimlessly, hopelessly lost.

After a visit to the Ben Youssef Madrasah, a sixteenth century Koranic university, we explored the *souks*. We saw stacks of camel hides being cut up to make bags and shoes; smelled the strong scent of cedar as it was cut, shaved, and carved; dodged a shower of sparks from the metal grinder's wheel; heard the knocking of the copper merchant's hammer as they turned sheets of metal into lamps and trays; all the while avoiding the scooters and motorcycles that pressed through the narrow alleys.

Of course there was a catch. Our tour included stops at friendly merchants who were most happy to display their wares. The possibility that we might not want to buy what they were selling did not seem to have occurred to them. As far as they were concerned, the only option was to bargain until an agreeable price had been reached.

At our first stop, we were served mint tea and shown at least a hundred absolutely beautiful handmade hand-dyed rugs.

"But we don't have a house to put a rug," we told the charming master of ceremonies.

"No matter," he said. "We must show you the complete selection." He told us that the showcase was operated by the government tourist office and that it was his job to show us the rugs, not to make us buy one. As we drank our tea, his two assistants brought out and unrolled rug after rug. He taught us two words of Arabic, roughly translated: "Put that one away," and "Put this one aside." When one hundred rugs had been reduced to a mere fifteen, those having been selected by our saying something polite, like, "Isn't that a pretty one?" the bargaining began. He wrote down a price on a piece of paper, which he handed to me. I was to write down a counter offer. He would then write down a lower number, I would respond with a higher one. We would proceed until an agreeable number was reached. His first number: 37,500 *dirhams.* $3,750. I told him that we were but poor pensioners and couldn't possibly pay one tenth of that. We thanked him, shook his hand, and fled. He didn't seem to mind.

Other seemingly mandatory stops (it didn't occur to us to refuse these little shopping visits) included Mubarek's favorite ceramic merchant (the very best prices, he assured us), where we bought a beautiful *tajine,* a covered ceramic dish used to serve couscous and lamb stews; Mubarek's favorite spice merchant (herbs and potions to improve the taste of your dinner or the appearance of your skin); and another rug merchant, this one, according to Murbarek, much more reasonable.

Let's Make a Deal

Our host, a Berber, told us to call him Ali. He was dressed in full desert regalia, from head wrap to *burnous*. A large man with an almost cherubic face, Ali was full of charm, joking and teasing. He praised Flannery's beauty and commented on how much like her father she looked. Clever man. He asked Flannery if she would like to go to the desert with him. He said he would give me fifty camels. I insisted on no less than a hundred. He smiled and upped the ante to a hundred and fifty.

Then we were served tea and Ali taught us to say, "Put that one away" and "Put this one aside," though this time in both Arabic and Berber. We told him that we'd already experienced the full selection and could only consider a rug small enough to hang on the wall. His assistant brought out thirty to forty rugs. We put away thirty and put aside ten for bargaining. We chose a one by one and a half meters blue rug of desert silk (the threads of a cactus plant), handmade by people of the southern desert.

Ali insisted that I sit by him on the floor while we bargained. He wrote down a number and told me that I was to follow with a counter offer. It was, as Yogi Berra allegedly said, déjà vu all over again. He wrote down 9,680 *dirhams*—$968, only about $918 more than we hoped to pay. Write down 500 *dirhams*, Kay mouthed. Embarrassed to write a figure that low, I wrote down 1,000.

"You are being difficult," Ali said. "I will write down another number, then you must write a higher number."

"We simply can not go any higher," I said. "We don't have the money. We are but poor pensioners." For some reason I like that phrase. I stood, thinking that the transaction was over. No way was he going to accept one tenth of the original asking price.

"I accept," said Ali, and had our rug bagged.

That night we celebrated my birthday in an excellent, although almost empty, French restaurant. For whatever reason—perhaps because we were in a French restaurant, maybe because we were not in the medina—we were able to order wine. The service was as enjoyable as the meal.

The next day we returned to experience the square. At least as large as three soccer fields, this enormous bare space was surrounded on three sides by the *souks*, on the fourth by a small park and its horse carriage-lined entranceway. The square and all its action could be viewed from several second-floor and rooftop cafés.

During the afternoon, throngs of visitors, mostly Moroccans but with a goodly number of French, came to see the action: cobras swaying to the sound of the snake charmer's flutes and drums, animated storytellers surrounded by crowds of eager listeners, colorfully dressed water men from the desert, and monkey handlers willing to pose for photos—all for a price. We tried to take it all in from the edge of a rooftop terrace, but there was so much and the crowds too thick.

"There, there, look over there," we urged each other, tugging on a sleeve to demand attention. It was bigger than a three-ring circus. It was a ten-ring circus.

After a while we decided we had to see it at ground level and we came down and wandered along the edge of the square, dipping into the *souks* from time to time and waiting for evening. Around five the performers began to disappear, to be replaced by carts piled high with metal tables and chairs. Soon the square was occupied by dozens of open-air restaurants. Cooking fires were lit, tables covered and arranged in squares, cooks and waiters on the inside, chairs and long, backless benches lined along the outside. Soon the smell of grilling chickens and lamb filled the air. Lights were strung from pole to pole and flickered through the smoke that blanketed the scene.

As sunset approached, crowds of diners filled the tables, waiting in anticipation. Suddenly there came the call of the *muezzin* and the breaking of the day-long fast began in earnest. This was a dinner rush of monumental proportions, as every able-bodied man in Marrakech wanted his dinner at exactly the same time. As for ourselves, we had dinner in a very pleasant second-floor café overlooking the square. Our dinner was delicious. The view was unforgettable.

We took the overnight train back to Tangier. We'd gone by the train station and upgraded to a couchette the day before, and we had a compartment with four reasonably comfortable bunks to ourselves. The train left at nine. We got to sleep around eleven, after a couple of drinks and lots of laughs. We arrived in Tangier at seven in the morning, were on the ferry by eight, back in Spain for lunch, and home by late afternoon.

Our rug looked grand hanging on our living room wall. Flannery forgave me for asking only a hundred camels for her. Kay was extremely pleased with the camel-bone framed mirror she'd bought. And I'd had a memorable birthday dinner. And best of all, we didn't get robbed. We declared the trip a success.

Thanksgiving

It's Not Just about the Turkey

With the exception of the trip to Marrakech, our first weeks in Granada were focused on carving out a new life. In addition to outfitting the apartment and making regular trips to the police station, we'd been learning the city, walking, walking, and walking. I'd folded and unfolded our city map so many times it was beginning to fall apart. We left the apartment every day with map and list in hand and returned every afternoon leg weary and ready for siesta. We weren't thinking much about our previous lives in California and thus far nothing in Granada reminded us of it. We missed our family and our friends, but generally speaking, California was drifting further and further away. Our days and thoughts were filled with Granada.

Nothing, however, promotes nostalgia like a holiday, at least for those for whom the holidays hold fond memories. Our first reminder of home came in late November: Thanksgiving, the quintessential American holiday. Not only would Thanksgiving be our first holiday abroad, it would also be the first time in years that Kay, Flannery, and I would celebrate it together. Who knew when we'd be together for Thanksgiving again, so ignoring it was not an option. We didn't know any Americans, so we wouldn't be receiving any invitations. Flannery, to whom the holiday had grown in importance while living abroad, wanted to create a traditional meal. Kay was in agreement. As third cook in a two-cook kitchen, I thought it wise to go with the flow.

I confess that Thanksgiving is not my favorite meal, not even close. I like mashed potatoes, rice, green beans, and carrots, but I can easily live without candied sweet potatoes, cranberries, jellied or whole, dry turkey breast, stuffing (well, not too bad if the gravy's good), and pumpkin pie. It's a meal held together not by the thoughtful combinations of contrasts and complimentary textures, colors, and tastes, but by history and gravy. Is there another American meal that includes mashed potatoes, sweet potatoes, rice, stuffing, *and* rolls? And there's just too much of it. No matter how hard I tried to take moderate portions, no matter how carefully I arranged my plate, the result was always a tall, unmanageable pile of food.

This Thanksgiving would be unique. We were together, at least three of us. We were in Spain. And we were cooking in an apartment that had no oven. We'd decided to have chicken instead of turkey, but we had no idea how to cook it. No roast fowl, no gravy. And how about stuffing, dressing, or whatever you wanted to call it? Not an item likely to be found at the local market. Could we find cranberries? Green beans? Sweet pickles? The search for ingredients promised to be as big a challenge as the cooking.

There were no Idaho potatoes in Spain. There is no Idaho in Spain. What they did have were the smoothest, tastiest potatoes, similar to Yukon Gold, delicious mashed or fried, though not as good for baking. Sweet potatoes were readily available, as well as green beans. Flannery found a recipe for stuffing on the Internet, so we were almost there. Eagle eye that she is, she also found both cranberries and sweet pickles at the upscale food market in El Corte Inglés.

The primary challenge remained the bird. We'd bought a smallish, medium-powered microwave. There was an illustration on the door showing a chicken being cooked inside, which implied that it could be done. What we didn't know was what it would taste like. And there was only one way to find out. By Wednesday all the supplies were laid in, champagne included, champagne being necessary for either success or failure.

Wallowing in the Glow

To me, the most memorable part of our Thanksgiving Day was an afternoon walk. The day was clear and chilly, as the day should be. There was, of course, no indication whatsoever that it was Thanksgiving; it was just another Thursday in Spain. Not one person on the street seemed to know that this was the only day of the year that tens of millions of Americans, sitting at millions of tables all over the world, ate the same meal. There's no other meal like it. Think of it. Americans across the globe—businessmen in Hong Kong, servicemen in Iraq, diplomats in France, students in Rome, basketball players in Greece, cruise ship passengers in the Caribbean, drug dealers in the South American jungles—were filling their plates with turkey, dressing, cranberry sauce, mashed potatoes, gravy, etc., etc.

We walked through Plaza Bib-Rambla and the shopping area and past the post office and down the wide tree-lined pedestrian *paseo* we called The Ramblas to the river, then turned and headed back. We stopped at our winter headquarters and took a table upstairs. We ordered wine. I don't remember now what the *tapas* was, but they were always good there. What I do remember very clearly was an overwhelmed feeling of well-being. I was tremendously happy. We'd been in Granada for only six weeks and life was proving to be even better than I could have dreamed. We were celebrating our first holiday together. The plan had worked. I was so full of the moment that I wanted to order another round of wine, enjoy a second *tapa*, and wallow in the glow. My dear ladies, knowing the tasks that awaited them, and knowing that another glass of wine would certainly diminish what little usefulness I might offer, convinced me that the glow was transportable, so home we went.

The dinner was, though not a total culinary success, a happy occasion. The table was beautifully set, the candles lit, the music carefully selected. The music was my job. Our microwaved chicken was, if not delectable, enjoyable, and even provided enough drippings for gravy. Flannery's deviled eggs were better than ever, her stuffing surprisingly good, the potatoes and vegetables superb. Flann made a flan for dessert. Afterward we flopped on the couches, full and reasonably pleased with ourselves.

The Spanish Inquisition-Part 3

The Marathon Continues

On October 16, at the conclusion of our last visit to the police station, we'd been told that in about thirty days we would receive letters instructing us to come in for our permits. Two certified letters, one for me and one for Kay, arrived the day after we returned from Morocco. We presented our passports to the postman and signed the forms. According to the letter, we were to return to the police station no sooner than fifteen days and no later than thirty days. We would need two photocopies of each letter and three photos apiece, our third set since beginning the process. We marked the date on the calendar.

Our Fourth Visit to the Police Station

On December second, seventeen days after receiving our letters, we went to the police station and waited in line at the window where we'd submitted our papers six weeks earlier. The wait was a relatively short fifteen minutes. First, the friendly lady informed us, we were in the wrong line. Second, we had come too early and our information was not yet in the computer. The letter, she pointed out, instructed us to come to the police station not less than fifteen days from the day we *received* the letter, not from the date *on* the letter. Come back next week to the other window.

I took deep breaths. I tried visualization, first of a peaceful meadow, then a burbling brook. When that didn't work, I decided that stronger measure were merited: a cold beer and *tapas* in the sun. It wasn't until the cold beer and *tapas* were actually in hand that I relaxed.

Our Fifth Visit to the Police Station

Due to another four-day holiday, it was nine days before we returned to the police station. The line reached across the courtyard to the entrance. It took one hour for us to reach the window. "You're still too early," the clerk informed us, "your information isn't in the computer yet." But, perhaps seeing an expression of desperation and despair on my face, she said she would give us the tax forms anyway. It seems there was a fee, or tax, on the issuance of a permit. We were to take the forms to any bank, pay the tax, and return with the stamped and signed forms the end of the following week. We were flying to Munich the next day to retrieve the remainder of Flannery's possessions and to see the Christmas markets, so waiting still another week worked out fine.

Even as I reminded myself that there was no reason to think that we wouldn't get our resident permits, I couldn't ignore what was becoming increasingly obvious: the Spanish bureaucracy was not designed to make this process easy. It could even be said that they were making it as difficult as possible. But why? We were not taking anyone's job; we were not depending upon the Spanish health care system; we were bringing into the economy thousands of American dollars. Why weren't we being embraced?

The following Tuesday, the day after our return from Munich, we went to a nearby bank to pay the tax.

"She didn't say how much the tax is, did she?" I asked as we walked toward the commercial district.

Neither Kay nor Flannery remembered any mention of the amount.

"We have no idea what it is," I said. "It could be €100 each. €200 each, for all we know."

Flannery shrugged.

"It couldn't be that much," Kay said.

"We paid $100 each in San Francisco, and we didn't even get a real visa. It could be €500 for a real visa."

"Relax," they shouted at me.

At the bank we waited in still another line. The man took our forms and looked them over. The tax was €6,31 each, less than $7.50. It was hard to ignore the shrugs and rolling eyes of my wife and daughter. But I tried. The man stamped our forms and instructed us to take the two white copies, along with two photocopies of each, to the police station. The blue carbons were for us.

Our Sixth Visit to the Police Station

We returned to the police station on a rainy Thursday morning a week before Christmas. Expectations were high. This could be the day that we actually received our resident permits. The champagne was in the fridge. The signs were auspicious: there was no line, and the lady at the window awaited us with a smile. We gave her the forms. "But where," she asked, "are your blue copies?" She needed the blue copies, not the originals, which were for us. Having been misinformed that the blue copies were ours, Kay had left them at home. Home she scurried, returning exactly eighteen minutes later. We turned in the blue copies, not the pink ones as we'd been instructed by the man at the bank, two photos each, not three, signed the forms, and had our fingerprints taken.

We waited breathlessly. Had the moment finally arrived? Our journey over? The long sought-for prize within our grasps?

We were then given a receipt. The receipt contained the following instructions: Come to window four at the police station with this receipt not more than thirty days from today to receive your foreigner's identification card/residency permit.

The champagne would remain on hold.

The Streets of Granada 2: Café Afternoons

Of Air Kisses and Strolling Minstrels

Once we'd decided that Spain would be our destination, we began reading about our new home. Rick Steve said in his guide to Spain, "People work to live, not vice versa. Their focus is on their friends and family. In fact, the siesta is not so much naptime as it is the opportunity for everyone to shut down their harried public life and enjoy good food and the comfort of loved ones. Nighttime is for socializing, whether it's cruising the streets or watching the soccer game on TV in a crowded bar. Spaniards eat to live, not vice versa."

Another particularly informative book about modern Spain is *The New Spaniards*. According to its author, John Hooper, "No other people I have ever encountered put as much effort as the Spanish into having a good time. Whatever its political and economic problems, their country is an immensely entertaining place."

A great deal of this "having a good time" takes place in public places: plazas, streets, and cafés. *Granadinos* love being out and about, and on sunny days the cafés are full; streams of walkers fill the plazas, sidewalks, and pedestrian lanes; and every bench in every plaza is occupied.

In Spain, people stroll, particularly in the late afternoon and early evening, when the streets come back to life after siesta, and on

Sundays before and after a mid-afternoon lunch. This strolling doesn't appear to be a nonchalant, spontaneous activity. No, a proper Spanish stroll, whether down the block, around the local plaza, or through the shopping streets, requires more than a little preparation. Looking good is important. Both Kay and Flannery assured me that a considerable amount of mirror time takes place before a public appearance. Young people are more casual, as they were everywhere, but it was a studied casualness, a sort of funky chic, a laid-back carelessness belied by the excellent application of makeup. Those a little older, say in their thirties and forties, tend to dress very stylishly, while those over fifty dress as if they were going to the theater. Well, in a way they are, but they're the ones on stage. Everyone, young and old, walks arm in arm, hailing friends and acquaintances across the street with shouts and waves. They stand in clusters, smiling, chatting, kissing cheeks, and blocking the sidewalk.

All this promenading and greeting and looking good is accompanied by a soundtrack provided by street musicians. It makes for a wonderful show. And the best place to take it all in is an outdoor café. People watching from a front-row café seat, a glass of beer or wine and *tapas* on the table, is without doubt one of the most enjoyable—and certainly one of the most inexpensive—of life's pleasures.

Wherever there's space enough for three or more tables, there's an outdoor café. The narrow streets and winding lanes of Granada's older neighborhoods rarely meet at right angles, leaving small, oddly shaped intersections. Rarely do they go empty.

Although many cafés put out their tables only when the weather was mild, which is to say dry and over 40° F, those in the major plazas have theirs out almost every day. One sunny, relatively mild January Sunday afternoon about three, Kay and I walked the upper Albaicín in search of a table in the sunshine. There are six plazas in the Albaicín *alto,* with a total of twelve outdoor cafés. I counted. Every table was occupied. Every one.

On rainy days awnings are pulled out over the tables, and umbrellas are erected. In historic Plaza Bib-Rambla, most of the cafés have their own awning-covered structure, all substantial, some quite ornate, which could be completely enclosed during chilly weather. A few even have heaters inside. The structures are seasonal, going up in the fall and disappearing in the spring.

Some outdoor cafés are seasonal; those that have no inside dining area simply close their doors for the winter. Here today, and suddenly, one cold rainy day in December, gone. I couldn't help but imagine that all over Granada thousands of tables and umbrellas and tens of thousands of chairs were stacked away under stairways, behind counters, and in storage rooms in anticipation of spring, when, on the first warm weekend, the entire city blossomed into an enormous outdoor café.

This outdoor blossoming happened in the most surprising places. One of the delights of walking the streets of Granada in the spring was discovering a café where the day before there'd been nothing. What yesterday was empty space—a wide section of the sidewalk, the corner of a small neighborhood plaza, the area behind a fountain, along the wall of a wide stone stairway up the hillside—now held several tables, each occupied by people enjoying a glass of beer and a *tapa*. It seemed as if it had always been there. One small restaurant in our neighborhood, one we'd barely noticed, had commandeered two parking places, erected a curb-high metal platform with a railing, and furnished the space with a half dozen tables, chairs, and umbrellas. Behold! Instant outdoor café. Some of these seasonal curbside-dining areas had no apparent source of food and drink. Only by watching the waiters as they raced to and fro did we discover that the food was coming from a café around the corner or through a door down the street.

Enough Kisses for Everyone

Watching the Spanish greet each other is a treat. The standard greeting in Spain is the double air kiss, one on each cheek, right cheek first. Sometimes the cheeks touched, sometimes not. There was also real cheek kissing, lips to cheek, but that was, I think, primarily between family and close friends. Even men, who generally shake hands, sometimes exchanged real kisses, though I'm guessing that they're related. Everyone else received an air kiss. When there are three couples, or two couples with children, this exchanging of kisses took awhile. Perhaps sweetest of all was watching the kids—eight, ten, twelve, fourteen years old, boys as well as girls—exchanging air kisses.

The Spanish don't stop at kissing. There's lots of touching. They enjoy physical contact. Women of all ages walk arm in arm, sometimes hand in hand. It's the exception to see two or three girls or young women walking together and not touching. Sons and daughters walked hand in hand with their parents and grandparents. Older couples walked along holding hands. Parents and relatives were abundant with their affections with children. They hugged them, squeezed their cheeks between their hands as they kissed them, tousled their hair, and then bent to kiss them again. The children didn't seem to mind, often turning their faces up for more. When two men meet on the street, they exchange a warm handshake, a slap on the back, perhaps a hug, and then they talk. And as they talk, there is a constant touching, a hand resting on a shoulder, a patting of the other's arm, fingers pressed against the other's chest, perhaps to make a point. When they parted, the handshake/back slap/hug is repeated.

It's catching, this physical contact. Kay and Flannery walked arm in arm almost all the time. Flannery and I often walked arm in arm, as did Kay and I. What a nice feeling.

One aspect that took some getting used to was physical proximity. I know that every culture has its own sense of private space. I've read, and observation supports this theory, that Americans require more personal space than most cultures. We feel uncomfortable when people stand just an inch or two closer than we're accustomed to as they talk to us, or when people we don't know very well touch us. I'm still not completely at ease with having my American space infringed upon, but I have overcome the impulse to step back.

Now, back to the soundtrack. Strolling minstrels—which sounds so much better than begging musicians—are as ubiquitous in Granada as, well, cafés. As a result, we heard a good deal of free music—free if you don't put anything in the hat—not only while sitting in a café but while passing through the plazas or just walking down the street. On a warm day, during the midday dining hours, say one to four, any outdoor café with five or more tables featured constantly changing entertainment. The musicians were reasonably accomplished and never overbearing, rarely playing more than three songs before moving on, and seemed to be quite happy with any coins you tossed in the hat. A large plaza might have two musical offerings, one at each end. The usual procedure was for a group to play one end of the plaza, then the other, before moving on to another location. Anyone spending an afternoon at one café would hear a lot of different music. Although most of the entertainers were Spanish, there was a sizable contingent from Eastern Europe, particularly, for reasons I've been unable to discover, the Czech Republic. The usual Czech group was composed of sax and/or clarinet, a guitar or two, and a tambourine. Their music sounded like a mix of folk music, Jewish klezmer, and swing. Our favorite group was composed of seven Danes and an Italian who played, in the true spirit of international music, Romanian folk songs.

Not all the music took place around cafés. Many played on the street. During our daily walks throughout the city, we passed through most downtown plazas and pedestrian streets several times a week. Some entertainers we saw week after week, others played for a few weeks and then suddenly disappeared, possibly off to another city and a new audience. There were a number of regulars: a Chinese man who played a stringed Chinese folk instrument; a teenager who played a small xylophone-like instrument with mallets; a group of Peruvians in full regalia who performed Andean flute music; a harpist and a handful of accordion players, one of whom couldn't have been ten. There was a singing guitarist who wore a funny turned down hat and specialized in Beatles songs; he seemed to know only three, "Norwegian Wood" being his favorite. There was a perky young woman, accompanied by a guitarist, who sang American jazz/pop songs in an almost perfect American accent. She even scatted pretty well. One day we came across a jazz duo playing inside one of the old city gates in the Albaicín. The domed, twenty-five-foot ceiling of the L-shaped gate produced a wonderful, rich sound. The saxophonist was Irish, the bassist German.

Street entertainment was not limited to music. There were, as there are in all cities, jugglers, mimes, clowns, and human statues, some excellent, some sadly desperate. The most original statue was a young man who wore a swimsuit, facemask, fins, snorkel, and an inflatable kiddy inner tube around his waist. Beside him was a small plastic child's wadding pool, little more than two feet across. Put a coin in the cup and he came to life, jumped into the pool where he stomped and splashed and cavorted like a kid for about ten seconds, then he stepped back out of the pool and refroze.

There was music going on somewhere every night—flyers and posters papered the walls—but we had a hard time adapting to Spanish time. Lunch takes place between two and four, dinner nine thirty or later, but nightlife, now that's really late. According to the flyers, the music was usually scheduled to begin at half past ten. In Spanish time, that's eleven o'clock. Or later. At the jazz/flamenco club just off Elvira—where I'd envisioned myself hanging out a night or two a week—shows began at midnight, which meant that the evening's entertainment would actually begin tomorrow. This cellar club was far too smoky for Kay to even consider. Too late, too smoky, it was enough to make a person feel old. If only we had retired in our thirties.

Our first night on the town we ventured out to hear a flamenco guitarist play at a Moroccan teahouse in the neighborhood. The poster said that the music would begin at ten. We arrived at 9:45, took a perfect table, moved once because of smoke, and then waited for an hour. At 10:45 people began streaming in. The music began around eleven.

The Wonders of Beauty

Almost every day in Granada was a café afternoon. And each café afternoon was enjoyable in its own way. But two remain particularly memorable. One took place in one of our favorite café areas: the Paseo de los Tristes, the broad esplanade between the street and the low wall along the River Darro. On the other side of the river, the Alhambra stretched along the ridge high above. At least six cafés on the street used the esplanade as their outdoor dining area. Each café's chairs and tables were different colors or styles, so there was never any doubt which café you were patronizing. The waiters had to cross the sidewalk, a busy one-way street, and then another sidewalk in order to deliver food and drinks to the tables and to return dirty dishes. We spent many afternoons in the cafés there and we never saw a waiter struck by a vehicle or stumble over the curb, though we did see a few dishes hit the pavement. Each café had its virtues and shortcomings: great *tapas,* poor service, abbreviated *tapa*-serving hours; some provided longer hours in the sun, while others slipped into the shade as the sun moved behind the Alhambra.

The spring day was sunny and warm. We were multi-tasking, which meant reading the newspaper, watching passersby, sipping our beers, and nibbling *tapas* as the same time. I watched as a family group of at least eight moved from café to café in search of two or more empty adjoining tables. Kay drew my attention to a young couple sitting on the river wall; they had been kissing without breaking lip contact for at least ten minutes, she told me. At a nearby table, an *ensalata mixta* and basket of bread was delivered to two extremely well dressed ladies. The salad was huge, and I watched as one of the ladies tossed and divided the lettuce, tomato, shredded carrot and beets, sliced boiled eggs, and chunks of tuna. Kay pointed out how far the shadows cast by the towers of the Alhambra had moved since we'd arrived. She predicted that the shadows would reach our table in less than an hour. Three young women, possibly university students, took a table at the next café. Two of them were beautiful. The third was breathtaking. I gulped my beer and tried to concentrate on the waiters and wondered if this might be the day one of them would be run over.

"Gorgeous, isn't she?" Kay asked and winked. I nodded, thankful that such wonders existed, both my lovely, loving wife and the presence of such beauty in the world. It felt good to be alive.

The music from the other end of the esplanade had stopped and I could see the musicians passing the hat before moving to our end, where they selected a spot from which they could sing to the largest number of tables, and began. I'd never heard anything like it. There were three men, not that young, maybe thirty. One played a guitar, another a stringed instrument resembling a lute, while the third pounded a very large tambourine. The beat was very strong and they sang/chanted at the top of their voices. The music sounded very old.

After they'd played three songs, they passed among the tables with upturned hats. When one of the men reached our table, I asked him if he spoke any English, as my limited Spanish was geared more to asking for the check than inquiring about the origins of music, which is what I wanted to know.

The musicians spoke some English, but the accent was definitely not Spanish. They'd been playing thirteenth century Italian tarantellas, he told me.

Well, of course, I thought. *What else?*

As we waited for our second beer and *tapa,* a young, bearded guitarist replaced the tarantella chanters. Before the guitarist had a chance to begin, a *Gitano* sitting two tables away from us asked to borrow his guitar, then commenced to play Flamenco. He was very good. The guitarist exchanged a few comments with the *Gitano,* retrieved his guitar, and played a few Flamenco licks himself. Then, facing the tables, he sang an American pop song, followed by Ellington's "Take the A Train," and a blues piece. He was talented and certainly versatile.

When he came by with his hat, I asked him if he spoke English. He sounded American when he sang, but you never know. So many of the street musicians learn American and English songs phonetically, singing them exactly like the record, but speak little, if any, English. As it turned out, the guitarist was from Alaska and living in Granada in order to study Flamenco guitar. He was the only American we ever heard playing in Granada.

Giving in to the Day

Another memorable café afternoon took place in February, only months after our arrival and during the second week of our Spanish lessons. Our class that week ran from ten to noon, two hours that often felt like four. When we left our apartment that morning for the short walk to class, the temperature was, according to our thermometer, 5° C, or 41° F. There was a light breeze, so it was chilly. I wore a T-shirt, flannel shirt, sweater vest, and jacket. Kay was dressed similarly and wore a scarf. The sky was a cloudless deep blue.

We emerged at noon to a considerably warmer day, the first warm day in a week. There was no question that we would lunch outside. We decided to eat at a café located in the upper Albaicín in a small plaza that was always sunny. We stopped for a newspaper and headed up the hill.

When we reached the café a little before one, only a few tables were occupied, primarily by tourists, as the Spanish generally don't show up till two. We took a table in the sun and ordered two beers. Our *tapas* were two slices of Spanish tortilla (egg and potato pie) plus a mound of olives and pickled vegetables. We removed our jackets, and I moved to the other side of the table to avoid the glare of the bright sun.

We finished our beer and *tapas* and ordered lunch. We'd eaten here before and knew what we liked. Kay ordered fried calamari and I the *boquerones*, fried fresh anchovies. Both meal included a pile of French fries, a large salad and basket of fresh bread, all for only €6 each. Of course, we had a second beer.

The sun grew stronger and we shed our sweaters. The café had filled and more tables were set up. A guitar player sang. There was so much food that neither of us had been able to finish our lunch. Although we had our materials, we knew that studying Spanish was out of the question. Instead, we looked around us at the setting: a small plaza behind a very old church, another café just over the railing, tourists and craft sellers milling about in the Mirador San Nicolás, and beyond that, a view of the Alhambra in the distance. We felt the warm sun on our faces. We looked at each other across the table and shrugged. What choice did we have? With a deep sigh, we gave in to the day. We ordered another beer. Our table was cleared. We read the *Tribune* in the warm sun. We watched as the waiters put out even more tables. In Spain, as in most of Europe, you are not rushed from your table; it is yours as long as you wish.

We finished our beers around three, and then slowly made our way back down the hill. At the apartment we fell onto our couches and were soon asleep. It had been a splendid day.

No Place Like Home for the Holidays

Especially When You Aren't There

Flannery had accumulated more during the two years she'd lived in Munich than she'd been able to bring with her to Granada. That three people can transport three times as much baggage as one provided an excellent excuse for a trip to Munich. Whatever she couldn't take with her to San Francisco in January, Kay and I would store and bring with us when we visited. On December 10, we bused to Malaga on the coast, then flew to Munich. Kay and I were particularly excited about seeing the *kriskindlmarkts*, Munich's famous Christmas markets. We were also looking forward to experiencing winter in Germany and meeting Flannery's friends.

Flannery, who stayed with friends, found a modest, though very satisfactory, hotel for us only a fifteen-minute walk from Marienplatz, the central historic district. Although we'd lived in Granada for only two months, the differences between life in Spain and life in Germany—perhaps I should say between Granada and Munich—was readily apparent.

Let us begin with breakfast. In Spain, the usual breakfast consists of a *tostada*, a sliced toasted roll, topped with either olive oil, tomato sauce, cheese, or butter and jam, along with coffee and juice. Not so in Germany, as we found out our first morning at the hotel.

The receptionist, in softly accented English (this is a second difference, as many Germans, at least in Munich, spoke English, while very few *Granadinos* did) directed us to the dining room. Breakfast, she informed us, was included. We took a table and looked around. On one table there was a display of cold cuts and cheeses, at least four of each, along with a selection of rolls, buns, muffins, toast and bread. A second table held containers of cereal, jugs of milk and juices, plus bowls of fruit and yogurt. A row of hot chafing dishes heaped with bacon, sausage, ham, and eggs—scrambled, boiled, or poached—lined a third table. A fourth table in the corner held an enormous coffee urn, carafes of hot water, a basket of teas, and a bottle of prosecco, a light, Italian sparkling wine.

I poured a cup of coffee and Kay made tea, which we took back to our table along with juice, toast, a boiled egg, and bacon. We watched as our fellow diners, who were all Germans, returned to the buffet, filled a plate from one of the tables, devoured it all, then headed for the next table, where they repeated the process. As best I could tell, the choice was not what to eat but how much. We watched as the bottle of prosecco was replaced twice. It was eight thirty.

What the hell, we agreed, when in Munich, so back to the buffet we went, only this time we returned to our table loaded with scrambled eggs, sausage, croissants, fruit, and glasses of prosecco. By the time we finished we felt very full and very, very decadent. The thought of eating again before tomorrow's breakfast was beyond imagining.

Another difference, though not a surprising one, was the weather. Granada can be quite chilly on winter mornings, but Munich was something different. It was a cold that made me acutely aware of those parts of my body not protected, like my ears and nose. I wondered if my eyelashes would break. But we were here to see the Christmas markets and that's what we were going to do, no matter how cold it was. Eyelashes will probably grow back, though I wasn't too sure about ears. It occurred to me that it would be impossible to freeze with that much food in your body, which led to the following revelation: the prodigious breakfast I had just witnessed being consumed was to Germans body-warming fuel. Though our fueling effort had been piddling, at least by German standards, we felt ready to confront the cold. Protected by hats, gloves, scarves, the heaviest coats we owned (which weren't very heavy), and 1,800 calories, we headed for Marienplatz, where we were to meet Flannery.

Although many districts in Munich have their own Christmas markets, each with its own distinct character, the city's main Christmas market was on Marienplatz, the square in front of City Hall in the heart of the pedestrian shopping zone. A one-hundred-foot tree with two thousand five hundred lights towered over the market. There were, our pamphlet said, more than one hundred forty booths, most selling ornaments and decorations. We wandered from booth to booth while waiting for Flannery. There were so many exquisite ornaments, many handmade, that the thought of decorating a tree with factory-made balls and tinsel seemed almost shameful.

Another Cup of Antifreeze, Please

"Have you had any *gluhwein* yet?" Flannery asked when we met at the fountain.

Kay and I looked at each other. We'd washed down our breakfast banquet with prosecco only three hours before. Were our bodies capable of additional morning imbibing?

"We though we'd wait till noon," I said.

"Twenty minutes," Flannery replied.

Gluhwein, pronounced "glue vine," is a hot, spicy mulled wine. In Marienplatz alone, there were at least a dozen stands selling *gluhwein*, along with sausages and fried potato pancakes. The lines leading to the stands wound through tall, chest-high tables, around which groups gathered with cups of *gluhwein* and plates of sausages. Many drank from personal *gluhwein* cups, just as some patrons bring their own beer steins to the beer halls. We were surprised how many took their morning *gluhwein* with a shot of brandy or rum. The temperature, which that day hovered around -7° C, or 20° F, wasn't particularly cold for Munich, but I don't think that colder weather would have made any difference to the holiday merrymakers. Eating a German breakfast, chased by a glass or two of prosecco, followed by a plate of sausages and potato pancakes, washed down by a few cups of brandy-laced *gluhwein*, would certainly fortify one against winter's harshest assaults.

We hadn't come all this way just to observe Christmas in Munich; we wanted to experience it, so we joined the line to the *gluhwein* stand. Flannery ordered three cups and paid the deposit on the cups, and there we stood, looking up at historic city hall through the fog of our breaths, sipping the hot wine mixture along with a throng of Germans. I felt only one sausage away from removing my coat. Properly warmed, we browsed a bit more and bought a couple of lovely, modestly priced ornaments.

Over the next three days, we visited a market that specialized in blown glass items, wooden toys, and nativity scenes; one that featured arts, crafts, and live music; and one in the English Gardens known for porcelain, china dolls, marionettes, and antiques. At every market the longest lines were those at the *gluhwein* stands. At the market on the Oktoberfest site, we sipped hot *gluhwein* while perched on tall stools outside the tents. Shivering in the cold, we realized that we'd allowed that day's caloric intake to fall under three thousand and pledged to do better.

The German breakfast was not the only meal with antifreeze properties. Flannery and her friends took us to a restaurant where the schnitzel portions literally covered the plate and the mound of fried potatoes underneath. Our efforts to fortify ourselves against the cold continued; we ate sausages, roast pork, dumplings, and sauerkraut and drank dark beer in restaurants patronized by Germans wearing lederhosen and mountaineer hats, where old men, beer steins held high, swayed back and forth as they sang along with an oompah band. It struck me that Bavaria was to Germany what Andalucía was to Spain: that picturesque area that contained the symbols the greater world identified with the entire country. Germany was no more about lederhosen than Spain was about Flamenco music.

Four days, twelve meals, and approximately twelve thousand calories later, we arose early in the morning, surprised that we were still able to do so, lugged our bags and Flannery's excess possessions down to the lobby, and waited to be picked up. Flannery and her friend Svenya were to pick us up at six thirty, which was, fortunately for us, half an hour before breakfast was served. They arrived on time and we waddled to the car. It was dark, cold, and rainy. A few hours later we landed in sunny, warm Malaga, and bused home to a cool, but not cold, Granada. For the first time we used the phrase *going home.*

That very night we attended a performance of *Messiah*. Back in November, we'd seen posters announcing a "sing-along" performance of *Messiah*. We'd rushed to the box office to find that the only tickets remaining were behind the orchestra. But the price was right and we'd snapped them up. Having gotten home by lunch, we'd had time to rest and have dinner before walking up the hill to the Manuel de Falla Auditorium, which is located on the hill by the Alhambra. It was wonderful.

The following day was bright and sunny, so off we went, as we did every day it wasn't raining, to walk the city, run errands, and continue our search for the perfect *tapas*. As usual the antique dealers lounged on the sidewalks in front of their stores. When they saw us coming, they smiled and nodded before we could get our *buenos dias* out. The merchant two doors down broke into a huge smile when he saw us and waved as if we were old friends. Our persistent American friendliness had paid off.

Christmas Balancing Act

Christmas presented the same dilemma that Thanksgiving had: to what extent should we try to recreate our traditional holiday. Both Kay and Flannery were leaning toward trying to make Christmas as traditional as possible. While I didn't have strong feelings one way or another, I did know that balancing expectations and reality was important. We had more than a few discussions about how we would celebrate the holiday and eventually agreed on the following guidelines.

The first thing we decided was to tone down the gift exchange. Flannery didn't have a lot of money and what she had she needed to get reestablished in San Francisco. So our gift giving would be modest but thoughtful. Besides, she already had more stuff than she could carry back to California, so any gifts would have to pass the portability test.

We agreed that there would be a Christmas card with a photo. Every year we'd included a family photo in our Christmas card, especially those we sent to friends and relatives we didn't see very often. This year's photo would be more important than ever. Look! Here we are, living in Granada! The day before Thanksgiving, we'd had a waiter take our photo while sitting in one of our favorite outdoor cafés. It had been a beautiful, sunny day. We were in shirtsleeves and sunglasses, our table covered with fried calamari, fried potatoes, salad, and tall glasses of beer. It was the perfect holiday photograph: three happy people in Spain.

Putting up a Christmas tree was a challenge. As far as we could determine, there were no Christmas tree farms around Granada. Other than olives trees, of which there were millions, there weren't many trees of any kind. Although streets in the shopping districts were decorated, and many of the store windows, Christmas trees as such did not seem to be an important expression of the holiday; we saw very few in the windows of homes. The absence of trees, as well as Santa, makes sense, when you think about it. We were in Spain, where gifts are delivered in January by the Three Kings on camelback. There was only one solution: a Christmas tree by declaration. If we declared it a Christmas tree, it was a Christmas tree.

Kay and Flannery bought a small spruce about two feet tall, and decorated it with one string of tiny lights and tiny red balls, and placed it on a small, round table on a carefully arranged white towel. They placed the tree before the window so it could be seen from the street. It was the only tree on Calle Elvira. The ornaments we'd bought in Munich would have dwarfed our small tree, so we hung them in the window.

We'd always hung stockings, stockings large enough to fit a giant, and stuffed with everything from ChapStick to mints, tins of anchovies, and smoked oysters, to miniatures of Jack Daniels. We decided that we could live without stockings. Kay, however, later decided that she could not live without doing a stocking for Flannery. Which she did, on the sly, name sewn on and filled to the brim. Flannery, for her part, decided to create an Advent Calendar. She tied red and green paper napkins into small pouches, strung them together with a long ribbon, and filled them with small candies and treats. She attached this to the shelving along the wall behind the dining table, and we opened one every day.

There had to be Christmas music. We bought two holiday CDs, one by Bing Crosby and one with medleys of familiar Christmas songs played in a ricky-ticky style by what sounded like a mad chipmunk on a synthesizer. It was so awful it was funny.

There would be no entertaining. We'd always thrown two or three Christmas dinner parties. Setting the table with Spode Christmas china and glassware, holiday tablecloth, napkins, and candles was as much a part of our tradition as decorating the tree. Alas. The Spode was in storage, and we had no one to invite. We would entertain each other.

On Christmas Eve, weather permitting, we'd taken a late afternoon walk. This was the easiest tradition to duplicate. A walk is a walk. We bundled up and walked through the city admiring the overhead decorations, then hurried home for our Christmas Eve supper.

Every Christmas morning Kay prepared ham biscuits (home made biscuits, sliced, buttered, and filled with thin slices of fried salt-cured North Carolina country ham) along with mimosas (champagne and orange juice). We had no oven to bake biscuits and Kay did not care much for *jamón* Serrano, Spain's nearest equivalent to country ham, so we settled for store-bought rolls and baked ham.

On Christmas morning we opened gifts, ate ham biscuits, drank mimosas, and listened, one time too many, to Bing Crosby sing "White Christmas." The little tree twinkled by the window. Gift wrap and ribbons fell from the coffee table. It was wonderful being together. But in spite of our best efforts, it just wasn't the same. Kay wore her best smiling face, but she wasn't fooling anyone.

We weren't gloomy or depressed. We'd enjoyed the holiday together. But we hadn't solved the problem of elevated expectations, which seemed to exaggerate every difference. The memories of those warm, wonderful Christmases back in California were too strong. It was a nice Christmas; it just wasn't the Christmas that Kay had hoped for. There was no way to compensate for the lack of friends to visit, parties, and, especially for Kay, kids.

Fortunately, we didn't have time to dwell on it, because one of Flannery's very best friends was joining us for New Year's. Flannery had met Martin, who was German, while living in Santiago, Chile, and had moved to Munich at Martin's urging. Kay and I had met Martin in Santiago and had renewed our friendship during our visits to Munich to see Flannery.

New Year's Eve itself was quite an affair. The main event took place in Plaza Carmen in front of City Hall. There was a bandstand and band; small stands selling splits of champagne (imagine that in the States); people handing out bags containing hats, noise makers, streamers, confetti, and small plastic cups containing the traditional twelve grapes. According to Spanish tradition, eating one grape along with each toll of the bell ringing in the new year brought good luck. We stood in the cold, packed in by the crowd, wore our hats, blew our noisemakers, and drank the champagne we'd brought with us. At twelve, we watched as local dignitaries standing on the balconies of city hall led the crowd in the eating of the grapes. Then people cheered and sprayed champagne on each other.

Flannery and Martin had met a group of Germans in the plaza and followed them to a party. Kay and I made our way back home through crowded streets. Other than a few officers diverting traffic (not even the buses were allowed on the downtown streets that night), there had been no police presence and no rowdiness or violence, just a noisy throng of very merry merrymakers.

Flannery spent the days after Martin's departure making arrangements for her new life in San Francisco. Although she'd completed much of the paperwork necessary for entrance into graduate school at San Francisco State, there were still a few loose ends dangling. Getting everything done from Spain wasn't easy, even using the Internet. She had arranged to move into an apartment in the city with an old friend, so at least she had somewhere to live.

On January 10, Flannery, with as many bags as allowable, left Granada for San Francisco. Our three months together had been happier than we had any right to expect it to be. Three months is a long time to spend together, particularly when our entire social world consisted of each other. Not that there wasn't a bit of friction from time to time. It was, I believe, more difficult for Flannery than us. Who could she complain to about her parents, her overly sensitive mother and sometimes-grumpy father? Kay and I were building a life that would not be hers. Making a life in a foreign country was, however new to us, old hat to her.

It had been, we agreed, a win-win situation. Without her help, arranging an apartment and getting our permits would have been so much more difficult. As for Flannery, living in Granada for three months, with side trips to Marrakech and Munich, having the time to read and relax, had been an enjoyable interlude before the grind of putting herself through graduate school.

We'd always been close. Now we were even closer.

The Spanish Inquisition–Part 4

Ever Hopeful, We Press On

Our Seventh Visit to the Police Station

On January 9, twenty days after being told to return to the police station no more than thirty days later, and the day before Flannery's departure, we presented ourselves at window four. We'd waited as long as we could, not wanting to be too early, but we wanted Flannery with us. If our visas were not waiting—there had been several holidays over the past eighteen days—we wanted to be sure that we understood what, if anything, we would have to do, knowing we would have to do it without Flannery.

We handed the clerk the receipts, as we'd been instructed. He looked through the drawer. There were no permits with our names on them. Then he looked at the computer. Everything seemed to be in order. Which was a relief. But we were too early. The actual cards hadn't arrived yet. Come back next Thursday with your receipts, the man said. We decided to wait until the Monday after that.

The next day we put Flannery on the bus to Malaga, where she would spend the night before catching her plane to Frankfurt, then on to California. Sadly, she would not be with us to celebrate reaching the end of our long pilgrimage.

Our Eighth Visit to the Police Station

At eleven o'clock, Monday morning, January 18, we delivered ourselves to the police station. Wrapped in nonchalance, Kay swaggered into the station exuding an air of sure victory. I expected to be arrested. The line was only six people long. The lady at the window wore a broad smile. Each transaction before our turn took no more than a few minutes. We reached the window in fifteen minutes. It was obviously a trap.

I handed the smiling lady our receipts. Kay stood with passports in hand. The lady asked for our cards. But we didn't have any cards, only these receipts. She asked again. No one had said anything about cards. I waited for hands to grasp my arms and drag me down the basement stairs. Then Kay realized that she was asking for our old cards.

"*Tarjeta primera*," Kay said. These were our first cards. Ah, the lady smiled. She quickly looked through a drawer of cards, then pulled ours out. Each *Permiso de Residencia* was the size of a driver's license and laminated.

"William," she said, using my first name, "and Kay." She lay the long-sought for prizes before us. Our pilgrimage was over.

"*Muchas gracias*," we said at least four times each.

We examined our cards carefully before leaving the window. The photos were of us. The names were ours. The address was correct. The expiration date was November 19, 2004. We were legal for ten months, at which time we would begin again. But November was a long time away, and we were only thinking of the moment. That night, at long last, we broke out the champagne.

Drowning in a Sea of Spanish Verbs

When a doe is not a deer, when a breast is not a breast

Although learning to speak Spanish at some level was part of our plan, I don't think either of us had any illusions about mastering the language. I couldn't imagine taking part in a conversation regarding the political ramifications of increased autonomy for Catalonia or the Basque country. And the thought of finding myself in a discussion comparing the films of directors Pedro Almodóvar (who directed *All About My Mother*) or Alejandro Amenábar (*The Sea Inside*) was beyond the pale, to say the least. Learning to pronounce their names, to say nothing of remembering who was who, was more than daunting.

Our Spanish-speaking goals were modest. We wanted to understand and be understood as we shopped, dined, and traveled, and to exchange a few pleasantries with our neighbors and the merchants with whom we dealt regularly. We needed to navigate bureaucratic and legal mazes, like renewing our visa or lease. Being able to communicate medical needs could be important; knowing the difference between *el culo*, the backside, and *el cuello*, the neck, could well prove important to making the correct diagnosis.

We'd studied a bit before leaving California, and we knew the alphabet, numbers, days and months, some rules of pronunciation, that sort of thing. But in all truth we hadn't advanced all that much.

Once we arrived in Granada, the need for Spanish was overwhelming. Unlike the coast, where much of the economy revolves around English and German tourists and retirees, very little English is spoken in Granada. Very little. Everything we needed to do during those first weeks, from renting an apartment to applying for our residency permits, required speaking Spanish. Fortunately, Flannery was able to get us through all the rough patches. Unfortunately, her presence allowed us to rely on her and eliminated any sense of urgency. We'd had every intention of attending Spanish classes, but we'd had plenty of excuses to procrastinate.

Actually, some of our excuses were more or less valid. Less valid included outfitting the apartment and learning the city. More valid was trekking to the police station two mornings a week. Valid were our trips to Morocco and to Munich. Signing up for daily lessons when we couldn't attend didn't make sense. Then the holidays arrived and the language schools closed. We finally signed up in early January, but the beginning of classes was delayed twice because the staff was slow in returning from their holidays.

Kay and I began an "intensive" course of Spanish in late January. The foundation where we took our classes described intensive as ten hours a week. And intense it was. There were also eight- and six-hour programs offered, but we felt the need to catch up. The school's advertisement stated that classes would have from two to six students. Because most students came to Granada to study Spanish in the spring and summer, winter enrollment was low. Our class had the minimum. That would be two: Kay and me. Our teacher, Anna, who was twenty-six, had moved to Granada from Barcelona to study Flamenco dance. Teaching English was her means of support. She was funny, charming, and absolutely lovely.

So began our life of being students. The first week we met from noon till two, the second week from ten to noon. January mornings were cold, and each morning we arose and went over the previous day's work in our chilly apartment. Then, after bundling up, we walked to class. Anna always looked great, but, because she'd danced into the morning hours, sometimes she was a bit frazzled. And although frequently she wasn't as prepared as she should have been, she was always perky and patient and we liked her very much. We spoke with students whose teachers were very well prepared but not as likeable, so we didn't complain. After the first two weeks, our class hours were changed to nine thirty to eleven thirty, which gave us less time to review before class and gave Anna less time to put on her face. She was usually five to ten minutes late. Only once did she arrive somewhat disheveled, so we knew that that night must have been an unusually long one. A long night in Spain would not end till dawn, just a couple of hours before class.

We soon discovered that a two-hour class requires two to three additional hours a day of study. We reviewed our assignment before class. After class, during lunch, we went over the vocabulary we'd learned since the class began. In the evening, we studied that morning's lesson. But that, plus studying over the weekend, was not enough. The vocabulary list kept growing and the number of irregular verbs was multiplying irregularly. We were dogpaddling like crazy and the big waves, the compound tenses, were still out there, gathering strength before they crashed down on us.

The book *501 Spanish Verbs* is, I was told, indispensable to anyone studying Spanish. Actually, the number five hundred and one is misleading, as the book contains one thousand six hundred and one verbs. The five hundred and one verbs, which are conjugated, one per page, are the most commonly used verbs. I learned that Spanish has fourteen tenses, seven simple and seven compound, plus two progressive forms. There are also two imperative moods, familiar and polite, so that commanding your child to "watch out!" requires a different verb form than the one used to warn the taxi driver. And I learned about reflexive verbs, verbs used when the subject and object are the same, like *vestirse*, to dress yourself, and *lastimarse*, to feel sorry for yourself, which described my feelings after trying to learn just fifty verbs.

The number one thousand six hundred and one refers to infinitives only. The number of verb forms is far, far greater. The English conjugation of *to speak* is: I speak, you speak, he speaks, we speak, you (plural) speak, they speak. Speak, speaks, just two simple words. *En español*, the conjugation of *hablar* (to speak) is: *yo hablo, tu hablas, el habla, nosotros hablamos, vosotros hablais, ellos hablan.* Six verbs forms. So already our one thousand six hundred and one verbs have become nine thousand six hundred and six verbs forms, and that's just the present indicative.

Granted, *to speak* is an easy verb to conjugate. But so is *hablar*, because it's a regular verb. The difficulty that Spanish poses is that there are so many, far too many, irregular verbs, the conjugation of which often defies explanation. The first conjugation of *ir, to go*, is *voy, vas, va, vamos, vais,* and *van.* The past tense is *fui, fuiste, fue, fuimos, fuisteis, fueron.* Commit *that* to your memory bank.

My Teapot Runneth Over

By the end of February, our minds had become so muddled that we were having difficulty communicating in English. There was so much material we simply didn't have time to review it all while adding new vocabulary and concepts every class. We hadn't moved to Spain to study Spanish and only study Spanish. I felt like a teapot whose spout is lower than the rim, so when you try to fill it to the top, the water comes out the spout. As the difference between *ser* and *estar* was poured in, the meaning of *hay* was dribbling out the spout. It was time to slow the pouring. I was having nightmares in Spanish, but I didn't know what anyone was saying, not even me. I didn't even know what the dream was about.

So, after four weeks of Spanish classes, Kay and I bid Anna, our lovely Flamenco-dancing teacher, a fond *adios* and launched ourselves into the calmer seas of "home schooling." We felt we had a reasonably solid foundation upon which to build, and Anna was impressed with the course book we purchased. The book was English, not American, so we knew we'd likely come upon a lorry parked outside a chemist's shop, but we were confident that by spending the hour or so a day that the course required, we'd learn Spanish. We'd learn a little slower, but we'd get there without drowning.

We were now on our own. Each day we followed our book's lesson plan and studied for an hour. We listened to the CD-ROM we'd brought with us in order to train our ears. And we tried to use the language as much as possible. This proved to be more difficult than we'd thought. The pronunciation, as heard on our CD-ROM and as illustrated phonetically in the book, did not sound like what we were hearing on the streets of Granada.

Language is a complicated, somewhat contentious issue in Spain. What we call Spanish (*español*) was called Castilian (*castellano*) well into the twentieth century. It wasn't until the 1978 constitution that Castilian was designated Spain's official language. Although Castilian is Spain's most widely spoken language, it is not the only one. For many Spaniards it is a second language. Interestingly enough, the three most prosperous regions of Spain, Catalonia, the Basque country and Madrid, have three different "first" languages. But Castilian is the unifying language, the one spoken across the entire country. Once simply the language of the central highlands of the Iberian Peninsula—Castilla La Mancha, Castilla y Leon, and Madrid—Castilian became the prominent dialect when Isabel of Castilla became queen. To the victor goes the last word, and always in their own tongue.

Spain is not, like France for example, a unified country with a relatively common identity. It is more like Great Britain, where Northern Ireland, Wales, and Scotland have their own distinct identities, languages, and aspirations of increased home rule, if not independence.

Spain has nineteen regions, political entities not unlike states, and most regions have several provinces, something like counties. Catalonia, with its capital in Barcelona, speaks Catalan as a first language and continually presses for increased autonomy. The Basque country, where Euskera, or Basque, is still spoken by a large number of people, sprawls across three regions lying on the southern side of the Pyrenees. ETA, a very small, violent terrorist group, has for years demanded full independence. Natives of Galicia, which lies north of Portugal on the Atlantic, speak Gallego, a mix of Spanish and Portuguese. In Valencia, just south of Catalonia on the Mediterranean, and on the Balearic Islands (Mallorca), a dialect heavily influenced by Catalan is spoken.

And there is Andalucía, which speaks its own version of Spanish. There are six provinces in Andalucía, including Granada, Sevilla, and Córdoba. There is also the Costa del Sol, which is not a province as such but a land of oceanside high rises, fish and chips, and sausages and kraut.

Spanish Spoken Here?

Just before moving to Spain, I bought a copy of *The Spanish Temper, Travels in Spain*, by V.S. Pritchett, the English essayist and short story writer. According to Pritchett, who'd traveled throughout Spain in the twenties and thirties, and again in the fifties, when he'd written the book, "The Andalucíans do not lisp the letter 'c' or 'z' in their speech: they drop out as many consonants as possible from their words and speak fast in shouting, headlong voices as if their mouths were full of marbles. They are very difficult to understand."

Pritchett did not exaggerate, and his description of the difficulty of understanding Andalucíans has been confirmed by other Spaniards. *Granadinos* don't merely drop their consonants, as Pritchett wrote, they fling them down and stomp on them.

But we tried our best, greeting our neighbors and other familiar faces in the Spanish we were learning. "*Buenos dias*," we said.

"*Bon dia*," they replied. Sometimes just "*Bon*" or "*Buenos.*"

"*Muchas gracias*," we said to the waiter when he brought our food.

"*Mucha gracia*," he said to us when we paid him.

"*Hasta luego*," we waved upon leaving. See you later.

"*Aluego*," we heard. Or perhaps, "*Adio.*"

"*¿Cuanto cuesta?*" we asked, wanting to know what something cost.

"*Doe*," comes the answer.

¿Doe? Doe? Isn't doe a deer, a female deer? What happened to "*dos?*" as in "*uno, dos, tres, cuatro, cinco?*"

Once, when Kay was buying cheese, she asked for three hundred grams, please. "*Quiero tres cientos gramos, por favor.*"

The girl behind the counter looked at Kay as if she were speaking a foreign language. Which, of course, she was, but that's not the point here. Kay repeated her request slowly and carefully.

"*Tres cientos gramos, por favor.*"

Another quizzical look. Then the girl held up three fingers.

"*¿Tray?*" she asked.

Tray? How were we going to learn Spanish if they refused to speak it to us?

Watching television, we were advised, is a good way to learn to hear Spanish, as the newsreaders spoke proper Castilian. We had a television. We watched. We listened. We recognized, possibly, one word out of twenty.

Sometimes, usually during a commercial, a written message accompanied the voice. This should have helped, but in order to keep up with the voice, the on-screen words whizzed by far too fast to read.

It was like watching movie credits on fast forward. Are the Spanish able to speed-read as well as speed-speak and speed-listen?

There was one weather reporter, a lovely young woman, who spoke clearly and slowly. She was wonderful. We were able to understand almost half of what she said. Unfortunately, she was replaced. My theory is that she spoke so slowly, compared to other newscasters, that Spanish viewers either fell asleep or changed channels.

Our understanding Spanish was made even more difficult because everyone spoke very loudly and at the same time. In America, competing monologues last only as long as it takes for one speaker to establish dominance. The loudest, most persistent voice wins, the others listen. Not in Spain. No one gives in; everyone simply speaks louder.

Once, after we'd lived on Calle Elvira for a few months, we asked Enrique, our English-speaking, upstairs neighbor to come down to our apartment while the landlord was there and do a bit of translating for us. At the conclusion of our business, they began a discussion of their own. They both spoke, simultaneously and at considerable volume, for at least fifteen minutes. Neither stopped once, yet both seemed to have understood everything the other said. They seemed so pleased by whatever it was they'd agreed on, they shook hands on it.

Make that Boned Bosom for Two

Of course we've managed to commit our own communication fender benders. On one of Kay's first visits to the central market, she asked the butcher for *seno filete*. What she wanted was chicken breasts filets. What she'd ordered, in Spanish, was boned bosom. The butcher didn't blink. He carefully boned and sliced the thick chicken breast and handed it over. The next time, having discovered her gaffe, she asked for *pechuga filete*. If he remembered her first order, he didn't let on.

I found that there's more to learning a language than studying vocabulary. That's the easy part. You've got to use it. The more you hear it, the more you'll be able to understand it even if they don't pronounce everything "properly." Kay was far more willing to mix it up with the natives than I was. I'm convinced that she has a far better ear. I've wondered if that has to do with being a woman, as women are supposed to be better listeners, an assessment with which I have no argument. I also wondered about my own listening abilities. Perhaps the difficulty I have remembering names of both people and foreign cities has to do with a failure to listen carefully. Living in Spain proved to be a continuous learning experience, though not all the lessons were ones I had anticipated.

I confess: I relied too much on Kay to do most of our communicating, like asking directions or reserving a hotel room. It's not that I couldn't ask the question, it's that I wasn't nearly as capable of understanding the answer as she was. But, Kay reminded me, how are you going to improve if you don't just do it? There were times when my reluctance to give it a go must have been irritating to her. But for the most part she was very patient. And I improved, slowly but surely.

There is one Spanish usage with which Kay has a philosophical difference. In Mexico, a married couple is spoken of as *el esposo y la esposa*, the husband and the wife; in Spain, *el marido y la mujer*, the husband and the woman. Why, she asked, is she *la mujer* and not *la esposa*? I looked it up and was delighted to inform her that *las esposas* also meant handcuffs. She did not find this as amusing as I did.

In all fairness—and to protect myself from charges of hypocrisy, cultural insensitivity, if not arrogance—I must admit that English, as I speak it, may be difficult to understand for someone learning English. I'm a native of North Carolina, have a Southern accent, though not a drawl, and speak very rapidly. It has also been said that my enunciation leaves something to be desired. I can't help but wonder how a Spanish Pritchett would describe how I speak. Knowing that my English could be as baffling as the Spanish spoken by Andalucíans should make me more understanding. It does. But being understanding hasn't improving my ability to understand. In the meantime I'll just have to rely on *mi mujer*.

Learning to Live with Elvira

To Sleep or Not to Sleep, that Was the Challenge

As the weeks, then months, went by, we gained a sense of the ebb and flow of the night on Calle Elvira. In the early evening, say between eight and nine, the arriving began, as crowds of people, lots of couples but mostly groups, prowled the street, laughing, talking, seemingly delighted just to be there. By ten the street was a sea of people. It didn't matter how cold it was, they were out there. Temperature near freezing? No problem. Up and down they paraded, wrapped in long scarves, heavy coats, and gloves—never a hat, as it would muss carefully coifed hair. Light drizzle, perhaps an umbrella. A downpour thinned the crowd, but never eliminated it.

By eleven o'clock the cafés and bars were crowded. One evening a few weeks after we'd moved in, I ventured out to see the extent of the revelry. I walked down to Plaza Nueva and back. Every bar was packed, and the streets were crowded with people drinking or waiting to get inside.

Midnight till two was the heart of the evening, when almost everyone coming to the party had arrived. Those who arrived late to our intersection had a hard time finding space inside a café. La Tortuga was usually packed, as was El Circulo, and neither had an outside area. Unfortunately for us, El Espejo did—just beneath our balconies.

People stood around, beer in hand or placed on one of the half dozen tall pedestal tables the café put out at night. About the size of a large pizza, these chest-high tables, found inside and outside of cafés all over Granada, were just large enough for four beers and possibly two *tapas*. New arrivals peered in, and either shrugged and passed on, or appointed one member of the group to worm inside for beer and *tapas*. Somehow the appointed member got inside to the bar, and then, perhaps even more miraculously, emerged some minutes later with a handful of beers. The group then pressed around a pedestal table, if one was available, and a loud, animated discussion began. If no table was available, they often used our stoop as a booth.

The parade home began around four. I knew that because earplugs, which we'd resorted to, had a way of working themselves loose, no matter how hard you pressed them in. There was also user error, like those mornings when I awoke around four or five and, hearing no noise, as was sometimes the case on a weeknight, removed the earplugs. It was a decision I rarely failed to regret. It represented, as Dr. Samuel Johnson said about remarriage, the triumph of hope over experience, for the quiet was always short lived, as Granada Ten released its music-crazed patrons onto Calle Elvira between five and six in the morning. As they walked beneath our window the music spilled out. The Spanish are a musical people and they love to sing. They are not shy about singing in public. Perhaps it's the practice, but they all sing fairly well, many extremely well. They sing with gusto and at full volume. They sing solo and they sing in groups. Everyone seemed to know the words. Sometimes they paused beneath our window to complete a particularly heartfelt chorus. It might have been delightful to hear if the concert had taken place at, say, eight in the evening.

It was curious, the way these homebound groups arranged themselves. Although sometimes they moved as a group, frequently they divided, some walking along one side of our narrow street, some on the other side, and shouting back and forth as they walked. And, in the Spanish manner, they all shouted at once. The acoustical effect could be quite surprising. More than once I looked out the window expecting to see a crowd of twenty or more, only to see a small, noisy band of four or five.

Occasionally a few stragglers passed beneath our windows after I'd gotten up. I'd look out and watch three or four young men as they made their way down the street, a liter beer bottle in each hand, a little unsteady, perhaps, but not staggering; or perhaps a couple walking very slowly, arms around the other's waist, head leaning against head.

Finally the street was quiet and remained so until midmorning deliveries began. After that there was a midday lull, which was in turn followed by two o'clock, siesta-break, horn-blowing traffic. The street was calm until the five thirty back-to-work traffic, then quiet again till evening, when it all began again, night after night.

In spite of the fact that Calle Elvira was lined with café-bars and filled every night with their customers, we never saw one violent incident or any vandalism on the street. Nor did we see any police presence. Think of it, thousands of young people walking up and down from café-bar to café-bar, drinking in the street, and there were few if any police patrolling. The thinking is, as I understand it, that the police provoke more problems than they prevent.

I think the primary reason for the lack of running amuck is that Mediterraneans almost always eat when they drink. *Tapas* are served with each drink. Mediterranean Europeans take their alcohol in cafés and café-bars, outside if at all possible, while Northern Europeans— and that would include most Americans—drink, for the most part, in bars, pubs, taverns, and saloons. And usually they don't eat. Spaniards drink mostly beer and wine. Although most café-bars in Granada have a full range of alcohol behind the bar, we rarely saw anyone order a cocktail.

The importance of eating cannot, I think, be overestimated. Two or three glasses of beer or wine (servings here are relatively small—beer is served in eight to ten-ounce glasses, wine servings are about five ounces), each accompanied by a snack, will get you full long before it gets you drunk. Drunkenness is definitely frowned upon.

Unfortunately, teenage drinking was becoming a problem in Spain. In Granada, during every fiesta thousands of teenagers and college students filled the plazas and streets, bringing with them bags, boxes, and even grocery carts filled with booze. In the mornings, the plazas were knee-deep in trash, not bodies. They made an awful mess and kept the town awake, but the fighting and vandalism that often accompanied youthful drinking in America and northern European countries was rare.

Actually, there was one incident of near violence on Calle Elvira. I was awakened one morning around five by the sound of a raging, threatening, obscenity-filled voice. This male voice was joined by a young woman's voice, begging him to calm down. I could understand everything they were saying. They were Americans, probably students.

Life in the Quarter

Within days of moving into our apartment, we discovered that our neighborhood was Granada's French Quarter, Calle Elvira its Bourbon Street. It was where the young Spanish, foreign students, and tourists came to party.

A lot of the action took place at El Espejo, the café-bar beneath us. Smaller than our apartment, with a short, L-shaped counter, three tables for sitting, and three or four pedestal tables, this deceptively innocent-looking place was one of the most popular watering holes on the street. Like every café-bar in Granada, it had a tiny kitchen that turned out *tapas*, which we tried and found to be nothing special. There was nothing unusual about the décor; in fact, there was no décor. The drink prices were the same as everyone else's. The only feature that might account for its enormous popularity was the music. The music was very loud.

Needless to say, our evenings were alive with the sound of music, plus the babble from the sidewalk, the honk of car horns, the roar of the crowd downstairs, and the slam of the café's back door in the lane. I guess the music had to be loud to be heard over the sound of forty or fifty shouting customers. And what they couldn't hear, they could feel. The boom, boom, boom of the bass pounded up through the café walls to the café ceiling and then up through the floor of our apartment. One night—well, actually morning, as it was well after midnight—I traced a bewildering ringing sound to the tinkle of wine glasses vibrating against each other in the living room. It was like living in a speaker. Not only did the music come up through the floor, it bounced off the buildings across the street and through our balcony windows. We were being tortured in stereo.

If we were watching television or listening to our own music, we could almost ignore it. Bedtime was a different story. We tried earplugs, learning, through trial and error, which ones were most effective. But even the best earplugs couldn't block out the thumping, the tremors that came up through the floor when the music really got cranked up. Earplugs pressed into our ears, pillows pulled across our heads—nothing worked.

Fortunately, most nights the music wasn't played at full volume. It was irritating but bearable. Although the café stayed open as late as four or five in the morning on weekends and holidays, it usually closed at two, so many nights we just waited them out. But there were those nights when the music was unusually loud, when the disco beat moved up through the floor and the bed and into my body, dictating to my heart what its beat should be. It was maddening.

We were losing sleep. We were getting grumpy. Our wonderful new life in Granada was becoming less wonderful. Discussing possible courses of action led to a bit of family disagreement.

Kay felt that something had to be done. She was awake half the night and she was miserable. Someone, she said, should go downstairs and inform them that there were people up here trying to get some sleep. Flannery, who'd lived abroad for several years and was sensitive to such issues, insisted that complaining would be in bad form. She thought that it would be arrogant for us to tell the Spanish to change their behavior for the benefit of American sleeping hours. My position—okay, fear—was that if we complained and pissed them off, they might turn the volume *up,* not down.

We asked our upstairs neighbor Enrique what he thought. Enrique said that the music didn't bother him. It was simply the Spanish way of life. There was even a verb for it, he told us: *trasnochar,* to stay up through the night. But, he advised us, don't call the police. He told us that when he'd lived downstairs in our flat, inspectors came to do a sound check. It seemed there was a law, though rarely enforced, regulating how much and how late noise could be disseminated from a commercial establishment into a residential one. If we called the police, the café people would be in trouble, which would present problems for Manuel, our landlord, who owned the building and was also a friend of the café owner.

Not long after this conversation, I read a story concerning this very issue in *El Pais*, Spain's national newspaper. Fortunately for us, the *International Herald Tribune* contained an eight-page English-language digest of *El Pais*, allowing us to keep up on the Spanish and international news from the Spanish perspective. It seems that, after several years of legal wrangling, a citizen of Barcelona had won his suit against the bar beneath his apartment for making too much noise after midnight. After midnight! The reporter concluded the article by stating that this was quite an historic ruling, since, "As every Spaniard knows, we are the loudest people in Europe."

Vindication! The problem wasn't that we were delicate, puritanical, early-to-bed, American whiney-butts. At least some Spanish wanted their sleep, too. Even we, Americans in Spain, had the right, along with every Spaniard, to a decent night's sleep. The battle lines were drawn. Now we knew we had a legal leg to stand on. When the time came, we would use it.

Living with Super Woman

The fateful night arrived shortly after Flannery had returned to California. We'd moved into the front bedroom, over the stairwell rather than the café itself, hoping for some small relief. The music didn't seem to be quite as loud, and our bed wasn't directly over the constantly slamming alley door. But this particular late January night surpassed all previous nights. It was New Year's Eve, Mardi Gras, and Saint Patrick's Day all rolled into one. I could swear that the bed was moving.

"I can't take it anymore," Kay cried. She sat up and turned on the bedside lamp. "I'm going down there right now! It's driving me insane." She did have a crazed look in her eyes.

"I don't think you should go down," I said. "What are you going to say? You don't even speak Spanish." In all truth, I was a little worried that she might start throwing glasses. She was, shall we say, in a state of extreme agitation.

"They'll understand, all right," she said. "Don't worry about that." She stood by the bed pulling on a sweat suit.

I lay there waiting for her to cool off in the chilly room, vent a bit more, then crawl back into bed. She continued to dress and growl.

"This is not a good idea," I said. "This is a very bad idea."

She sat on the bed long enough to pull on socks and sandals. Part of me thought I should go with her, though there was no reason to think there was any danger other than being embarrassed to death. I'd never heard of it, but there's always a first time. The other part of me hoped that she'd come to her senses, as defined by me, and return to the warmth of our bed. Look at the positive side, I almost said, recklessly flirting with danger, in a motel you have to pay for a vibrating bed. Fortunately, wiser survival instincts prevailed and I kept my mouth shut.

She left the room and slammed the bedroom door. I heard the door from the salon to the foyer slam. There was a pause. Then I heard the front door slam. She was now on the stairway. I waited. Then I heard—as well as felt—the heavy metal entrance door slam. At least she dressed, I thought. Confronting one's adversaries in your underwear would most certainly undermine any potential effectiveness.

Suddenly the pounding stopped. Well, not really stopped, but it had diminished to the point where I had to listen for it. My God, she did it! Hell hath no wrath like a sleep-deprived woman. That'll teach 'em.

I listened to the doors slam in reverse order, entrance door, front door, salon door, and then the bedroom door. I waited while Kay sat on the side of the bed and undressed. Finally, I could wait no more.

"What happened?"

"It wasn't easy getting through the crowd to the bar. But I did. And they knew who I was." She sounded very calm. She wasn't even breathing hard from running down and back up the stairs.

"What did you say?" We often practiced a phrase we knew we were going to need, like: "I'd like four thin slices of lomo, please," or "Two first class round-trip tickets." But never: "The music is driving me crazy!"

"I didn't know the words for too loud, so I shouted 'musica,' and pointed up at the ceiling. Then I put my hands over my ears like I was being tortured."

She turned off the light and slid down beneath the covers. Her feet were cold.

"And how did they react?"

"Like they were really, really sorry and hoped that we wouldn't turn them in. They know it's not supposed to be that loud." I could feel her smile of triumph in the dark.

"Good for you." I congratulated her. "I feel like I'm living with Super Woman."

"You're a lucky man," she said.

And then we went to sleep, blessed sleep.

The volume remained at a tolerable level for a couple of weeks. Then one night, there we were again, back in thump-thump land. And down one of us would go. (Yes, I was finally shamed into making the journey.) By March, all we had to do was to show our face through the window or at the door. A look of dismay would cross their faces, and they would rush to the volume control and turn it down. Nothing had to be said.

A couple of months later, after we'd made a few trips downstairs, I thought it would be wise to make a social call to let them know that it wasn't personal. It wasn't about them; it was about sleep. So one afternoon we dropped by for a drink. Paco, the café manager, was a nice guy. He was a student at the university and spoke some English. He felt, or at least seemed to feel, badly about keeping us up. He promised to do his best to keep it down. He tried. But there were occasions when he wasn't there. And there were times when he forgot. And down, once again, one of us would go.

Our first four months in Granada had been wonderful—except for the nightly concert. There was so much that was right about where we lived, both the location and the apartment itself. But we weren't sure how long we could live with the nightly disruption. Our lease wouldn't end until September 11, and if we moved we'd lose our €400 deposit. All we could do, at least for the present, was to shrug, endure, and stock up on earplugs for the string of visitors we expected through the spring.

The Streets of Granada 3: Walking the City

Clasp Hands Behind Back, Remain Alert

One of the earliest decisions Kay and I made regarding our foreign adventure was to live without an automobile. Applying the Less-Stress Test made the decision easy. Admittedly, getting around Spain without a car requires an investment in time. It's a large country and cities are scattered. Buses provided an excellent alternative. Service was frequent and affordable; buses were modern and comfortable. Trains served most cities, but routes were often indirect and time consuming. So traveling the country by car does make sense. The Spaniards we knew who owned cars used them primarily for trips. But for us, buying, insuring, maintaining, and parking a car that we'd seldom use did not seem a wise choice.

Although driving from city to city made some sense, driving within the city made none. It's not because traffic was bad. It was often so light that it was possible to safely jaywalk at midday on the city's main boulevards. The main difficulty was that so much of the city was simply off limits to vehicular traffic. In addition to the downtown pedestrian-only shopping zone, there were plazas and pedestrian-only streets all over town. The majority of the streets in the historic Albaicín and Realejo neighborhoods were streets in name only, being too narrow or too steep to be driven by anyone except cinema action stars.

As far as navigating Granada itself, walking was the only way to get about, though it wasn't the only option. The bus system was efficient, inexpensive, and quite useful when taking home the groceries. The rough cobblestone streets and hillside stairways were not bicycle friendly, even if we were so inclined, which we weren't. In fact, especially compared to other European cities, there were very few bicycles on the street of Granada.

What filled the streets were scooters, motorbikes, and motorcycles. These were the bane of pedestrians, and they were everywhere, mostly small motorcycles—a Harley would be very impractical on the hills— and the screeching whine of their small engines was quite annoying. I'm sure that these two-wheeled menaces outnumbered all the cars, taxis, and buses put together. Their popularity is easy to understand. They can get the rider just about anywhere, through streets and lanes far too narrow for cars, even up steeply stepped hillsides. They can be parked almost anywhere. Forget the almost; they *were* parked everywhere: sidewalks, plazas, stairways, even across doorways.

Their third attraction was that, at least as far as I could tell, they were not bound by traffic or noise abatement regulations. They drove with immunity on sidewalks, down pedestrian streets, across plazas, and down one-way streets the wrong way. They drove far too fast, weaving through crowded streets as if they were figures in a computer game. I'm amazed that we never saw one plow into strolling pedestrians.

But back to walking. In addition to the pleasures of putting one foot before the other while feasting the eyes, walking lends itself to one of the great indulgences of retirement: solo tasking. Gone were the days of trying to balance three or four chores because there wasn't time to do them individually. Now we filled an afternoon by walking to the train station to pick up a schedule; to the post office for stamps, or two afternoons getting a roll of film developed, one taking the film in and one walking back the next day to pick it up. Of course these trips were always punctuated by a *tapas* stop at a favorite café.

You Are How You Walk

One of the challenges we faced in Granada was learning to walk European style. Strolling. We did not stroll. We've always walked for exercise and we walk very fast. I used to run until my knees declared their age, which was apparently ten years older than the rest of my body, at which time I joined Kay as an exercise walker.

Even as we stormed through the streets, weaving through slow-moving pedestrians, we told ourselves to slow down. We weren't in a race. The only reason to ever rush was to make it to a store before the two o'clock closing time. We were retirees; we had all day to do whatever it was we had to do. And what we didn't get done one day, we could get done the next. But still, it wasn't easy breaking the pace developed by years of walking. Our brains might be in stroll mode, but our legs followed their own metronome.

Then I read a newspaper column written by a similarly afflicted American with advice on how to stroll. The secret was in the arms. Do not swing your arms by your sides. Instead, lock your hands behind your back. You immediately slowed down. You also appeared to be lost in thought, as if pondering the great questions, like: Will people ever learn to live together peacefully? Or, where shall we take today's *tapas?* I found that holding hands with myself behind my back worked. The trick was remembering to do it.

There was another question that tickled my curiosity. Every once in a while—in situations when we were sure we hadn't given ourselves away by speaking English—someone said, "hello" or "excuse me." I didn't think it was our physical appearance. I'm six foot tall, weigh just over one hundred eighty pounds, and have graying hair. Kay is five foot nine, with high cheekbones and a wide, girl-next-door smile. To my eyes, we looked pretty much like everyone else, *Gitanos* excepted. It wasn't the way we dressed, as we'd bought much of our wardrobes in Granada. We didn't wear cowboy hats or fringed buckskin jackets or bright white tennis shoes (wearing white "trainers," we'd been told, is like wearing a sign declaring American). No little American flags or buttons declaring "Save the Redwoods" adorned our collars.

One evening the usher at the theater said, when taking our tickets, "Thank you." There was no line behind us, so I had time to ask him how he knew we were Americans.

"I didn't," he answered in clear, if heavily accented, English. "But I could see you are not Spanish, so I think maybe you are English. Or German. Either way, you speak English."

So, we didn't look American after all. Just not Spanish. I'm still unsure of why we don't look Spanish. Perhaps it was the way we walked, not just the pace but our style of walking, long strides, arms moving freely, that gave us away.

Granada is like an enormous maze, a gigantic board game whose primary objective is to avoid getting lost. All you have to do to win is to get home. We played almost every day, which is how we learned the city. One day we turned right at the church, the following week left. Some days we took the steps up the hill, other days a narrow street. Eventually we got our bearings. Trying every option is the only way to figure it out. This was particularly true in the medieval hillside districts, where the streets and alleys twist and turn, zig and zag, often acquiring a new name after each twist. Sometimes the name change was just a variation; one route down from the Albaicín alto began on Cuesta Algibe de Trillo and proceeded through Placeta Algibe de Trillo, at which point one could choose to continue downhill via Callejón Algibe de Trillo or by Calle Algibe de Trillo. The most traveled route from Plaza Nueva up to Mirador San Nicolás, a fifteen-minute walk at most, changed names at least twelve times.

This aimless wandering led to all sorts of little discoveries: a small, shady plaza hidden away in a neighborhood we'd never explored; still another spectacular view of the Alhambra and the Sierra Nevada, the mountain range twenty miles to the east; a neighborhood café with fantastic *tapas* at incredibly low prices. More than once we stumbled upon a small neighborhood festival, usually in honor of Saint Somebody.

Not all our walks were in the city. One of our favorites began just beyond the Alhambra, then climbed into the hills above the Rio Darro. There was a wonderful riverside walk along the Rio Genil through the countryside to a small, nearby village.

Alert! A Land Mine

Walking in Granada required both patience and caution. Patience was necessary because on every street, from the narrowest lane to the widest boulevard, there were human obstructions. These obstructions took two forms. The first I called "the incognizant," in which a group of five or six people, believing that they are the only people out and about, sauntered five abreast down the sidewalk arm in arm while the rest of us, apparently invisible, were forced against a building or out into the street. The other group I named the "squatters." These were clusters of people who stood in the middle of the sidewalk chattering away, air kissing, cheek kissing, seemingly unable to pull themselves away from each other. Both these groups appeared completely oblivious to everyone else. And they were ubiquitous. Neither of these obstructions, however, seemed to bother the Spanish at all. They simply walked around. I never saw an expression of irritation. I suppose they're used to it. It was simply the Spanish way, and I constantly reminded myself to relax; "when in Rome" and all that.

Caution, however, was even more important than patience. First, in the older hillside neighborhoods, most of the sidewalks were made of small stones embedded in cement and sand. The stones were carefully set on edge by hand, a fascinating process to watch. The edges protruded above the cement, so the surface was not smooth. In addition to being uneven, there were often missing stones, or even sections, so we had to be careful not to stumble.

A second reason for caution was that on all streets and sidewalks, great and small, hillside and downtown, little brown piles of, what shall we say, canine remembrances, lurked like land mines ready to explode under your feet. I became aware of these underfoot dangers our first week in Granada when I placed my foot in the very center of a land mine so large we could only wonder at the size, if not species, of the animal. I spent half an hour later that afternoon on the stoop with a pot of hot water and an old toothbrush returning my shoes to usability. From that day on, we called that street Dog Poop Street.

I became so sensitive to the dangers of not paying attention to where I placed my feet that I found myself hopping over leaves. Kay and Flannery also became much more careful, so some benefit was gained by my suffering. At any rate, we developed a walking strategy designed to prevent a second pedal disaster. That strategy was to make the lead walker, or point man, responsible for keeping an eye out for these land mines. "Alert," the leader said, and those following knew to look down. It worked, though it makes for rather strange conversations.

Leader: "Shall we go to the square with the view of the—alert—cathedral for lunch?"

Follower: "We ate there last week."

Leader: "How about the place—alert—with the calamari *tapas*—alert—and the delicious avocado salad?"

Follower: "Sounds good!"

Leader: "But first—alert—we need to go—alert—to the post office. Alert."

Alerts and sidewalk squatters weren't the only obstructions to sidewalk travel. Sidewalk merchants, by setting up their shops where foot traffic was heaviest, created maddening bottlenecks. These shops consisted of a piece of material or tarp strategically placed to block the most traffic. The most common "tarp shop," almost always tended by Africans, sold pirated copies of the latest CDs and DVDs. When I say latest, I mean the movie was currently playing in the local theater; sometimes it hadn't even opened yet. CDs sold for €3, DVDs for €10 to €12. They also sold sunglasses on sunny days, umbrellas on rainy ones. The Chinese specialized in scarves, pashminas, gloves, hats, and sweaters, while Spanish street merchants usually sold mechanical toys and dolls. And there were, as in every other city in the world, street people, hippies, whatever one calls them, selling handmade jewelry.

Why didn't the merchants demand relief? Occasionally the police made a sweep, but, this being Spain, racing down the street with clubs held aloft was not the way it was done. Instead, a policeman or two strolled (yes, in Granada, even the police strolled) down the street, while ahead of them, as word traveled much faster than a strolling policeman, the merchants picked up the corners of their stores, dropped their bundles into large fabric bags, and walked quickly away. We never saw anyone arrested, though once we witnessed a panicky tarp merchant as he raced down the street, leaving a trail of sunglasses and knocking down a woman who hadn't moved out of the way fast enough. He'd brushed past me just before decking the woman, and I, on instinct, began pursuit. I'd only run a few yards when I came to the following realizations: there was one of me and ten of them, all far younger than I. What made me think I could catch him? And what in the world would I do if I did? I stopped and turned back. The woman was on her feet, unhurt, and brushing off the concerns of those who'd gathered around to help.

There was one other obstruction, that being the news kiosk, at least one per block on major streets. They used the sidewalk to display their wares—newspapers and magazines, telephone cards, books, CDs, DVDs, toys, and girlie magazines—sometimes reducing passage to single file.

After a while, sidestepping dog droppings, skirting tarp shops and "squatters," and dodging racing motorcycles while treading carefully on uneven sidewalks became second nature. We'd even learned to stroll. What I never learned was why we couldn't pass for Spaniards.

The Roar of March

New Friends, First Visitors, and Terror in Madrid

By early March Kay and I had experienced a significant amount of togetherness. Since Flannery's departure in early January, neither of us had exchanged more than two sentences with anyone except our Spanish teacher. This was an unexpected development. Although we'd chosen Granada because it was not, like the Costa del Sol, overrun with expatriates, we'd assumed there would be a few. We'd also assumed that they'd be primarily British, but that was fine, as most spoke an English dialect that we could understand if we listened carefully. As we walked the streets, our ears were always on alert for the sound of English. Anyone who spoke the language would do, but other than university students and a few tourists, we heard none. There were three Irish pubs in Granada—at least they had Irish names—two of them just off "Bourbon Street," only blocks from our apartment, and we dropped in a few times for a pint and in hopes of meeting a resident English speaker. Other than a handful of students, we encountered no one. One afternoon we struck up a conversation with the bartender, who, as it turned out, was Irish/Spanish. He'd grown up in Ireland, hence the brogue, but had returned to Spain a few years before and preferred living in Granada. Was there a place, we asked, a café or reading room or tearoom, where the English-speaking community hung out? There was no English-speaking community, he said. There were English people living in Granada, but there was no community.

Apparently, unless we somehow stumbled upon some English speakers, we would forever serve as the other's sole companion. Not that extended periods of togetherness was new for us, as Kay's being a flight attendant had given us as much time together as apart. It had been, in many ways, the best of both worlds. When flying to Hawaii, she was gone for four days with a night home in the middle. Trips to Hong Kong, Sydney, or Japan, or to London, Paris, or Frankfurt, usually took several days. Extended periods of togetherness followed; upon her return, she would be at home for four or five days. Now, however, we were together all the time, 24-7 as they say. I couldn't spin an amusing, possibly enhanced tale out of what I'd done the day before; she'd been there with me. The subjects of most conversations took place in "real time," as we shared observations on the spot.

That being attached at the hip worked as well as it did was more to Kay's credit than to my own. To describe Kay's outlook on life as positive is an understatement. Her attitude is so upbeat and so optimistic that I sometimes call her Pollyanna, Polly for short. For example, she has the tendency to discount even the possibility that things might not turn out wonderfully. For Kay, misfortunate does not exist in the future tense.

Misfortune anticipation is my job, one that I'm pretty good at. Kay considers me overly cautious, though I prefer the term "forearmed." I don't *expect* the worst, but I like to be prepared just in case. I think about what problems we might encounter and try to have a contingency plan ready. It's a matter of degree. To fear that every situation carries within it the seeds of destruction is destructive in its own way, so I try not to carry contingency planning too far.

Fortunately, combining our two outlooks resulted in a guarded optimism, a practical and useful approach to living in a foreign country. Believing that everything will turn out well can get you through anxious times, especially when you aren't in command of the situation. Accepting the possibility that things might not go as planned prevents being blindsided by misfortune.

In short, our first few months in Granada presented unexpected challenges, even for an enthusiastic, upbeat person like Kay. Remaining so with no family, no friends, no neighbors, no garden, and no proper kitchen was a test. In addition, she had to contend with me, Mr. Impatience, who, after finding out he'd been standing in the wrong line at the police station for forty-five minutes, wrapped himself in a gray cloud of doom, gloom, and muttered deprecations. But contend she did, so that little more than a half an hour later, Mr. Impatience had become Mr. Equanimity, and was sitting in a café laughing at the absurdity of it. Believe me, the benefits of living with Polly far outweigh the drawbacks.

The Beautiful Sound of English

Our English-conversation drought ended the first week in March, not long after our final Spanish lessons. We were poking around at the morning market in Plaza Larga, in the Albaicín *alto,* or upper Albaicín, when we heard the unmistakable sounds of American English. For some reason, they did not strike us as tourists, so we introduced ourselves. Steve and Anne had recently moved to Granada from Kansas and lived not far from Plaza Larga. We exchanged phone numbers and parted, promising to call soon.

"Let's invite them over," Kay said.

"I think we should meet for coffee or drinks first," I said. "I'd like to know more about them."

"I thought they were nice enough."

"What if they turn out to be members of some kind of cult? Or believe in flying saucers?"

"You're being silly."

"What if they're the kind of people who are always wanting to borrow our telephone card or use our washing machine? You find out things about people when you meet for a drink. Like you and I order a beer and they order French champagne and then want to split the bill."

"What if you just relax? They seem like perfectly normal people."

"They could be radical vegetarians, or teetotalers. Or believe that the Alhambra is a holy place where you can get in touch with dead ancestors, and they'll invite us to their apartment, which instead of being a cocktail party would turn out to be a séance or something, and we'd be stuck for hours sitting on the floor drinking herbal tea and talking with people with names like Moon Garden. And every time we'd see them they'd invite us to their apartment, and we'd have to come up with a new excuse, and when we ran out of excuses we'd have to start wearing a disguise or avoiding Plaza Larga. You never know what you're getting yourself into."

"Sometimes I wonder if I knew what I was getting myself into."

We called the following week and met for coffee, and the weekend after that we walked out to the flea market together. Anne and Steve were not weird at all. In fact, they turned out to be normal, friendly people with similar tastes and values and we became friends.

The second week of March marked the beginning of a string of guests we would be hosting throughout the spring, which was another reason we'd terminated our Spanish lessons at the end of February. Kay's brother Mason and his friend Monte were our first visitors and we were eager to have them.

Mason and Monte arrived on March 9 for a four-day visit. Crossing the Atlantic for only four days may not seem worthwhile, but both were airline employees, so the cost of flying was next to nothing. Although we had a second bedroom—the decision to take a two-bedroom apartment had been made not only because Flannery would be living with us, but because we thought that being able to provide lodging would entice our friends to visit—the two M's decided to take rooms at a nearby *hostal* where they would have their own beds and bathrooms. "We're too old to share a bed," Mason told us.

We tried to pack in as much into their four days as possible. The weather, which had been cool and wet, cleared, and we were able to mix the sightseeing with sampling *tapas* in the afternoon sun.

Early Thursday evening, relaxing at home after a day tramping the city, we turned on the television, more from curiosity than a search for news. But news we got, on almost every channel. What we saw were pictures of a train that had wrecked or been bombed. All we were able to determine was that whatever had happened had happened in Madrid. We heard the word *terrorist* but didn't know if this was suspected or factual. Spanish television newsreaders speak even more rapidly than people on the street, so try as we might, we were getting only a few words. Then there was George Bush on the screen, and we heard him say, beneath the Spanish voice-over, that America stood with the Spanish people. Whatever had happened was big, but we knew no one in Granada who we could call for information, except for our upstairs neighbor Enrique, and he was out of town. We assumed that CNN must be showing in a hotel or restaurant somewhere in Granada, but we didn't know where. I guess we could have called someone in the States, but we didn't know enough at that time to be alarmed.

Kay and I had moved to Spain knowing that if a disaster took place in the States, an earthquake in California, a hurricane in Florida or North Carolina, staying informed could be difficult. Getting through by telephone can be tricky under normal conditions; after a catastrophic event, it might be impossible. What we had not anticipated was the difficulty of finding out what was going on right here in Spain.

We rushed out Friday morning to buy the *International Herald Tribune* with its *El Pais* insert. The photos of the bombed train were horrifying. According to the papers, the conservative government blamed the Basque separatists. In fact, the Minster of the Interior stated that there was no doubt that the ETA was behind the attack. Other sources suggested the possibility that al-Qaida was responsible. Unfortunately, both the *Tribune* and *El Pais* insert are printed in Madrid the evening before and what we were reading was already half a day old.

Walking into History

Still very much out of the information loop, we went on with our day. We walked over to the bullring and peeked through the gates into the ring. About six-thirty, more than a little leg weary, we decided to walk home along Calle Grand Via de Colón, the broad boulevard that runs parallel to Calle Elvira. We immediately noticed that the sidewalks were unusually crowded and that almost everyone was walking in the same direction. As we walked the number of people increased and traffic rapidly decreased. Within blocks the crowd spilled out into the almost empty boulevard.

Many walkers wore a white sticker with a black ribbon. Spanish flags, each with a black ribbon attached, stretched across business fronts and hung from the apartments above. Shops and offices, which normally reopen at five thirty after the afternoon siesta, were closed. Even the cafés and bars were shuttered.

We assumed that whatever was happening had to do with the train bombing. The atmosphere was electric. More than simply curious, we felt compelled to be part of it, so we joined the crowd. Every small cross street had become a stream feeding a growing river of people.

The wide boulevard was strangely quiet. There were no cars, no buses, no motorcycles, and the normally very loud Spanish spoke in hushed voices. The dominant sound was marching feet.

Grand Via de Calón ends at Calle Reyes Católicos, another major boulevard. There the two rivers of marchers merged, and we turned and headed down Católicos toward Puerta Real, the city's central intersection and one end of Granada's largest open space. Once there, we watched as people poured in from every direction, forming a sea that stretched toward the river in the distance. Movement was reduced to a shuffle. The tightly packed crowd—families, matrons in furs, jean-clad students, groups of older men in dark suits, well-dressed workers from the surrounding banks and offices, even old ladies with walkers— pressed slowly forward.

A man pushing a baby carriage bumped me, then excused himself in English. I guessed he'd heard us talking. I asked him what was going to happen. He told me that there would be a few speakers and then a march. The march would begin at the far end of the already-packed plaza, proceed back through where we were standing, and then continue along Calle Reyes Católicos and Grand Via de Calón, the route we'd just walked.

Unlike most demonstrations and marches in the States, there were no expressions—signs, banners, leaflets—of political opinion or agendas, mainstream or fringe. This massive gathering was not seen as an opportunity for free publicity. The impressive cross section of Spanish society that surrounded us had gathered solely to express their sorrow and outrage.

We were within minutes of being blocked in, so we quickly gathered to decide whether to continue or to head for home. We'd been walking all day, were very tired, and both Kay and Mason were beginning to feel claustrophobic. Home it would be. We worked our way through the crowd toward the pedestrian shopping area, then through narrow lanes lined with shuttered stores toward Calle Elvira.

During the evening we watched televised demonstrations and marches taking place all over Spain. Millions of Spaniards had taken to the streets. I later read that an estimated one-quarter of the population of Spain had participated. We'd never seen anything like it.

Mason and Monte left early Saturday morning, not knowing if events would affect their trip home. That morning's *El Pais* accused the government of withholding information and placing responsibility for the attack on the ETA in order to influence the election. Although surveys showed that ninety percent of Spaniards were against the war, the governing Popular Party (PP), which supported the war, had been running several points ahead, although recent polls had showed that gap closing. An attack by al-Qaida could further inflame opinion.

That afternoon, we checked our e-mail, where we found notes of concern and inquiries as to our safety, but no new information. We went to bed without knowing who was responsible for the attack.

Sunday was election day. All campaigning had ceased after the attack, cutting Spain's mercifully short four-week election campaign even shorter. That afternoon I ran into Enrique, our upstairs neighbor. He was very upset. There had been arrests and al-Qaida had claimed responsibility for the bombing, he told me. The PP had tried to suppress the information so as not to damage their re-election prospects, but news of the arrests had leaked, and the Socialists had demanded a statement and explanation. Demonstrations were going on in Madrid, he told me, and people were calling for the government to step down.

"We have to vote them out," Enrique shouted. "We have to!"

That night Kay and I watched the election results, which, amazingly, were completed before eleven. The incumbent Popular Party lost. The Socialist Party candidate, José Luís Rodríguez Zapatero, had promised during the campaign that he would pull Spanish troops out of Iraq in the absence of a United Nations mandate. The Spanish may have voted against the Popular Party because of the war in Iraq and terrorist attack, possibly because of the pre-election cover-up, perhaps both. For months, both sides continued to accuse the other of twisting the truth.

Those days in March were historic ones for Spain, perhaps for the world, as it was increasingly obvious that there were no safe zones. The hope that we were entering a time of relative peace, a possibility engendered by the demolition of the Berlin Wall, the demise of the USSR, the thaw in US-China relations, was dying. There would be, no doubt, little wars, lots of little wars, as nationalism, religion, and tribalism replaced capitalism versus communism as the driving conflicts of the twenty-first century. But those nasty little wars, I thought, would take place "over there," on the Soviet rim, in Africa, the Balkans, possibly the Near East, as those artificial countries created fifty to one hundred and fifty years ago began to break apart. Otherwise, with the exceptions of a few diehard terrorists, like the ETA and the IRA, much of the world could look forward to a future with little fear of war. Well, so much for my career as a political pundit. No one was safe, though the danger is no longer worldwide conflagration; it's being blown up while commuting to work.

Kay and I were, I admit, a little apprehensive. Many of the businesses in our neighborhood were Moroccan, and we heard almost as much Arabic spoken on our street as Spanish. But we reminded ourselves that Morocco had also suffered terrorist attacks, and that the majority of Moroccans were as horrified by what happened in Madrid as we were.

Hello twenty-first century. Goodbye illusions.

No Longer Franco's Spain

Our friends Bob and Penny arrived the week after the attack and were with us as we watched a televised national service of mourning, which took place in the cathedral in Madrid. Taking part were King Juan Carlos, Queen Sofia, Prince Felipe, his then-fiancée and now-wife, Letizia, and other members of the royal family. Also in attendance were Prime Minister-elect Zapatero, Prime Minister Aznar, Tony Blair, Colin Powell, and other foreign dignitaries. The majority of the congregation was composed of the families of the slain and injured.

At the conclusion of the service, the queen, who had been visibly weeping, the king, and the rest of the royal family moved out into the cathedral to offer their personal condolences to the families. They walked the aisles and moved into the pews, shaking hands, touching cheeks, holding hands, exchanging kisses, patting backs, even hugging those who reached out, pausing time and time again to share a few words with mourning family members, who numbered in the hundreds. This emotional and tearful personal contact went on for some time. This was not a rushed "photo op." The king and his family took as much time as was required, while the attending dignitaries waited quietly.

We found the royal family's dignity and sincerity very moving. King Juan Carlos, who is very well liked and respected, seems to hold a special status as a non-partisan national figure. The royal family reached out to the victims' families as representatives of Spain and the Spanish people, not as representatives of any political party. Neither Aznar nor Zapatero, as representatives of their respective parties, nor their families, could have fulfilled this function. I tried to think of a national figure in American life whose statue transcends politics, but no name came to mind.

We were aware that many people in the United States, particularly within the government, considered Zapatero's insistence on pulling Spanish troops out of Iraq as capitulating to the terrorists. This I never understood. Nor did the Spanish, who were quite indignant at being accused of appeasing the terrorists. There were two very important points they felt the American public didn't understand.

First, Zapatero promised to remove Spanish troops from Iraq long before the attack and the election. His position was that the war in Iraq was an ill-informed response to terrorism, that its management had proved to be a fiasco, and that it had made the world not safer but more dangerous. This view was shared, according to a Gallup poll, by the Spanish people. It is also important to remember that Zapatero promised to remove the troops *only* in the absence of United Nations leadership. How could he break such an important campaign promise and hope to govern? Perhaps his critics expected him to say to the Spanish people who had elected him, "Sorry, folks, I know I promised to bring back our troops, but they're calling us chickens and we can't allow that."

A second point overlooked by those eager to criticize is that Spain has suffered more than eight hundred deaths to the Basque terrorists. To question the bravery of the Spanish government and people is absurd. The government's response has been to get tougher. Not appeasement, get tougher. In fact, some thought that the response had been so excessively combative that it's escalated the conflict.

The election and its aftermath taught Kay and me a lot about Spain. Many of the assumptions we'd brought to Spain were turning out to be false, mainly that Spain remained Franco's Spain, a conservative, puritanical, reactionary, church-dominated society. We were discovering a considerable amount of evidence to the contrary. We'd noticed, for instance, that young girls were not escorted by elderly, black-clad aunts but were instead riding around on motor scooters, mini-skirts hiked high on the thighs. We learned that even teenagers stayed out until the morning. We couldn't help but notice that the newsstands carried a surprising number of naughty magazines, and that they were not hidden on the back wall. On the few occasions that we'd watched late-night television, meaning after midnight, we'd seen sexually explicit shows not shown even on cable in the States.

If you find this surprising, especially for a Catholic country, consider this: 68 percent of Spaniards favor some form of gay marriage. Spain's gay community is active and vocal and individual drug use in the home is tolerated. The Spanish consider the Puritanism of American politics, like the Monica Lewinsky affair, laughable. Even the wife of conservative Prime Minister Aznar, a devout Catholic, was quoted as saying about politicians who commit adultery, "It doesn't matter if someone has one or two or three or four affairs."

What we were quickly learning was that Spain, in the quarter century since Franco's death, had surpassed most European countries as a progressive, open-minded society. According to an article in the *New York Times*, "Of all the countries in Europe, Spain is already among the most cultured, tolerant, and socially liberal." As a result of the Socialist Party coming to power, Spain has become even more progressive. After the election, the Zapatero government announced plans to legalize some form of gay union, eliminate compulsory religion classes and Catholic dogma from public schools, free medical research from religious restraints, allow women to terminate their pregnancies during the first twelve weeks for any reason, and create a nonpartisan state television. Also high on the agenda were efforts to pass laws protecting women and eradicating sexism in Spanish society.

We'd moved to Spain in spite of believing that it was a conservative country. What a bonus to discover that we were wrong, and that our new home was tolerant and progressive.

The Rain in Spain

Praise the Lord and Pass the Wine and *Tapas*

April 10 marked six months since we'd arrived in Granada. Half a year. It seemed momentous, a watershed of sorts. Although we'd never doubted that we could make a new life here, we also knew that anything could happen. Would we miss our family more than we could bear? Would we suffer relationship stress? Illness or injury—involving us or our family back in the States—could shorten the duration of our adventure. There'd been challenges; there continued to be challenges, but so far we'd met them all and felt confident about the future. We had our residency permits, our apartment was outfitted and comfortable, and we had enough Spanish at our disposal (a self-flattering way of saying that although we didn't actually speak it, we could use it) to handle our everyday needs. We knew the city pretty well and had become, we felt, quite proficient at hosting and touring our visitors. We'd already made two trips, one to Morocco and one to Munich. We'd made friends. All in all, we felt pretty good about the lives we were living. The unforeseen could happen, but we weren't worried about it.

Granada had become an enormous classroom, with lessons coming daily. April was no exception. We learned that it rains a lot in the spring. We learned that every celebration, no matter how religious its context, is an excuse for a big fiesta, or party. And we learned that the former, the rain, has no appreciable impact on the latter, the party.

The Spanish love a festival. It seemed to us that no month passed without at least one celebration. In addition to national fiestas and holidays, there are regional and even municipal events. Any reason, religious or secular, is sufficient. The most important religious celebration of the year in Spain, the one of longest duration, and the one we'd most looked forward to experiencing, was *Semana Santa*, or Holy Week. Beginning on Palm Sunday, for eight days religious processions would wind their way through the city streets. The processions in Andalucía are the most spectacular in Spain, and Granada's are said to be second only to those in Seville. Visitors from all over the country as well as Europe crowd the cities to view them, racing around the city in an attempt to see as many processions as possible. Hotels and restaurants are packed. If you became leg weary from climbing the hills, or if it rained and local processions were cancelled, you could watch televised coverage of processions taking place in other cities in Spain.

Thirty-four processions were scheduled to take place our first spring in Granada. Each procession left a church in the afternoon and went on into or even through the night. Many didn't end until early morning. The *Gitano* procession began at five thirty in the afternoon and ended at five thirty the next morning, a twelve-hour walk up the hills and through the night. If this sounds somewhat painful, it's supposed to be. The marchers are, after all, paying penance.

We bought a guide listing the times and routes of each procession. We were in double luck; the very first procession of Palm Sunday would be coming down our street and would pass our apartment around 6:00 p.m., and a second would come by at nine that night. We invited our new friends Steve and Anne, and Tom and Nancy, fellow Californians we'd just met but who were, unfortunately, nearing the end of a one-year stay in Granada, to join us for wine, *tapas,* and viewing. As Calle Elvira is very narrow, the figures on the *pasos* would pass at eye level only feet from our three balconies. Not even the viewing stands by City Hall or the cathedral afforded a better view.

The day was sunny and warm, and Calle Elvira was so crowded I wondered if there would be room for the procession to get through. There were no police cars leading the procession with flashing lights to clear a way. It just happened. The crowd parted like the Red Sea as the band approached.

Although every procession is distinct in its own way, almost all included some basic elements. The most important is the *paso*, what we'd call a float. They are quite ornate, with sides made of intricately carved wood or bas-relief images of bronze or silver depicting saints or scenes from the bible, and the top covered with flowers, not unlike a Rose Parade float. There are almost always two. The first carries Jesus and often depicts a scene that happened on that day of the holy week, Jesus entering Jerusalem on a donkey, for example. There may be disciples or Roman soldiers. We saw one depicting Jesus being visited by an angel while sitting under the olive tree. Yes, a real olive tree. Mary is carried on the second *paso*. She is protected by a canopy with rays of purity emanating from her head, and there are often tears on her face.

The *pasos* are not wide, perhaps eight feet, as they have to pass through the church doors and narrow lanes of the city. They are about twelve feet long and perhaps twenty feet tall. Approximately thirty men carry each *paso,* which can weigh up to two tons. Heavy drapes hang from the side of the *paso* to the ground, so all you can see of the *confradías*, or carriers, are their feet, which are usually identically clad.

Accompanying the *pasos* are church dignitaries and the penitents, whose long robes and tall pointed hoods are strikingly similar to those worn by the Ku Klux Klan. This can be a disturbing sight to Americans, especially Southerners like Kay and me. The hoods are almost two feet tall and have two small eyeholes. We saw a number of colors: white, black, purple, blue, gold, green, and red. A few hooded figures, acting as parade marshals, moved back and forth through the ranks keeping the lines straight and eliminating gaps.

Also walking the route are "The Ladies in Black," each wearing a black dress, black high heels, black lace gloves, and a tortoise-shell *peineta* (tall hair comb) from which a long black lace mantilla falls as far down as the knees. They walk two abreast and carry rosary beads in one hand and an enormous candle in the other. Walking up and down cobblestone streets in high heels for ten hours or more is a modern expression of medieval self-mortification.

There were children: altar boys and girls swinging incense, robed children scurrying about re-lighting candles, sometimes small children in costume, tiny shepherds, for instance, many walking hand in hand with their parents. I never followed a procession to its end, so I have no idea how long the children walk, but I hope not for hours. What need could they have to pay penance?

And there were bands. Most processions had two bands, one near the beginning, the second near or at the end. Every band we saw wore traditional marching band uniforms. Most bands had a bugle section, a trumpet section, and a drum section; a few processions had only drums. The music was unlike anything we've ever heard, the bugles mournful and shrill, the drums pounding. There wasn't always music. We were told that the sound and sight of the *Gitano* procession as it marched silently through the night—the tramp of feet, the flicker of hundreds of candles—was a dramatic and never to be forgotten experience. Another unforgettable experience, according to someone who lived on a procession route, was hearing the blare of bugles outside your bedroom window at two in the morning.

Bringing up the rear were the balloon sellers that trailed every procession. The passing of the procession by our balconies lasted about thirty minutes.

We'd been told that seeing the *pasos* come out of the church was a must. According to our guide, one would be leaving the church on Gran Via de Colón on Wednesday afternoon, and we planned to be there. It had rained the day before, canceling that day's processions (rain could damage the *pasos;* climbing wet cobblestone streets would endanger the marchers), but the afternoon was sunny and warm. The procession was scheduled to begin at five thirty. The street had been blocked off and thousands of people packed the wide boulevard and sidewalks. People stood on the balconies and hung out the windows of the surrounding buildings. Television platforms had been strategically placed. By five o'clock it was almost impossible to move.

At the appointed hour, a hooded figure approached the closed door of the church and pounded forcefully, as if demanding to be let in. The tall doors opened, and the hooded figure entered. Moments later, the procession began to emerge from of the church, led by hooded penitents holding aloft crosses. They walked three abreast through the narrow lane that opened in the crowd.

Now the real drama began. The *pasos*, while being carried, are taller than the church doors are high and almost as wide, so they must be lowered by a foot or two to get through. The carriers do this by carrying the *paso* through the doors on their knees. It is extremely important that the carriers work in unison, so black-suited directors accompany each *paso*, shouting instructions through screened openings. They also signal to the carriers using something akin to a giant doorknocker located on the edge of the *paso*.

We could see the *paso*, which was still inside the church, moving oh so slowly toward the doors. Once there, the carriers went down on their knees. The *paso* cleared the doors by inches. They moved very, very slowly through the doors and down a ramp that had been built over the steps. Imagine coming down a ramp on your knees carrying three to four thousand pounds. Once on the street, the *paso* was lowered and rested on its supports while the carriers gathered themselves for the lift. I've never been able to see if they sit or crouch. After perhaps two minutes, the director alerted the carriers to be ready, then signaled them with a series of knocks, usually one, two, three and UP! The *paso* popped up as if it on a spring, and the crowd applauded its approval.

The *paso* made a gentle turn onto the street, then joined the waiting procession. The carrier's feet moved in unison, left, right, left, right, producing a side to side sway. Following the first *paso* were another hundred or so penitents and children. The procession moved very slowly. Every two hundred meters or so, the *paso* was lowered so the carriers could rest, then the signal was given and up it came again. Every lift was greeted with enthusiastic applause. Everyone knew how difficult it must be to get three thousand pounds or more up again.

All through the evening and into the night, the processions weaved their way through the city. At some point on its route, each procession passed in front of City Hall, where viewing stands had been erected, and continued on to the cathedral only blocks away. There the procession passed between another set of grandstands, where it paused to hear comments and a blessing from the bishop, then proceeded up a ramp into the cathedral, then out another door and back out into the city. Midnight, one o'clock in the morning, then two, three, the drums beat, the bugles blared, the procession made its way up and down the cobblestone streets.

It rained again Thursday. We went out that night after the rain had stopped, hoping that the last procession, scheduled to enter the cathedral at eleven thirty, hadn't been canceled. It had, so we walked around. The area around City Hall and the cathedral had been closed to traffic, and although it was midnight, the streets were thronged with people walking through the vehicle-empty downtown. Every café, restaurant and bar was filled, and diners and imbibers spilled out onto the sidewalks and streets, beers and *tapas* in hand. Groups of teenagers, handholding couples, and three-generation families promenaded down the boulevards, children joyfully tightrope-walking the center line of the street.

A Mystery Parade

There were also unexpected pleasures. One came about ten thirty on a Thursday night in late April. First we heard the drumming. To hear drumming—or guitar playing, singing, tambourine banging, chanting, even shouting—was not unusual on Calle Elvira, so we tried to ignore it. It didn't take long for us to realize that this was not the usual street drumming. Something was going on. Kay opened the doors to our balcony and stepped out.

"You're not going to believe this," she called to me.

Coming down Calle Elvira was a parade of sorts. First came a police car, so we guessed that whatever was happening was sanctioned. Or that the entire parade was being arrested. Next came a flatbed truck carrying five African drummers in colorful African dress and masks. The truck stopped just below our balcony and they waved up to us. Twenty or more masked dancers dressed in black leotards swirled and pranced from curb to curb as they followed the truck. Next came three costumed stilt-walkers dancing to the rhythm of the drums. They wore masks identical to those worn by the dancers and the drummers. Their heads came up almost to the level of our balcony. A large crowd followed, perhaps a hundred or more, then another group of drummers on foot.

Just below our windows a half dozen costumed and masked people ran wildly back and forth across the street, literally leaping up and pushing off the walls of the buildings. They waved bright torches that flung white sparks high in the air over the crowd, so that sparks rained down on our balcony, sending Kay fleeing back into the apartment. But only for a moment, as she returned to see one more group of drummers, a trailing police car, and a crowd of marchers who seemed to be tagging along for the fun of it.

Just down the street, the parade paused for some minutes, and through our open windows we heard the sound of the drums echo off the buildings of our narrow street. Then it moved on. I felt as though we'd been extras in a Fellini film.

We never found out who they were, or why.

We also discovered that city-sponsored events and concerts were going on all the time. Finding out about them was the challenge. So we became conscientious, if not compulsive, poster readers, which was how we found out about a series of evening concerts taking place in the plaza facing the entrance to the cathedral. The concert was to begin at nine, and we walked down at eight thirty. The plaza was filled with rows of chairs, and a microphone and stool were placed on the landing just below the steps into the cathedral. We took two seats near the aisle on the third row.

While we waited, we looked up at the cathedral. The sky was a dark blue and the top of the bell tower glowed in the last rays of the setting sun. We watched the cathedral slowly change color as the sun dropped below the horizon. A quarter moon emerged from behind the adjoining buildings. At 8:45, few of the chairs were filled. How sad, we thought, that these city-produced concerts were so poorly attended.

Suddenly, as if by signal, people began streaming in from every street. By nine, every seat was taken and the rest of the square filled to capacity with standees. The last-minute appearance of the audience happened at every event we attended in Granada. It's obviously in the *Granadino* Operating Manual: "Thou shall never take your seat more than five minutes before the beginning of any event." We've attended the jazz festival, the symphony hall, Flamenco shows, even the opera, and without exception, at least three quarters of the seats were empty five minutes before the beginning of the concert. Because it takes ten minutes for everyone to get inside and seated, all concerts begin five minutes late. Except for clubs, where the show starts forty-five minutes later than the announced time. I shouldn't complain, as we early-arriving Americans always got a good seat.

That night's concert featured three guitar-playing singers, all very good and all enthusiastically received by the large crowd. Sitting there listening to Spanish popular songs on the balmy spring evening, the cathedral as a backdrop—well, what can I say?

We left early, around ten thirty (arriving early does make for a long sit), and walked for a while, passing through several of our favorite plazas to see what nightlife was all about. We were rarely out after eleven. Calle Elvira wasn't, we discovered, the only gathering place in town; there were a lot of people out and about. On the way home we passed by the cathedral. It was almost midnight and the music was still going on and the plaza was still filled. The streets were far busier than they had been when we'd begun our evening. Saturday night in Granada, where midnight is actually mid-evening.

Any Excuse for a Party

It seems that every Spanish city has a festival or fiesta of some sort a few weeks after *Semana Santa*. In Granada it was *Día de la Cruz*, Day of the Cross, celebrated the first weekend in May. The festival had two very different manifestations.

By day the festival is both a citywide celebration of the cross and a community fundraiser. There were thirty-five participating organizations that year, and each erected a large cross, some more than ten feet tall, almost always in a plaza. The crosses were flower-coated, usually with red carnations, and were the centerpiece of a carefully arranged display of traditional and symbolic items: overturned urns, local ceramic pottery, Flamenco dresses, shawls, guitars, and, the most puzzling, a pair of scissors piercing an apple. The displays were judged and the results shown on television at the festival's conclusion.

The idea, apparently, was for people to stroll from plaza to plaza, viewing as many crosses as possible (and some were quite remarkable constructions), pausing frequently for a libation and *tapas*. Enormous canopies covered the fundraising booths and the surrounding area to protect customers from the rain. Even though there were occasional showers both days of the festival, the plazas were filled with families. Many of the children were dressed in traditional Andalucían outfits.

Spanish music blasted from the speakers, while around the plazas people danced the *Sevillanas*, a Flamenco-inspired folk dance. The atmosphere is relaxed and family oriented.

But evening is an entirely different event. By six o'clock the families and "persons of maturity" began to drift away and rivers of young people flooded in, not by the hundreds but by the thousands. They brought with them plastic bags filled with bottles of wine, beer, rum, and mixes. Some pushed grocery carts filled to the brim. These outdoor drinking events, known as *botellón*, during which the young drink and party the night away, have become a problem in Spain, not that they usually result in rioting, fighting, or serious vandalism, but because they keep entire neighborhoods awake all night, turn the area into an outdoor latrine, and leave piles of trash. After every major *botellón*, the authorities and media cried, "What's to be done?" No one had an answer.

By evening, all the major downtown streets had been closed. Central Granada had become party central.

The small food stores which dot the city had lines of young people waiting to get in to buy booze. Some stores had erected makeshift counters across their doorways in order to handle the customers. Sidewalks were stacked with cases of beer and wine; the stores simply didn't have enough storage room inside. Opportunistic entrepreneurs sold beer and wine out of car trunks.

One large plaza we visited was filled with several thousand kids. It was so packed we could only circle it and observe. There didn't appear to be one person over twenty-one. Each plaza seemed to attract a specific age group, the under twenties, university students, mid- to late twenties, and so on. If Spain had laws concerning alcohol and minors, they certainly weren't enforced.

Plaza Nueva, just down the street, was packed to capacity. As the canopies stretched over the three beer booths could protect only a small number of people, most revelers stood in the rain, drinking, singing, and dancing. It didn't seem to bother them at all.

Around eight thirty, after an afternoon of wandering and observing, we walked home against a steady stream of partygoers, all smiling and carrying their plastic bags as they headed to the plazas in the rain.

How long, we asked ourselves, could this go on? Can they drink for eight hours? Ten? Although the night did become one of the noisiest we had experienced, it was not the longest, a gift for which we can probably thank the rain.

The garbage trucks and street sweepers began their rounds before dawn and by late morning all evidence of the massive party had been erased. Amazingly, the event was repeated the next day. It was hard to believe that Spain had once been a straitlaced, puritanical culture.

The Streets of Granada 4: Pollo Asado

Take Out It Was, Fast Food It Wasn't

Although Granada's population was roughly two hundred thirty-seven thousand people, plus some sixty thousand students, there were relatively few fast food outlets. Walking the city, we came across only a handful of Burger Kings, McDonald's and Pizza Huts, and one brand new Kentucky Fried Chicken on the far edge of town. The lack of fast food joints wasn't that surprising. For one thing, the Spanish don't seem to be in a big hurry. And, because almost all stores closed from two till five thirty, they didn't need to be. There was plenty of time to eat lunch. As for convenience, it was almost impossible to walk more than two blocks without coming upon a café or café/bar, so getting a bite to eat was never more than minutes away. And the drive-through, a feature car-loving Americans particularly enjoy, simply wasn't possible. If you've ever spent time in an older European city, you'll know why. Where ever would they put a hamburger joint, parking lot, and drive-through? There was one drive-through in Granada, a Burger King located in a parking lot on the outskirts of town.

Although there weren't many fast food joints, there were take-away options. For pizza lovers, Tele-Pizza delivered pizza, chicken wings, and even beer right to your door. There was the *schaurma*, the Moroccan wrap, and the *bocadillo*, a sandwich made on an eight-inch baguette filled with cold cuts or sliced pork or cheese or even fried calamari. Well, perhaps "filled" is an exaggeration as they're mostly bread. But they were cheap. One mini-market advertised a *bocadillo* and a liter of beer for €1,50. Beat that, McDonald's.

There was another, and in my opinion, better option, one we discovered on a long Sunday walk. Sundays were very quiet in Granada, as commercial activity was almost nonexistent. Even the supermarkets were closed. Although the city center still bustled with Sunday strollers and tourists, streets in many neighborhoods were virtually deserted.

We were on a Sunday walk through a quiet neighborhood, and had just commented on how it seemed that every business was shuttered, when we noticed a line of people on the sidewalk in the next block. What, we wondered, could this be? As we got closer, we could read the sign in the window. "*Pollo Asado.*" Roast chicken.

This was not a restaurant. It was take-out only. No larger than a room, the *asador's* back wall was one large stainless steel rotisserie. On the rotisserie dozens of deep brown, dripping chickens rotated slowly before the hot flames.

For roast chicken lovers, especially chicken lovers without an oven, this was an important discovery. Our search for the best *pollo asado* began. We tried the roast chicken wherever we could find it. We learned that although *asadores* were open five or six days a week, Sunday was the day of long lines. Perhaps the idea was to give mama a break. We learned to be on time, because they all closed by four. One day we waited for more than half an hour before being turned away. They'd sold out.

The serving process was pretty much the same everywhere. Using poultry shears, the proprietor cut the chicken into three or four pieces so that it could be packed in a heavy tinfoil container, which was sealed either by hand, or in some places by a mechanical foot-operated device that firmly crimped the top down. Before the top was closed, the customer was asked if he or she wanted sauce, which was nothing more than the drippings collected in a trough below the rotating chickens.

"*Si,*" we always said enthusiastically.

The proprietor ladled in a cup or so. "*¿Mas?*"

"*Si, mas.*" There's no such thing as too much sauce. The container was filled to the brim and sealed. Alas, some might say, this "sauce" was nothing more than chicken fat. True. Just as sweetbreads are but a more palatable name for thymus or pancreatic glands. It might be chicken fat to some, but it was liquefied essence of chicken to us.

We found our favorite chicken in a tiny *asador* in Plaza Romanilla behind the cathedral and central market. This place was so small that customers waited in the plaza. But it was worth it; it was delicious. Plus it was the only *asador* that made an actual sauce, as opposed to simply pouring liquefied essence over the chicken. Their white sauce was perfect with either mashed potatoes or pasta.

We'd walked by it several times before trying it out. One Sunday, having decided not to cook, and remembering the lip-smacking aromas emanating from this poultry palace, we headed toward Plaza Romanilla. We arrived about two thirty. There was no line, just a dozen or so people standing around, all facing the counter, so neither of us was sure about the ordering procedure. Kay, whose Spanish was coming along quite nicely, asked a gentleman standing near the back of the crowd what to do. "Just go up and order," he replied. Kay made her way through the small crowd, which was growing as we stood there, and approached the man standing at the counter. "*Un pollo*," she said.

"*¿Pan? ¿Patatas?*" he asked. Bread or potatoes?

Kay shook her head. "*Con salsa*," she added.

"*Solo pollo con salsa*," he said loudly, and wrote it down on the clipboard he held in his hand. The counterman was a bit of a character. About forty, I'd guess, he had short hair, a thick mustache, a wide smile, and a very loud voice. He seemed to enjoy performing for the crowd.

Kay returned, and we waited and watched the show. As I said, the *asador* was very small; three people behind the counter would have been one too many. The menu was posted on the back wall above a cooler filled with soft drinks, juice, and beer. On the left side there was a counter over which the food was delivered, on the right a glass case filled with huge potato chips, which are sold by weight. *Granadinos* eat a lot of potato chips. The food was prepared upstairs and brought down the narrow stairs by a young man. The counter man shouted the orders up the stairwell.

In addition to *pollo*, one could order paella, croquettes, soup, Russian potato salad, bread, and desserts. And people did. We watched as they picked up their orders. Each order was declared loudly by the smiling counterman as he sealed the top of the tinfoil container, put the container in a plastic bag, carefully tied the bag closed, then put that bag, along with any other bagged food, into still another bag. The last bag was tied in a way that provided a handle for carrying. Some people left with three or four bags, all neatly tied.

Whenever there was a brief lull, which is to say that no chickens were coming down the stairs, the counterman would look over the crowd, point people out in the order in which they had ordered, and shout out their order as if it were their name. Perhaps he was confirming orders so as to avoid any confusion later. It didn't matter how many things they'd ordered, he knew what person went with what order. I'm not sure why, maybe he'd noticed the enjoyment we were taking in his performance, but every time he got to Kay, whose order was slowly rising to the top of the list, he grinned even more broadly and shouted even more loudly, "*Solo Pollo.*"

We waited for half an hour before Kay's order came up. The day was cold and getting colder and we buttoned up to the neck and stomped around to keep warm. Finally our chicken appeared.

"*Solo Pollo!*" he shouted and smiled at us. The chicken was so big he could hardly get the lid to stay on. It was swimming in white sauce. He bagged it neatly and gave it to Kay. It cost €6. We could feel the heat from the bag all the way back to our apartment. It tasted every bit as good as it smelled and provided us with two complete meals.

A week or so later we walked through the Plaza Romanilla. It was early afternoon, about one thirty, and the *asador* was open, though there were no customers. The counterman was at his station, smiling broadly. He seemed to recognize Kay and she gave him a wave and they exchanged *holas*.

I waved and pointed to Kay. "*Solo pollo,*" I shouted.

He laughed. "*Solo pollo!*" he shouted back in a voice that resounded through the plaza.

At Long Last Spring

Mountains, Weddings, and a Pilgrimage

There is no spring in Granada, the man at the photography shop told us when we commented that so far May had been chilly and rainy. And no autumn, he added. He held his hand out. "*El invierno.*" Winter. He flipped his hand over. "*El verano.*" Summer. He turned his hand again, palm up, and then down. "Granada," he said, and shook his head as if at the delightful impossibility of it.

We remembered autumn as being warm well into November, then, it seemed within days, turning cold. Maybe that's what he meant. Granada is very hot in the summer. So when would the warming begin? So far, spring had been a continuation of winter, not quite as cold, but certainly every bit as wet; two or three chilly rainy days followed by a couple of mild sunny ones, then cool and rainy again.

We were getting restless. Except for one overnight trip to Córdoba to see the amazing Mezquita, once the largest mosque in the world, we hadn't been out of town since our December trip to Munich. It was time to see a bit more of Spain. Our next guests weren't expected until the end of May, and there were no festivals between now and then, so all we needed was good weather.

A few days later, with the promise of a couple of days of dry weather, we headed for the bus station, destination: Las Alpujarras, the mountains on the southern flank of the Sierra Nevada. With the exception of paved roads and the coming of electricity and small-scale tourism, mostly hikers, Las Alpujarras supposedly hadn't changed much since Gerald Brenan lived there in a small village during the 1920s, which he described in his classic book, *South from Granada*. The land is rugged, with steep gorges and narrow river valleys, the villages small and poor, the winters cold, and the mountaintops snow blanketed.

One of the most popular destinations, and one easily accessible without a car, as three buses a day left Granada, were the three *pueblos blancos*, or white villages, that overlook the Poqueira Gorge. The bus ride to Capileira, the highest village, where we planned to stay, took two and a half hours. After an hour or so driving south on the highway circling the Sierra Nevada, our bus left the highway and headed up into the mountains. The ride was not for the faint of heart. Kay sat by the aisle.

"Look down there," I said to Kay. "You can see the village we passed through earlier. The cars look like ants."

Kay, whose eyes were closed, shook her head.

I decided not to mention that there was no barrier preventing our bus from joining the ants down below.

We arrived intact, found a suitable hotel, and had lunch. May, we discovered, was an excellent time to visit Las Alpujarras. Snow still covered much of the popular hiking country, so the tourist season wouldn't begin until July. Many restaurants and hotels hadn't opened, and we had the place almost to ourselves. The afternoon was warm and sunny, so we decided to walk from Capileira down to Pampaneira, the lowest of the three villages. The trail wound across sheep-filled meadows, around ancient stone buildings, through the middle village of Bubión, for short stretches along the road, always overlooking the gorge. The hike down, which took less than two hours, was unlike any hike we've ever done before.

Leaderless Expedition

Pampaneira, like its two neighboring villages, was very small, and it didn't take long to explore every street, so after a café stop, we headed back up. That's when the trouble began. The trail was not marked, and I had not been as attentive to each twist and turn as I should have been. In short, I'd once again led us astray. How far astray became apparent as we struggled up a steep hillside on all fours, hands digging into the dirt in search of roots to hold onto. The "trail" I'd followed had ended and the only options were retracing our route back or climbing this hillside, a hillside that hadn't seemed nearly so steep from below.

"I do not like this," I could hear Kay's litany from just above me. She insisted on my being behind her to catch her if she slipped. "Why do I let you get me into these things? I do not like this at all."

"It looked like the trail to me," I grunted in reply. "How could I know the hill would get this steep?"

I heard her mutter something.

"I never saw a sign. Did you see a sign of any kind?" This was an excuse she'd heard a number of times in the past, so she didn't answer.

Finally, sweating, panting, hands and knees caked with dirt, we reached the top, then continued to make our way upward toward the sound of the road till we crossed the trail, then walked on to Bubión, where we stopped for a much needed wash and well deserved beer. The café had a small deck out back that overlooked the town and gorge. It was late afternoon, and we watched as shadows slowly crept across the other side of the gorge, leaving portions a golden yellow as others areas fell into a deep green dark shade. It was beautiful, and we watched it unfold without speaking.

Until I, seeking redemption, asked, "It was worth the climb, wasn't it?"

She gave me a look that I interpreted as: yes, it may have been worth the climb, but there better not be a next time. Then, after a long sigh, she smiled. The day was warm, the beer cold, spring was here. All was well.

Sitting on the deck above the town gave us a view of the rooftops, which were flat and covered with slabs of grey shale, nothing like those in Granada or the rest of Andalucía. The low stucco houses, I was to learn, were built in the Berber style, a style common in the Atlas Mountains of Morocco.

The existence of North African architecture is explained by the fact that Las Alpujarras were the very last refuge of the Moors. In January 1492, Boabdil, the last sultan of Granada, surrendered Granada to Isabel and Ferdinand. The Moors were neither slaughtered nor driven from the country. Instead, Boabdil and his followers were given thirty thousand gold coins and exiled to Las Alpujarras. As Boabdil, who had come to power after a civil war between his mother and father (the existence of the Moorish harem resulted in a complex and often volatile fight for succession) entered his new mountain home, he turned and looked back at the Alhambra and Granada, a paradise that had been Moorish for almost eight hundred years. Boabdil wept and breathed what is now known as the Last Sigh of the Moor.

Upon hearing his weeping, his mother responded. "You do well to weep as a woman for that which you could not defend like a man." This was not the kind of mother you ran to when you'd skinned your knees.

Boabdil and his followers were not the only ones who lost their homes. The Inquisition, renewed in 1478 primarily to deal with false converts, mainly Jews, was gaining power. This is not to be confused with the Inquisition as suffered by Kay and myself in San Francisco, as suspects really did get the rack. Just three months after the fall of the Alhambra, Jews were ordered to be baptized or be gone. This included, most conveniently for Isabel, the very Jews who had financed her war. An estimated fifty thousand "converted," and two hundred thousand left, mostly to North Africa *(Sefaradh* is the Hebrew word for Spanish), Italy, and Greece. Thousands were killed.

In 1502, ten years after Boabdil's chastisement, the treaty between the Moors and the Catholic monarchs was set asunder by the Inquisition. Moslems, who had been guaranteed the right to continue practicing the religion and using their language and customs, were now ordered, as had been the Jews, to convert or leave. Many "converted," and were henceforth known as Moriscos.

Identifying false Moriscos became quite an art. Cleanliness was, and still is, very important to Moslems. Bathing is a religious expression. As a desert people, water was a precious commodity to them, and their fountains and *aljibes* (cisterns) still exist across Granada. Christians, on the other hand, in an effort to prove their Christian identity, stopped bathing. Bathhouses were destroyed. The very act became suspect. Being accused of excessive bathing could lead to a death sentence. Christians became very dirty, very smelly people and were proud of it.

The eating of pork became another badge of Christianity, as it is forbidden to both Jews and Moslems. Devouring pork became a public display of faith. Whether this contributed to the Spanish love of pork—not only does it hold a central place in the national cuisine, it is absolutely delicious—is a point of debate.

There is one last twist to the story of Las Alpujarras. When the last of the Moors was expelled from Spain in 1610, Las Alpujarras, and in fact much of Andalucía, was left depopulated. Settlers from poverty-ridden Galicia, located in the northeastern corner of Spain, were moved to the mountains, bringing with them their Celtic and Visigothic customs, clothing (kilts), and music (bagpipes), but retaining the Berber architectural style. The result is a culture unlike any other in Spain.

Princess for a Day

For months, the Spanish newspapers and television had been filled with news of the upcoming royal wedding. We do not have royal weddings in America, Kay reminded me, and there was no way that she was going to miss it. It was the opportunity of a lifetime. Supplies were laid in, champagne chilled, the television screen cleaned. Saturday morning we rose and took our places in the living room.

The marriage, on May 22, 2004, of Prince Felipe de Bourbon, Prince of Asturias, son of King Juan Carlos I, and heir to the Spanish throne, was the first royal wedding in Spain since 1906, when Felipe's great-grandfather, Alfonso XIII, married Victoria Eugenia of Battenberg, granddaughter of Queen Victoria. For Spain, the wedding was an important event, both culturally and politically, not just another tourist oriented television spectacular. In fact, the couple had even requested that the extravagant celebration planned by the city be canceled, and that the money budgeted for the event be donated to the fund for the victims of the March 11 terrorist attacks.

First, a little background as to why no royal wedding had taken place in Spain for a century. For almost four hundred years, from the Catholic reconquest through the Hapsburg dynasty, followed by the Bourbon dynasty, Spain had been a monarchy. The constitution of 1876 created a government ruled jointly by king and parliament. This lasted until the 1920s, when General Miguel Primo de Rivera assumed dictatorial powers over an increasingly violent and chaotic Spain. In

1931, King Alfonso, in disgrace for supporting Rivera, fled the country, and Spain once more became a republic.

This progressive, left-leaning Second Republic was short lived. In 1936, Generalissimo Francisco Franco seized control of most of the army and plunged the nation into war. The Spanish Civil War ended in 1939 when Franco's Fascist Falange forces took Madrid. Although the war was over, the bloodletting was not. Many republican leaders, artists, scientists, and intellectuals fled; those who did not were assassinated or imprisoned. Thousands were slaughtered all over Spain. The following forty years of harsh dictatorial rule is now called the National Tragedy.

In 1969, Franco announced that Juan Carlos, and not his father, Don Juan, would become his successor and Spain's king after his death. Franco died in November 1975, and the thirty-seven-year old became Juan Carlos I days after. Juan Carlos had been Franco's protégé, but not even his mentor knew that he had strong democratic ideals. Only months after becoming king, Juan Carlos relinquished power and started reforms. A national election took place only one year after Franco's death, and in 1978, Spain adopted a new constitution, creating a parliamentary monarchy.

In 1962, Juan Carlos married Princess Sofía, daughter of King Paul and Queen Frederika of Greece. The wedding, a grand, royal affair, with kings, queens, and presidents from around the world in attendance, took place in Athens, not Spain. By the time Juan Carlos became king, the royal couple had three children. Felipe was their third child, and first and only son.

The Spanish king is not a ceremonial figurehead. The constitution of 1978 delegated to the Spanish crown certain fundamental duties. The king is the highest representative of the state to other countries. He may disband congress, call for new elections, or postpone them in the case of a public emergency. He is also commander in chief of the armed forces. In 1981, during the attempted coup, he ordered rebellious troops back to their barracks. They obeyed. Juan Carlos is widely respected and seen as a unifying figure in Spain.

Now back to the wedding. Felipe, thirty-six years old and never married, is tall, dark, and handsome. His fiancée, Letizia Ortiz, a thirty-two-year-old divorced journalist and news anchor, is blonde and beautiful. Someday he will be king of Spain. She is a commoner who will become queen. This could well be *the* ultimate princess story.

Kay planned to devote her entire Saturday to watching the event, from the first arrivals at the cathedral in Madrid to the final toast. The day had the makings of a transcendental experience, better by ten than the best chick flick ever made, better than *Bridget Jones' Diary*, *Love Actually,* and *Pretty Woman* all rolled into one.

Although the wedding guests wouldn't begin arriving at the cathedral till nine thirty, Kay was stationed before the television by nine. Five thousand citizens who had been admitted on a first-come basis lined the plaza to watch the arrivals. Invited guests—friends of the couple, we guessed—were the first to arrive; most were young and outrageously beautiful. They were followed by distinguished guests (thirty heads of state were in attendance), and royalty (forty royal houses were represented). The men wore tails, the women lovely dresses and fabulous hats. Many of the titled men wore metal- and ribbon-decorated uniforms and carried swords. The royal family arrived last, walking the two hundred meters or so from the palace to the cathedral. Felipe escorted his mother, Queen Sofia. Letizia arrived at the cathedral alone in a carriage after everyone was in place, where her waiting father met her.

The United States was represented by its ambassador, President Bush having declined to attend. Some attribute his absence to presidential pique at the new premiere's decision to pull Spanish troops out of the "coalition" in Iraq. I could imagine him saying to Dick Cheney, "If they won't come to our war, we certainly aren't going to go to their fancy dress ball."

The arriving took two hours. Then the ceremony began. It was very high church, a good time for me to run errands. Leaving Kay misty eyed and moon struck, I walked down to Gran Via de Colón, Granada's main boulevard, to find the street closed and lined, block after block, with *Gitano* wagons.

Another Day, Another Procession

The *Gitano* once lived and traveled in such wagons. Not so long ago horses pulled these little houses on wheels. Now each of the fifty or so trailer/wagons was attached to a very large enclosed tractor, John Deere being a favorite. The wagons were painted in bright colors and decorated with flowers. All had roomy balconies on the back with wrought-iron railings and fold-up steps. They were furnished like living rooms, with couches and chairs, photos on the wall, lamps, and tables. Most seemed to have a party going on inside.

The presence of tractors did not mean a lack of horses. At least one hundred horsemen rode through the street, which was, as usual, blocked off. The riders wore traditional Andalucían black or gray collarless suits and large-brimmed black hats. The horses were magnificent, prancing and high-stepping down the street. The sidewalks were filled with women and children dressed in tradition Andalucían dresses and suits. The children seemed happy to pose for photographs.

I quickly returned to the apartment to tell Kay. Fortunately, the wedding ceremony had ended and the procession from the cathedral had begun. Kay, confident that the event would be shown afterward on television (which it was, in its entirety, over and over, on almost every channel), left her tiara on the coffee table and joined me.

What was happening, I found out, was not a parade as such. All over Andalucía, similar caravans were beginning the Romería del Rocío, a multi-day pilgrimage to Almonte, a small town near Seville. The purpose of the journey was the veneration of the *Virgen del Rocío*. Typically Spanish, it is part religious observation and part fiesta. Each night the pilgrims stopped at dusk, circled the wagons, then spent the night sitting around campfires singing, dancing, and drinking till dawn. Staged versions were shown on television.

A little before noon, they headed out, led by dozens of horsemen, followed by a two-wheeled, silver-gilded, flower-covered cart pulled by two massive, flower-draped oxen. Next came a large crowd of marchers, most in costume, who sang loudly to the accompaniment of guitars and tambourines. Most of the walkers, we found out, as well as many of the horsemen, only escorted the caravan as it passed through the city and did not continue the journey. More horsemen followed, and after them the fifty or so trailer/wagons. Mini-street sweepers roamed up and down the street cleaning up after the horses.

We decided to follow the procession as it proceeded through the heart of Granada. It was early Saturday afternoon, and every street through the commercial district was closed. The procession stopped in front of the basilica, where a large crowd filled the sidewalks and promenade. The oxen-pulled cart was also there, as well as twenty or so horsemen. We thought that perhaps a wedding was taking place in conjunction with the procession.

The doors of the church were open, and we could see that a service of some kind was taking place. Being tired and thirsty, we adjourned to a sidewalk café opposite the church and waited. Suddenly the bells (and these were awfully big bells) began to gong. The crowd in front of the church broke into song. The horses neighed and pranced. People applauded. Then the horsemen, followed by the oxen-pulled cart, slowly moved on. The crowd thinned. What had taken place had not been a wedding but the blessing of the statue of the virgin carried in the cart.

That evening we watched the highlights of the royal wedding on television. According to the broadcast, there had been hundreds of weddings all over Spain that day, a dozen or more in Granada alone.

A lot of history had taken place in Europe during the seven months we'd lived in Granada. There had been the celebration of the twenty-fifth anniversary of the Spanish Constitution, the terrorist attack in Madrid, the election of a new Socialist government, the enlargement of the European Union, and the first royal wedding in a hundred years. It was an exciting time to be living in Spain.

We went to bed late that night, tired but too filled with the day to fall immediately asleep. Beside me, even in the darkness, I could feel Princess Kay shimmering with pleasure.

Our First Visit Home

Along a Surprisingly Bumpy Road

We'd lived on Calle Elvira for seven and a half months, and the irritations, aggravations, and deprivations were beginning to outweigh the advantages. We loved the apartment's sunny brightness and Kay enjoyed the kitchen, even without an oven. Manuel was a friendly and helpful landlord. The nearness of the central market, Tienda de Oro, Plaza Bib-Ramble, and the pedestrian shopping area allowed us to get almost everything we needed within minutes. We could make the climb to the upper Albaicín in fifteen minutes or be in the Alhambra in twenty.

All these advantages were sinking beneath a film of dust and nighttime bedlam. There was construction up and down the street, and trucks picking up and carrying away dumpsters of dirt and debris constantly rumbled past our windows, windows that were, now that it was getting warmer, sometimes open. We could write our names in the dust every morning, wipe it away, and write them again in the evening. The music from downstairs wasn't as bad as it had been before Kay's first trip down—we went down only every three or four weeks—but it was still very irritating. The buildings across the street and to the right were long abandoned. What if demolition and reconstruction of those were to begin?

We decided that we had to move. Our lease would not expire until September 10, but if we had to pay double rent for a month or more, so be it. Our move wouldn't have to take place immediately, as we would soon be making our first visit back to the States. We needed to reacquaint ourselves with our three-year-old grandson before he forgot who we were. We'd planned on a visit every eight or nine months, and the time had come. Leaving now would also allow us to avoid a good deal of Granada's infamous summer heat.

Our friends Steve and Anne had used the services of an English-speaking rental agent to find their apartment. They took us to his office and introduced us. We told Guillermo what we wanted. I even prepared a printed list of requirements, listing them under mandatory or desirable. Under mandatory we listed quiet (meaning quieter, as quiet doesn't exist in Spanish cities), at least one balcony, and two bedrooms, as we expected more guests. Under desirable we listed oven, the neighborhoods we thought we would enjoy, and a maximum rent of €450, €50 more than we were now paying. We told him we were going back to the States and would return in late July. We left the list with him and told him we'd call upon our return.

The last two weeks of May were busy with preparations for the trip and entertaining guests, Dan and Dolores, longtime Mill Valley friends. We missed our families, but we were seeing a trickle of friends coming through. In fact, we were seeing more friends than we thought we'd see at this point. Perhaps, we thought, they felt we might not stick it out and they wanted to visit while we were still here. Oh, ye of little faith, we laughed to ourselves. The days were mild; the days were cold; there was sun; there were deluges. Then suddenly—on May 28, to be exact— summer arrived. On that day, for the first time, I lowered the blinds to block the sun. In forty-eight hours, our strategy had changed from keeping the apartment warm to keeping it cool. Our photo man had been right: the transition from winter to summer had taken only a couple of days.

Because United Air Lines flew from London to cities all over the United States, London would be our departure city. It was early in the season—we were to leave on June first—so we didn't anticipate any difficulty in getting on a flight even if it wasn't to San Francisco. Once in the States, we'd get to San Francisco one way or another. Flying standby is a great benefit, but it does require flexibility, as either the departure date or destination may have to be changed on short notice. We always fly with a contingency plan or two.

There was a second reason for flying through London. We'd purchased roundtrip tickets on a discount airline from Malaga (Granada was not yet an international airport) to London, but flying standby and arriving in London on the day of our scheduled return flight to Malaga could be tricky in July. It would be far less stressful to fly to London several days before our departure, and then train up to Yorkshire, where we could stay with Rusty, our English-American Mill Valley neighbor who lived there half the year. On the day of our flight to Malaga, we'd simply train back down to London.

Getting from Granada to London required busing to Malaga, spending the night, arranging a taxi pickup for seven so as to check in for a nine thirty flight, flying to Gatwick airport, taking a bus to Heathrow (at a staggering devalued-dollar fare), then standing by in Heathrow for our flight to San Francisco. None of this was made any easier by the fact that, in addition to our own luggage, we were carrying the rest of Flannery's.

We made the connection and, nine time zones later, arrived in San Francisco, where Flannery awaited us. She'd brought the tiny Tracker, into which we stuffed ourselves and the six bags we'd left Granada with thirty-six hours before. We dropped her things off at her apartment in the city, then drove north to Novato, where Bax and Renée had the crank-up camping trailer, now guesthouse, open and stocked with champagne. It felt great to be back after so many months away.

We stayed longer in California than we should have. We'd left Spain early to get ahead of the summer rush, and we stayed as long as we did because we wanted to celebrate Kay's sixtieth birthday on July third with the family. Even though we had a wonderful time with the family, a month is a long time. We walked, we cooked, we re-bonded with our grandson Gray, and we spent long summer evenings on the patio under the California oaks sipping wine and talking with Bax and Renée. We enjoyed a long weekend in the city at Flannery's. We visited old friends and neighbors.

Social Calendar Overflowing

Our home visit proved to be difficult in ways we hadn't imagined. This was more my fault than Kay's. The problem was my insistence that we see every friend and every former neighbor. We'd made lots of friends during our twenty-five years in Mill Valley and I wanted to see them. I felt obligated to see them. Kay wanted to see old friends, too, but she didn't feel the obligation to see every single person.

"It's not like we're never coming back," she said. "We're here mainly to spend time with our family. There's only so much time, and if we don't see someone this trip, we'll see them next time. They'll understand."

"But," I insisted, "How can we see Jack and Jill and not see Hansel and Gretel?" I'd e-mailed almost everyone we knew that we were coming back for a visit, and every phone call we made resulted in an invitation.

I persisted and Kay went along. We met friends, almost always for lunch or dinner, two or three times a week. A couple of days we were out for both lunch and dinner. There were days when we felt like relaxing on the patio with a book, but we were expected somewhere.

Of course everyone wanted to hear all about our new life in Granada. This entailed telling the same stories over and over. To make this even more difficult, both Kay and I, talkative, gregarious people that we are, felt compelled to correct and interrupt each other. Sometimes the correction added information that the interrupter felt was crucially important to the telling. When this was the case, the interruption might be appreciated. But more often, the interrupted did not appreciate the efforts of the interrupter at all. Dirty looks were exchanged.

We discussed this and promised to make an effort to avoid further conflict. We tried taking turns. Sometimes Kay gave me the story. "You tell them about the mystery parade down Elvira," she'd say. Sometimes I left the room on some pretext. But try as we may, we just weren't able to control ourselves, and before the end of the afternoon or evening, visual daggers slashed through the air. Our only peace was found at Bax's. But I'd already filled the calendar with appointments, so we slogged on.

The constant driving was also taking its toll. Kay and I get along extremely well—except in the car. We don't fight, but there's sometimes a low level tension. The problem is that I have little patience with bad driving. I don't respond by driving aggressively or flinging obscenities. I simply informed these bubbleheads—in the voice I would use speaking to someone across the room—as to their shortcomings as drivers. Occasionally I tooted the horn, though, not being Spanish, I never held it down. And I asked irritating questions, like, "Did you see that idiot?"

This behavior did not endear me to my wife. "Why," she asked, "can't you relax and enjoy the drive?"

"I'm releasing frustration before it turns into stress," I responded. "I'm not shouting or cutting people off, so what's the problem?"

"The problem is …"

There were times when we reached our destination already out of sorts.

In short, we enjoyed seeing our friends, but we weren't enjoying each other. It wasn't that we never bumped heads in Granada. Making the move and setting up the apartment had had its inevitable tensions. But on those days when we were not the other's greatest fan, we could get away, take a walk, read a book. And we didn't drive. In California, however, when we were expected for lunch, we had to drive, and we had to be together regardless of how we were feeling.

But we got through it without a major blowup. The California portion of our trip actually ended on a high note with Kay's birthday celebration. Kay's brother Mason came from Florida to join us for the party, which began on the patio at Bax and Renée's, then moved to one of our favorite restaurants, a delightful French bistro in Sausalito. That day alone made the trip worthwhile.

Two days later, we flew to North Carolina to visit my family determined to relax and break out of the unpleasant little dynamic we'd found ourselves in. Our ten days in Durham were easier, though there was still a bit of driving and visiting to do. My mother and stepfather have a small cottage behind their house, so we were able spread out a little and have some time alone. We have only a few friends in North Carolina, so we weren't faced with thrice-weekly social events. My sister and two brothers lived within an hour or so of Durham, and we spent a night with each of them. Nevertheless, we were wearing down. We were ready for our return to Granada, but there was nothing we could do but keep on keeping on.

We left for Knarsborough, in Yorkshire, earlier than anticipated. We hadn't planned to stay more than a few days with Rusty, but when Kay found available seats on a United flight to London leaving six days before our Malaga flight, we took it.

There is an advantage to visiting one person for a few days; you can get the stories out of the way on the first day and go on from there. We didn't know anyone other than Rusty and her friend Rosemary, whom we'd met when we'd stayed in Rusty's place a few years earlier, so the retelling and stepping on each other's lines didn't take long. And we weren't driving. We took English country walks, enjoyed a few day trips, and contributed to the local pub economy. We relaxed. We were happy.

The Price of Getting Home

For some reason, getting to Granada was never easy for us, our initial trip taking some twenty-seven hours. It's as if we had to pay some dues before we could enjoy our good fortune.

This trip began well enough. Rosemary picked us up at Rusty's and drove us to the York train station. This forty-minute drive was followed by a two-hour train trip to London, a one-hour ride to Heathrow on the Underground, a two-hour wait, then a two-hour flight to Malaga on the coast.

The flight landed twenty minutes late. We'd checked three bags and had to wait twenty minutes between retrieving the first two and the last. We knew we didn't have all that much time to get to the bus station, so we rushed out to the taxi stand. The last bus to Granada left at 9:00 p.m. The bad news was that it was 8:35. The good news was that a taxi was waiting. The bad news was that traffic began to slow well before we reached the city.

"*¿Taxi a Granada?*" the driver asked as we slowed to a crawl.

How much? He handed us the rate sheet: €142, about $170. No thanks. Plus we only had the €130 we left Spain with. We decided to take our chance with the nine o'clock bus. Then traffic stopped. Just ahead of us was the beltway that skirted the city. It was also the highway to Granada.

"*¿Nueve?*" the driver said, rocking his hand back and forth. Getting to the bus station by nine didn't look good. I looked at my watch. We had seven minutes. Even if we made it, there was no guarantee that there would be available seats.

"Granada," he said again. He held up his hand and wrote €118 on it. I'd already done a little mental arithmetic. If we missed the bus, the cost of staying the night in Malaga—hotel, dinner, a morning taxi to the bus station, the bus tickets, plus this taxi—would be well more than €100.

Kay and I looked at each other. We were tired and wanted to go home. We did not want to schlep our five bags around anymore. We wanted to sleep in our own beds.

"On to Granada!" we shouted. And off we went.

We made what took the bus one hour and forty minutes in one hour flat. Traffic was light, the driver skilled, and the ride was *muy rapido*. We tightened our seat belts, clutched hands, and watched the countryside fly by. Occasionally we looked at each other and tightened our grips. We would live or we would not.

I had the driver drop us off a block from home on Gran Via de Colón, as getting down Calle Elvira at ten o'clock could take half as long as the trip from Malaga had. I gave him €125 for the speedy trip (I don't want to think about the conversion), keeping €5 for a sandwich and a beer.

That Wednesday night in late July wasn't so noisy, perhaps because the students were gone. It was hot, but the air conditioner quickly cooled off the living room and front bedroom. We slept well, happy to be home, carless, and with only Anne and Steve to tell our stories to.

We looked out the windows in the morning to find a wide gap in the line of buildings facing our apartment. The abandoned, sagging building across the street had disappeared. In its place was ten-foot-deep hole in the ground. In the hole, four young people, brushes, and small digging tools in hand, crouched on boards as they carefully poked through the remains of whatever had been there before. In history-rich Granada, every building site goes through an archeological research stage before construction begins. Having an archeological dig across the street would at least be quiet, but the hole and the makeshift surrounding fabric fence were certainly unsightly. And eventually construction would begin. Our balconies were coated with dust and dirt, giving us an idea of what the apartment would look like when the balcony doors were left open. We had to get out of there.

Kay called Guillermo immediately and told him we had returned and wanted to begin our search as soon as possible. He told Kay that he wouldn't be available until after siesta tomorrow afternoon. That would be five thirty Friday afternoon.

"We'll be there," she told him.

Now Living High in the Albaicín

We Move from Bourbon Street to Casa Tranquility

That very afternoon Kay saw our landlord Manuel on the stairs. He seemed concerned about something and tried to explain the situation, whatever it was, to Kay. Communication did not take place. Our neighbor Enrique had moved out the week before we left for the States, and we thought that perhaps it had something to do with the vacant apartment upstairs, which Manuel had offered to us before our trip, explaining that it would be quieter. But we knew we'd be moving and had declined.

That evening the doorbell rang. It was Manuel's wife and English-speaking daughter. Although not fluent, she was able to tell us what Manuel had been unable to.

"There is a problem on the roof," she said. "The city says we have to repair. It will be very noisy. And scaffolding outside the balconies. It could take a long time. It will be better if no one lives here." She shrugged an apology. "We have other properties but nothing is available." She shrugged again.

"Not to worry," I told her. "We were planning to move anyway." She told her mother and they smiled and nodded, as in relief.

"Move anytime you want," she said, "and just pay for the time you are here. The lease is no problem."

"Thank you," I said, clasping my hands behind my back so as not to applaud with glee. I thanked them again for coming by and for their consideration.

Hallelujah! We would not be paying double rent for August and the first ten days of September, which would save us some €530, at that time about $657. Optimists that we were, and still are, we dreamed of living elsewhere within the week. The stars were aligned, all system indicated go.

We were standing outside Guillermo's office Friday afternoon when he arrived. He didn't say anything about our priority list, but he said he had several places to show us. The first place he wanted to show us was a *casa*, or house, in the Albaicín *alto*. We hadn't placed the upper Albaicín high on our priority list because we feared that having to climb the hill might dissuade us from taking our daily walks. Would we want to climb that hill everyday? In the heat? It was very hot, high nineties to a hundred everyday.

"Just take a look," he suggested. "It has six balconies." And he laughed. At least he'd remembered how much we wanted at least one balcony. And after that he had a few apartments to show us down the hill. A house? We'd never considered a house. Why not take a look.

"It's too hot to walk up," Guillermo said, so we took the bus.

The house was actually what we would call a flat, in that it occupied an entire floor of the building. There was a cafeteria downstairs—more a coffee shop and ice cream parlor than café-bar—and it was closed. Guillermo called it a *casa* because it was the only living unit in the building and had its own private entrance. There were six balconies evenly spaced across the building. Guillermo took us in through the heavy wrought iron front door, through the entrance foyer, and up the stairs. The front door was very large and the doorknob was in the center. So far, so good.

An L-shaped hallway ran the length of the house, with an entrance to every room except the front bathroom. The living room, or *salon*, had two couches, an enormous hutch filled with dishes and glassware, a dining table with four chairs, and an arched brick inset in the wall facing the balcony. There was a large TV in the arch and storage cabinets below. There were two nicely furnished bedrooms: a master bedroom in the front with two balconies and large bathroom with a tub; and a smaller bedroom at the back of the house with two single beds. Off the hall there was a laundry room with a washer and a dryer and a smaller bathroom with a shower. The kitchen was small, but it had a relatively new refrigerator and, best of all, an oven. There was even a small pantry.

I was confused about the balconies. I'd counted six from outside, but once inside I'd seen only three. When I asked Guillermo, he grinned.

"Yes, there are six balconies," he said. "You could see them. But only three of them are yours." He laughed again. He obviously thought our love of balconies most amusing.

Then Guillermo took us up to the rooftop terrace. The floor was tiled and there were walls all around. The front area was long and narrow and overlooked the cafeteria's small courtyard below. The room-size back area was two steps up, and had a corrugated metal roof. We took in the view. Up the hill we could see the ancient hermitage; downhill the bell towers of two very old churches dominated a sea of tiled rooftops.

Very nice, we said. How much? The rent was €480. We wanted to see more, we told him. We couldn't just take the first one we saw without some comparison. So down the hill we went, where Guillermo showed us three apartments. These were apartments, not houses. They were small, the rooms were tiny, and the furniture cheap, rental apartment stuff. The only one worth considering was a third floor walkup. We did not like them at all. The rent ranged from €420 to €460.

"I had a perfect apartment for you last week, but it was taken immediately," Guillermo told us. "Good places go fast. I will have more next week to show you."

We said goodbye and walked back to Elvira.

That night we considered our options. We wanted out as soon as possible. Although Calle Elvira, *número cuarente,* was where our stuff was, in spirit we were already gone. Neither of us was up for a long search, particularly in the summer heat. We talked about the house in the Albaicín. It really was nice. A little more than we'd planned to spend but still within our budget. What if someone else took it? What if all we could find were apartments like the ones we'd been shown that afternoon? What if it took weeks to find something we liked? We promised each other that if we took the house, we would never let the hill be a deterrent to walking the city. We called Guillermo, who was, as he'd told us he would be, at his own birthday party. But he didn't seem to mind being called. We were putting €480 in his pocket. He told us to come to his office Monday morning to sign the lease and meet the landlady.

We assumed that we'd have to come up with four months rent, as we'd had to do on Elvira, one month in advance, a security deposit equal to two month's rent, plus the realtor's fee of one month. On Monday morning, looking as clean, responsible, and upright as possible, our pockets bulging with €1920 euros, we arrived at Guillermo's office, where we were informed that Conchita would not be able to meet with us until six that afternoon. We were dying to see the place again, and Guillermo agreed to meet us there later, which he did. We checked it out carefully this time and asked more questions. It was fabulous.

We met Conchita at six. She spoke not one word of English, but we found out through Guillermo that the house had once been her home, that she had raised her family there, and that she now lived in a small village on the outskirts of Granada. The water and electricity were in her name and she would come by every other month with the bills and collect. And, she told Guillermo, we could move in immediately, and she wouldn't charge us for the six days in July.

I pulled out our euro-stuffed envelope.

"That will be €960 for her," Guillermo said, taking the money and giving it to Conchita, "and €480 for me." We assumed that we'd pay August rent on the first. We signed the lease.

It was too late to begin moving that day, but we had every intention of making that night our last on Calle Elvira. It had served its purpose and we'd never regret living there. But we now had a new home: Calle Pagés, *número vientidós,* high in the Albaicín. All we had to do was get our things up there.

Porters Would Have Helped

Every step of the twenty-five-minute walk from Calle Elvira to Calle Pagés was uphill. The most direct route was up the lane by our apartment. The climb began immediately, all steps except for a short stretch that was just as steep. The task facing us: getting all the stuff we'd bought up the hill. Fortunately the short couch could be dismantled—the six cushions were attached with zippers and Velcro—and it wasn't that heavy. Neither was the television. There were the books and the microwave and all the dishes and all the plants and suitcases of clothes. The temperature would be in triple digits. This was a challenge that Kay and I might have taken on twenty years before, but Kay had just turned sixty and I was sixty-one, and we were both somewhat wiser. We turned to Guillermo for help. Fortunately, he had a friend, Leon. He called. Leon was available and would transport as much as his small van could carry on Tuesday afternoon for €30. That morning Kay and I filled six boxes—I'd saved all the boxes, TV, microwave, etc.—with glasses, dishes, and household items. Kay called for a taxi, but after being put on hold three times, gave up. So I walked to the taxi stand on Plaza Nueva and took a taxi home, loaded it, and we went up the hill. We emptied the boxes and walked them back down the hill. It was very hot, and we walked in the shade whenever possible. The temperature was one hundred degrees—a very dry one hundred, but one hundred nevertheless.

Steve and Anne, having taken leave of their senses, offered to help. We dismantled our short couch and took it downstairs, then refilled the boxes, concentrating on what we'd need right away. Next came things too awkward to carry on foot, like plants, then full suitcases and bags, each item carefully carried down the stairs and arranged along the curb. The rest could wait till later. Then we sat on the steps in puddles of our own perspiration and waited for Leon.

Leon arrived at five. We strapped the sofa and cushions on top, then filled the van with far more than I ever dreamed it would hold. Kay, Ann, and Steve carried suitcases and as many bags as they could and headed to the taxi stand. I went up with Leon.

After unloading and carrying everything up the stairs, we thanked Anne and Steve profusely and promised to take them to dinner. Kay and I had now reached a condition well beyond bushed. We were done in. Unfortunately, we discovered that somehow our toiletries, towels, and linens had not made the trip, so back down the hill we staggered, and back up, one more time, what seemed ten thousand steps. This time the climb back up took far longer than twenty-five minutes, but we made it. That night we slept, a long, deep sleep in our new house, only five days after our return from the States.

Over the next few days, Kay and I walked down the hill each morning with empty suitcases and bags, filled them with items we hadn't needed right away, like blankets, winter coats, decorations, and knickknacks, and either walked or taxied back up, depending on the load. Where did we get so much stuff? We saved the books for last. We filled two suitcases and two bags and walked to the taxi stand. I could hardly get the big suitcase into the trunk. By Saturday the move was complete. We cleaned the old apartment on Monday.

Once moved in, we were able to get to know our new home a little better. We discovered that in addition to three balconies, there were seven beautiful interior doors, three with etched-glass panes. The master bathroom was nothing less than a little piece of Las Vegas, with gold-plated fixtures, a huge sink, and a large, step-up tub with a nonfunctioning Jacuzzi. It was so *not* us, but we loved it. There was something almost decadent about it.

The stove, unfortunately, was electric and not all the burners worked, but we hoped to have it repaired. There was a dishwasher, but it didn't seem to work. As on Elvira, the water heater was gas fueled and ignited only on demand. Both bedrooms had wide, multi-door wardrobes with additional storage above.

All the floors were tile, and each room had a different pattern. Like the doors, all the closets and storage areas were made of beautiful dark wood and had heavy brass fixtures. The rooftop terrace definitely needed improvements, but nothing that couldn't wait.

Plaza Larga, the so-called heart of the Albaicín, was only a minute away down a narrow, shop-lined pedestrian lane. A produce and clothing market filled the tree-shaded plaza five mornings a week, café tables the rest of the time. In the evenings old ladies from the neighborhood sat on the benches that lined the plaza, gossiping and fanning themselves. There were several markets and a number of shops, and, of course, a multitude of cafés and restaurants, all to be explored with time.

What was missing was a neighborhood phone center. This required changing tactics. While we still received calls on our cell phone, we would have to call home on a public phone in the plaza across the street. We could see the three phones, which were in frequent use, so we knew when one was available. Of course, availability did not mean the phone was working. We usually determined through e-mail a time to call the

States, but if the phones were being used or out of order at call time, down the street we went to another set of public phones. These phones were all right on the street and often traffic noise made hearing almost impossible.

On Friday afternoon, by chance, we saw Guillermo across the street with a client. We rushed out before he got away. He hadn't told us how to pay the rent yet, which he'd promised to do. The rent was to be paid at the local bank, but we needed Conchita's account number.

"There is no hurry," he said. "You have till September."

"But we only gave her €960 for the two-month deposit."

He smiled. "Conchita requires only a one-month deposit. You've already paid August's rent." He laughed, obviously delighted to be giving us such good news. "Now you are almost €500 richer than you thought you were."

We were actually richer than that, as Manuel would be returning our €800 deposit on the Elvira apartment.

Life was good. We now lived in a fabulous, beautifully furnished house in a relatively quiet, very historic neighborhood. We had two bathrooms. We had a tub. We had a terrace. We even had an oven. We had three balconies overlooking the plaza. On top of that, our pockets were full of euros.

¡Que contentos estamos! How happy we are!

August on the Hill

Surviving the Heat, Listening to the Street

The move had been difficult, especially in the heat, and it took a few days to recover. Relaxing in our new home or wandering the neighborhood, we discovered that although Calle Pagés was the main street of the Albaicín, it was, compared to Calle Elvira, very quiet. On the midnight-noise scale, Calle Elvira easily earned a ten, the front bedroom on Calle Pagés a two, the back bedroom a zero. So we switched bedrooms, moving the double bed to the back and the two single beds to the front, making it the guest room. Our new bedroom was as quiet a bedroom as we'd ever slept in.

Our new house was much better equipped than the old. If anything, there was too much stuff. Conchita asked if we would store things we weren't going to use in the storage areas over the wardrobes. I packed away dozens of glasses, boxes of small figurines, and a number of religious articles, leaving us with only three sets of dishware, five frying pans, and enough platters to serve a banquet.

Not that everything was perfect. There were a few loose ends. Our first look at the house had been cursory at best, as we hadn't been, at least not at that time, favorably disposed to living in the upper Albaicín. We'd walked through with Guillermo, looked around, and moved on to look at another apartment. Our second walkthrough, which we'd requested after deciding to take the house, had also been with Guillermo, who, as it turned out, wasn't all that familiar with the house.

Ah, we'd said during our second tour: a washing machine! a dryer! a dishwasher! an oven! How wonderful! Guillermo had smiled at our enthusiasm and agreed that it was indeed wonderful.

What we discovered after moving in was that the washing machine had three small dispensing drawers and there was no indication of what—detergent, bleach, or fabric softener—went into which. The door of the dryer couldn't be closed and from all appearances, the dishwasher was a decorative item. But our major problem was the stovetop; there were four burners but only two control knobs. It wasn't simply a matter of missing knobs, one stem had been damaged and the other broken off. We couldn't phone Conchita and request that she have the stove repaired; she spoke no English and our Spanish didn't include stove repair. And we couldn't ask Guillermo for help because he, like all proper Spaniards, had closed the office for the month of August and gone to the beach. We left a message on his answering machine asking him to call us when he returned.

Hotter than Hot

We'd been in the United States for all of June and the first three weeks of July, so we'd missed much of the summer. It took only a few days to learn that what we'd read was true: Andalucía is the hottest region in the hottest country in Europe. Fortunately for us, Granada is almost twenty-four hundred feet above sea level and only twenty miles from the Sierra Nevada, so it wasn't as hot as Seville. But it was still very hot. From the end of July, when we returned to Granada, through mid-September, the daily highs, with few exceptions, ranged from thirty-five to forty degrees Centigrade. That's ninety-five to one hundred four degrees Fahrenheit. There were days when the temperature exceeded 105° F. Even the nights were surprisingly warm, rarely below 75° F.

A conference on global warming in Europe warned that temperatures in Spain could rise by three to four degrees Centigrade in the decades ahead. This meant that temperatures in Seville, which normally top out at around 110° F, could reach 115° F or higher. The report stated that temperatures that hot could "impact" tourism. Impact? Surely the prospect requires a stronger verb, perhaps incinerate. Other words come to mind, like "simmered" sightseer or "toasted" tourist.

Living in that kind of heat may sound terribly unpleasant, and I won't pretend that it wasn't. I'm not and have never been a hot weather lover. To me, lying on a sandy beach in the hot summer sun is about as comfortable as sleeping on gravel. Kay and I are Southerners by birth and well acquainted with tropical weather. Kay grew up in Memphis, Dallas, and Columbia, South Carolina, and I'm from Durham, North Carolina. We both have relatives in Florida, and we've spent many summer days there. Believe me when I say that summer in any of the above-mentioned places is far, far more uncomfortable than summer in Granada. The difference is the humidity. Granada is so dry that clothes hung on our rooftop line dried in two hours or less, including towels. If I didn't comb my hair immediately after taking a shower, I was in store for an extremely bad hair day, for within minutes it had dried into an unmanageable fright wig. Plants had to be watered at least once a day, sometimes twice, and skin frequently moisturized. A baguette purchased in the morning could be used as a weapon that evening.

Low humidity allowed us to live a reasonably active life in spite of the high temperatures. By reasonably active, I mean going about your business without worrying about sunstroke, dehydration, or being poached in your own perspiration. Reasonably active did not mean spending the day, as we had in the South, moving from air-conditioned house to air-conditioned car to air-conditioned destination. I remembered all too well hotfooting it across a hundred yards of shimmering black tarmac and weaving through lines of heat-radiating cars to reach the entrance to the mall, where, shirt plastered to my body, eyes stinging from perspiration, I found myself suddenly chilled to the bone by a temperature at least thirty teeth-chattering degrees cooler than outside. This cannot be good for your body.

Tactic One: Café Hydration, then Siesta

We developed a series of little tactics to deal with the heat that first summer. Because the hottest time of day is the late afternoon, not midday, we began our errands in midmorning. During the course of the day's journey, we made it a point to "hydrate," which is to say we stopped twice for a cold beer and *tapas*. Even when the temperature reached 100° F, sitting under an umbrella with just a bit of breeze was not unpleasant. Staying out of the sun was the key thing. Returning home, we walked slowly back up the hill, sticking to the shady side of the streets and lanes.

By the time we got home, usually between one and two, it was hot. But the house, which had been closed, was, as they say in the South, "right tolerable." We switched on the fans, stretched out on the couches with a book or magazine and eased into siesta.

We awoke around five and had iced tea. Kay made gallons of this traditional Southern American heat-beating potion. Outside, the street and plaza were almost deserted, with not one human being or vehicle in view. People began to venture out around six, and by seven life had returned to normal: shops and markets were open, shoppers streamed up and down the narrow streets, the cafés began to fill, and the taking of *tapas* had begun. At eight thirty the restaurant across the street began putting out tables and chairs in the plaza, and by nine thirty every table was occupied. By ten the street had become a crowded promenade, a procession of couples, families, and baby strollers that continued, especially on hot weekend nights, till midnight.

Tactic Two: Fans, Manual and Electric

Spending hot afternoons inside behind closed blinds and cooler evenings outside in a café or plaza weren't the only Spanish means to combat the heat. Another was the famous Spanish fan. Although some are quite ornate and expensive, they are not simply an affectation. They work. And they are used. Sitting on a bus, in a restaurant or café, or at an outdoor concert, when the air ceases to move, out come the fans. Hearing dozens of fans going at once brought back youthful memories of sitting in church on hot summer Sundays, and the sound of those round cardboard fans, with their wooden tongue-depressor handles, a colorful picture of Jesus holding a lamb on one side and an advertisement, usually for a funeral home, on the other.

The efficiency of this low-tech cooling device was demonstrated to us after a long August walk beyond the city into the surrounding *vega*, or plain. I was curious to see what all that green was that we could see from the heights. It was, we discovered, corn. We'd begun in the morning, but the day was hot, and after walking for a couple of hours, we turned back. Eager to get out of the sun, we picked up the pace, and when we reached the city's outskirts, we ducked into the first café we came across. In spite of the dry air, we were red-faced and sweaty. An older Spanish woman sitting across the café looked our way, smiled, and then offered her fan to Kay. Kay declined, but the woman insisted. It took only minutes for Kay to cool herself and me before returning it. She purchased two fans the next day.

Our apartment on Elvira had an air conditioner. Our house on Pagés did not. So we bought a small fifteen-inch electric fan that could be put on a table or chair; then an oscillating, pole fan for the bedroom; and finally a large metal fan, which sat on the floor and seemed strong enough to propel a small airplane. This fan had three settings, but we only used the slowest speed, for even at that setting it made the pictures and plates on the wall rattle. Perhaps it was intended for a larger space, like a gymnasium. Unfortunately, there was nowhere to put a fan in our small kitchen, so we weren't able to use the oven until October. But using a fan in the bedroom turned out to be very soothing, where its quiet whir had a nice lulling effect.

The ultimate summer survival strategy, one very popular among Spaniards, was simply getting out of town. All over Spain (all over Mediterranean Europe, for that matter) businesses, shops, even cafés and restaurants, simply closed their doors for the month of August, as owners and workers headed for the coast or the mountains. On the Spanish coast, they were joined by hordes of British, German, and French tourists. Prices were high and the beaches crowded. That didn't seem very inviting, so we stayed at home with our fans, sticking to the shade, hydrating in the cafés, and taking siesta.

Tactic Three: Evening on a Rooftop Terrace

Even closing the shutters against the sun wasn't enough to retain what little cooling the night had offered. We had a southern exposure, and we could feel the sun's heat through the shutters. So in the early evening, as the day cooled, we fled the still-warm house for the sanctuary of the covered rooftop terrace. Sitting in the shade under the roof with even the slightest breeze was comfortable. When we moved in, the terrace was sparsely furnished: four metal chairs, one of those broken, and a metal coffee table. Making the terrace a comfortable retreat became a priority. In addition to plants, comfortable furniture, and some decorative lights, it needed painting. Badly.

So we bought white paint, brushes, rollers, and a pan. There existed, much to our delight, a paint called Albaicín *blanco*. Not knowing how much paint stucco walls required, we bought a gallon. One gallon covered just one wall, so we bought another. We began in the morning and worked until midday when the heat became unbearable. As we worked, we reminded each other that painting a wall on the roof in North Carolina or Memphis, with the August temperature well into the nineties, would have been suicidal, while here we were merely uncomfortable.

We scrubbed the tile floors and dismantled and cleaned the filthy but very handsome iron and glass wall lamp. Once our painting and cleaning jobs were completed, I replaced the wire clothesline that zigzagged just above our heads with a series of strategically placed clips that allowed me to put up and take down a cord clothesline in minutes. Next, we bought a white resin table and chairs, a barbecue grill, and a bamboo shade, which could be moved to block the late afternoon sun. Every week Kay met Anne, a knowledgeable gardener, at the Saturday morning market in Plaza Larga, where they picked out the right plants to fill the large pots and flower boxes we'd bought at the *tiendas*. I ran a long extension cord up through the window in the washroom so we could plug in a radio-CD player and a lamp.

By the end of August, the terrace was complete. We thought it looked great. We invited Steve and Anne to our grand opening. As we climbed the stairs to the terrace, I instructed them as to the appropriate response on seeing the results of our labors. That response should be a long, drawn out *ooooooo*, followed by an equally long *aaaaahhhhh*. They complied beautifully and with great enthusiasm. For our first terrace dinner, I grilled pork chops and vegetables, and we ate by the light of the small lamp. The sunset was spectacular. The evening was splendid.

Observed from Our Balcony

Like Calle Elvira, Calle Pagés had a daily rhythm of its own. But unlike Elvira, the ebb and flow were not dictated by the café-bar scene. There was a busy Sunday afternoon café scene, but that was altogether a different thing.

The neighborhood was extremely quiet until seven in the morning, when the delivery trucks began unloading their wares. Our block of

Calle Pagés was one of the few places where the street was wide enough for a truck to park without completely blocking traffic. So the first sounds of the day were the clang of hand trucks being thrown off the trucks, followed by the drivers shouting at each other across the street. Cases of produce and dairy products, boxes of beer and canned foods, large crates filled with chickens and meat were stacked on hand trucks and carts and rolled down to the shops, cafés, and markets of Calle Aqua del Albaicín and Plaza Larga, where they were left by the store's door. There they remained till midmorning when businesses opened. Nothing, at least as far as we knew, was ever stolen.

There was a primary school nearby and each morning around eight thirty the children were walked to school by their parents or grandparents. The kids, say five to eight or nine years old, held the hand of their escorts—and almost every child had an escort—tightly and chattered away as they walked. A goodly number of escorts were what I guessed to be fathers. When they encountered someone they knew, they stopped, and the child was kissed, his or her hair tousled and cheeks pinched. The children didn't seem to mind at all. They waited patiently as the adults exchanged kisses and a morning greeting, then off they went. This little morning parade was without doubt the sweetest sound I heard all morning, and I often stepped out onto the balcony to watch them go by. Around two in the afternoon the parade, escorts and all, flowed by again, this time in the opposite direction.

Somewhere after nine, the man we called "the yeller" entered the scene. We guessed him to be in his mid thirties. He strode rapidly through the streets of the neighborhood shouting loudly as he came and went. Now we heard him, now we didn't. His shouts consisted of two or three short declarations of just a few words each. The only words we could make out were *señor* and *señora* and various numbers. I wondered if he suffered from Tourette's syndrome, as he also appeared to be a bit agitated. He went in and out of all the shops, talking to people on the street, and no one reacted as if he were doing something strange.

Several times the yeller burst into exclamation right behind us as we were walking, sending Kay several inches off the pavement. In response, Kay made it a point to greet him every time she saw him. Like the antique dealers down the hill, it took a while for this approach to sink in, but once it did, he began returning her greeting, never more than *hola*, but at least he responded. Once she'd established herself on his radar, he seemed to become aware that his shouts startled her. We'll never know for sure. But he stopped shouting while walking behind her, much to her relief.

We eventually learned that he sold lottery tickets and ran errands for local businesses. Because only the disabled were allowed to sell lottery tickets, usually the blind, it seemed to confirm that he suffered from something.

The yeller wasn't the only one whose voice was heard. Around midmorning the "deal maker" made his appearance at the café across the street. He didn't look like a deal maker, as he was usually dressed in jeans, sneakers, and a sweatshirt, but deal making is what he seemed to be doing. Two or three times each morning he came out on the sidewalk from the café across the street and held a highly animated conversation on his cell phone. He got very excited, walking up and down the sidewalk, out into the street, waving his arms, shrugging his shoulders, and looking quite exasperated. These "dealings," which often lasted five to ten minutes, were frequently interrupted as he greeted almost everyone who passed by, whether on foot or in a car. He seemed to know everyone in the neighborhood. When our windows were open, he sounded as if he were standing on our balcony.

On Tuesday, Thursdays, and Saturdays, somewhere around eleven, the gas truck arrived. The young driver parked his *bombona*-loaded truck wherever there was space and began hand-trucking the heavy tanks through the neighborhood. Just as on Elvira, I listened for the clang of the empties being flung on the truck, and then scrambled to get our *bombona* down to the street before he left.

Every week or two the knife sharpener parked his small van at the end of the street and signaled his presence by blowing on a small mouth harp. The trill it produced could be heard for several blocks. I don't know whether the sound of the harp was the signal used by all Spanish knife sharpeners or only this one.

Unfortunately, at least for us, Calle Pagés was the primary route into and out of the Albaicín. As the sole two-way street in the Albaicín, it was the only route for large construction trucks. Construction, which in the Albaicín was always preceded by destruction, presented significant logistical problems, namely, the delivery of building materials, as most streets were either extremely narrow, extremely steep, often stepped lanes, sometimes all three. As best I could determine, the procedure was for a large truck, as large as could negotiate Calle Pagés, to bring material in and unload it as close to the building site as possible. From there, mini-front loaders took the material as far as they could, and then, when necessary, wheelbarrows took over. Debris removal simply reversed the process.

Not so long ago, this hauling in and hauling out was done by burro and mule. They were still occasionally used; we'd seen heavily laden mules ready to ascend to hillside sites otherwise inaccessible. For the most part, animals have been replaced by mini-front loaders, smoke-belching, diesel-powered, muffler-stripped monsters whose drivers, when picking up a cup of coffee from the cafés below, never, ever once shut the ear-splitting engine off.

Calle Pagés, however, presented a rather unique problem. Just beyond our building the street abruptly ended, then continued through a wide gap to the left. To navigate this, trucks and cement mixers had to hug the extreme right side of the street before turning diagonally between the buildings. If a car was parked on the right, the angle was reduced, so progress was limited to eight inches forward, then six inches back. Sometimes the truck scraped the buildings; about four inches of the buildings on both sides of the gap had been scraped off up to a level of twelve feet or so. As there were no alternate routes, traffic was backed up in both directions for the duration.

This little street scene took place two or three times a week, usually between eight and ten. When it did, I usually stopped what I was doing and stood on the balcony with my coffee to watch the show. As the truck inched back and forth, blocked cars, horns blowing, tried to back out or turn around, while motorcyclists and old ladies pushing shopping carts squeezed between bumpers. Some drivers simply left their cars to order coffee through the window from the café below. Pedestrians were also trapped—getting around the truck required a detour of approximately four blocks—and they milled about, talking excitedly, shouting advice and encouragement, and waving their arms. Across the street in the plaza, the old men sat chuckling at the confusion. Occasionally they looked up, caught my eye, and shrugged at the foolishness of it all. I shrugged back.

Around one o'clock, Casa Torcuato, the café on the plaza across the street, put out its tables and umbrellas, which stayed out until four thirty or so. At eight thirty out came the tables again. Casa Torcuato was one of the Albaicín's most popular restaurants, and its tables were always filled.

Musicians entertained during both lunch and dinner. Each group or individual took a three-song turn, then made room for the next group, so the music was constantly changing. The place where the musicians performed was well back from the street, so the music was not all that loud, and it always stopped at eleven. Dinner on the plaza produced a lovely sound: the soft babble of dining voices, the clink and clatter of dishes and glasses being delivered and taken away, a serenading guitar, clarinet, or singer. Listening to it through our open windows proved a delightful way to end the day.

The Streets of Granada 5:
Beauty but No Beasts

Of Gorgeous Women and Civilized Men

Spanish women are among the most beautiful in the world, perhaps the most beautiful. Of course beauty is in the eye of the beholder and every eye sees through a lens of cultural bias, so I'll settle for "among the most beautiful." But I'll also look, once again, to V.S. Pritchett's *The Spanish Temper* for concurrence: "The evening *paseo* in Almería reveals the great beauty of the women. Many are superb, almost all are fine. So many beautiful woman are there that the senses are bewildered and quietened; one finds oneself in a state of exalted contemplation."

It's not unusual for people who haven't visited Spain to think of the Spanish as somewhat swarthy Mediterranean people. Think Carmen, Flamenco dancers with the black, shiny hair and dark, flashing eyes. That is, however, but one, minor aspect of the Spanish physical character. Spain is, in fact, an interesting mix of physical traits. Even in Granada, in the south of Spain, the ratio of blonds and brunettes was about what it is in America; the streets crawl with tow-headed kids. True redheads, as opposed to the chemically induced, unnatural red we sometimes saw, are rare.

This variety of traits reflects the Iberian Peninsula's fascinating history. The original Iberians are thought to have been darker people. Around 900 BC Celtic people, who were fair, began arriving. They were joined, particularly along the Mediterranean coast, by the Phoenicians, a Semitic people, and then the Greeks. The Romans responded to Hannibal's march across the peninsula by conquering it and making it a province, and ruled Hispania for six hundred years, from around 218 BC to AD 409. When the empire fell, the Romans were replaced by the "blond barbarians" from the north, the Visigoths, who spent the next couple of centuries flexing their muscles, tossing their dirty blond tresses about, and brutalizing the natives.

When four hundred Moors first landed on the shores of Hispania in 710, they discovered what they described as "women of rare beauty." The booty they returned to North Africa with included a number of these beauties. To stir up enthusiasm for the venture, the Moors took several hundred beautiful women to Damascus as an example of what awaited the conqueror. Whether the ten thousand Moors who returned did so for the women is not known, but return they did, quickly conquering the Celtiberians (as these original inhabitants are called), who displayed little enthusiasm for defending their Goth masters.

The beauty of the women was not the only attraction. According to Muslim legend, when Allah created the earth, each place was given five wishes. The land of Al-Andalus asked for clear sky, a beautiful sea full of fishes, ripe fruit, and fair women. These four wishes were granted in abundance, an abundance that continues to this day. A fifth wish, for good government, was denied; having all five wishes granted would have created paradise on earth, which was not allowed. As a matter of fact, Andalucía, as well as Spain, was plagued by bad governance for a millennium and a half, though considerable improvement has taken place since Franco's death. Now that Andalucía has been granted its fifth wish, I think it reasonable to declare it as close to paradise as any place on earth.

The Moors brought no women along on their invasion, so the subsequent generation was mixed. Each succeeding generation continued to dilute the Arabic and Berber blood; eventually many of the ruling Moors became so fair that it was not unknown for emirs to dye their hair and beards darker in order to emphasize their Arab ancestry.

This little history lesson behind us, suffice it to say that there is an extremely high level of feminine beauty in Granada. Every day I saw not one woman but sometimes dozens of breathtakingly beautiful women.

This observation was not mine alone, and was duly noted by my wife, daughter, and many of our visitors. A second observation worthy of mention concerns what I didn't see: crude responses by Spanish males to a passing beauty. In this city of beautiful women, not once did we hear or see anything that sounded or looked like an insulting or vulgar remark.

This is in sharp contrast to the behavior one might well see in Italy or America. I don't think I've ever spoken to an attractive woman who didn't mention the rain of whistles and entreaties endured while traveling in Italy. And as for America: ever observe a pretty, curvaceous, mini-skirt wearing woman walk by a construction site? The reaction is often wolf whistles, catcalls, and smutty suggestions.

Now to Granada. One day as Kay and I walked down Calle Elvira, we passed a construction site. Walking just ahead of us was an absolutely sensational looking woman, a woman so beautiful that it was difficult not to stare, a circumstance which increased the danger of walking into a post or stumbling over the curb and falling into the street. She was wearing a short skirt and a T-shirt with bare midriff. She was bathed in a golden light, an aura that proclaimed to all who would see: This Is A Woman! As she passed the site, the workers paused in their work and looked at each other out of the sides of their eyes and smiled. One actually shook his head in wonder. This was the strongest response to a beautiful woman that Kay or I ever witnessed in Granada. It was so subtle the woman didn't appear to notice.

Kay caught their eyes and smiled. The men looked at each other, as if embarrassed at being caught looking, and grinned.

"*Muy guapa*," Kay said. Very beautiful.

"*Si*," they all nodded. "*Muy, muy guapa.*"

Kay then stopped to help me to my feet, as I had walked into a post, stumbled over the curb, and fallen into the street.

Why the difference? Have Spanish men become so accustomed to being surrounded by beautiful women that they don't even notice? Are they not even interested in women? I don't think so. We saw affectionate, caressing, kissing couples everywhere. I don't think the matter has anything to do with the appreciation of feminine beauty. It has to do with acceptable behavior. It seems that Spanish society does not approve of vulgar behavior—at least not outside the soccer stadium.

Madrid via the Scenic Route

A Tale of Best-Laid Plans Gone Awry

In addition to learning our new neighborhood and refurbishing the terrace, there was other business to attend to. Back in June, while in California, we'd paid a visit to the Social Security office to inquire about applying for benefits while living abroad. Our visa tribulations had taught us a lesson, and we didn't want our ignorance of the application process to cost even one month of payments. Our master plan had been for Kay to begin taking Social Security at age sixty-two, while I would wait until I was sixty-five and ten months to begin collecting full benefits. As Kay's pension would not grow, my Social Security payments would serve as our "inflation fighter."

The Social Security office was located in downtown San Rafael, a few miles from my son's home in Novato. A friendly security officer greeted us. There were chairs to sit on, a water fountain, and a restroom. Two windows were operating and only eight people were waiting. After no more than ten minutes, our turn came. The lady at the window smiled and seemed eager to help. How incredibly different from the resident permit process in Granada. She informed us that US citizens living abroad were required to apply at the consulate in the country where they lived. She said that Kay should begin the application process ninety days before her birthday.

"But what about you?" she asked. "Why aren't you taking your benefits early?"

I briefly explained our plan to her, that we were saving my payments to compensate for inflation and the decreased buying power of Kay's pension.

"I'd look at those numbers again, if I were you. It could be to your advantage to begin taking benefits at sixty-two."

I promised her I would.

I'd already run the numbers as part of the twenty-year income projection (I confessed earlier to having been a bit compulsive during our planning), and I knew that taking Social Security at sixty-two put more money in the pocket until the age of around seventy-eight, when those who had waited caught up. Our goal was not to gain the maximum Social Security benefit over our lifetimes; it was to live as well as possible *now*. And what was happening now was that the dollar was losing value by the day. When we'd arrived in Granada, the exchange rate had been $1.14. It was, at the time we moved up the hill, around $1.24, and the experts were predicting a continued decline. To us, the difference amounted to about $150 a month, not a huge amount but it added up to $1,800 a year. Our rent was €80 a month higher on Pagés than Elvira, an increase of another $1,200 a year. We decided that I would apply in mid-August, ninety days before my sixty-second birthday. Little did we know that the dollar would fall to $1.37, so our decision turned out to have been a good one.

The consulate nearest to Granada was in Seville. Although we hadn't visited Seville, the idea of spending four or five days there in mid-August was not appealing. Going for the day was even less so. We decided to go to the consulate in Madrid, which was located in the embassy. Madrid, over two thousand feet above sea level, wasn't nearly as hot.

When I called the consulate on August 10 to make an appointment, I was informed that the process would be transacted by phone and mail and that I did not need to come to Madrid. They made it very clear that they did not want me to come to Madrid. I learned later that getting through security and into the embassy was no easy task, so I assumed they did as much by mail and phone as possible. Such is life in the early twenty-first century.

But we wanted to go to Madrid. Why should we let a mere technicality, like lack of purpose, be a deterrent? Not only would we go to Madrid, we would go by train, which took an hour longer than the bus and, for some strange reason, cost twice as much.

We went to the train station on Friday the thirteenth (a rather ominous beginning) to purchase tickets for our Monday trip. There are two trains a day, one in the early morning, the other in mid-afternoon. We asked for two non-smoking roundtrip tourist-class tickets on the morning train. The fare was €91. According to our tickets, however, the Monday morning trip was on a smoking car. The *no fumar* car was sold out, the agent said. We were disappointed, but what can you do?

But the more Kay thought about it, the less happy she became. The Spanish are heavy smokers, and she knew she would be miserable. She'd developed an allergic reaction to smoke; her eyes watered and her sinuses closed. She decided that paying for first class would be worth it. First, because life is short, and second, according to Kay, it was kinda, sorta still her birthday. Did the celebration of a July third birthday, even a sixtieth, extend to August 16? She insisted that it did.

We returned to the train station Saturday morning. There were first-class non-smoking seats available on the Talgo, the express train. But in order to receive the roundtrip discount, we would have to travel first class both ways. Kay nodded eagerly. It was only €30 more. *No fumar*, our new first-class tickets said. Departure time, 7:55 a.m., arriving in Madrid at 2:00 p.m.

We left the house a little before seven Monday morning for the short walk to the bus stop. The bus took us within two blocks of the train station, where we had breakfast in the crowded café. The train to Madrid arrived on track two at seven thirty. Even though the train was fairly long, we easily found our car and seats. I stowed our bags. We sat, smiles on our faces, tickets in our hands. Everything had gone like clockwork.

Suddenly another couple stood in the aisle. They had the same seat assignments. I found a conductor who came to sort things out. We compared tickets. Ours were for Sunday, the day before. The ticket agent had, for some unknown reason, changed our Monday tickets for Sunday.

Ouch! We raced for the ticket office to explain our plight. Our Monday tickets had somehow been exchanged for Sunday, we told the ticket agent, and we hadn't noticed. He listened, then looked at the computer. The train was sold out, not a seat left, not second-class smoking, nothing. He left and conferred with the manager. We might, we knew, have to eat the tickets and buy another pair for that afternoon. Even though the agent had made a mistake, it was our responsibility to check our own tickets. We were at their mercy. We looked up at the station clock and waited.

All Aboard for Barcelona

It was 7:50 a.m. when the agent returned to the window. Here's what we can do, he told us. Or Spanish words to that effect. This whole transaction was going down in Spanish, and we were concentrating as hard as we could. We were being put on the eight thirty train to Barcelona. We wouldn't be in first class, but it would be non-smoking. We were to change trains in Alcazar de San Juan about one o'clock. The train to Madrid came an hour later. We had two minutes to board the train. Unfortunately we wouldn't be sitting together. We would arrive in Madrid at 4:00 p.m. He shrugged. That was the best he could do. That will be another €24, please.

The best he could do? This goodhearted Spanish ticket agent had saved the day. Would this have happened elsewhere? Knowing that we were getting to Madrid that day—only two hours later than planned and on non-smoking cars—was more important than the fact that we were paying first class fares, plus a supplement, to ride tourist class in a regional train.

The train to Alcazar de San Juan was very short: one car and one engine. The sign on the car said Granada-Barcelona, so we felt reasonably sure we were on the right train. The car was comfortable but nothing fancy.

An hour later the train stopped. According to the sign, we were at the Linares-Baeza station. Our conductor changed into overalls and disconnected the engine, which was driven away. The conductor took off his overalls and walked away. Our solitary car remained on a sidetrack. Surely there was some explanation. I hadn't brought a map and had no idea where Linares-Baeza was. But then I didn't know where Alcazar de San Juan was, either.

About twenty minutes later, another engine arrived, hooked up, pulled our car along the track, then stopped and backed up toward the station. Was something wrong with the car? I watched from the observation platform as we approached the station. There our solitary car was attached to the long Barcelona-bound train we'd seen from our sidetrack. Off we went, destination, we hoped, Alcazar de San Juan.

The trip was quite nice. We relaxed and ate the lunch we'd packed. During our wait in Alcazar, we had a beer and *tapas* in the station café, a huge room with a twenty-five-foot ceiling and walls covered with historic train and track equipment. The *tapas* were small chunks of organ meats in a tomato sauce over toast. My loving and most generous wife gave hers to me.

The two-hour ride into Madrid was uneventful. We got off the train at the Atocha station, where the terrorist attack of the previous March had taken place. There's a memorial there, but we didn't see it.

We had a wonderful time in Madrid. Our hotel was only two blocks from the *triángulo de arte*, where Madrid's three great museums, the Prado, the Thyssen-Bornemisza, and the Arte de Reina Sofía, are located. The weather was mild, almost cool, and it rained twice. Madrid is truly a great walking city, with clearly designated pedestrian routes, huge parks, interesting neighborhoods, and beautiful historic buildings. It is also more expensive than Granada.

We left Madrid Friday afternoon from the Chamartín station. The reclining first class seats were very comfortable with lots of leg room. They handed out headsets and showed two movies. *Lost in Translation* proved interesting even in Spanish. We had a drink in the bar car and watched Castile La Mancha roll by. Yes, there are windmills in La Mancha.

For some reason the train was forty-five minutes late arriving into Granada. Although we didn't get home until almost midnight, the square across the street was still filled with diners.

There's no getting around the fact that we'd been lucky. In spite of our oversight, we'd arrived in Madrid the afternoon we'd planned without having to purchase another pair of tickets. And we learned a few valuable lessons. Although we'd bought our tickets in advance (as advised in the Less-Stress manual) we hadn't examined them. Never again would we leave an agent without looking carefully at every bit of information on the ticket. And we decided to always pack a map. It's good to know where you are when you find that you're not where you thought you were going to be.

Guillermo called back at the end of the August and agreed to arrange a visit with Conchita. In early September the contingent arrived: Conchita, who'd brought along a neighborhood friend, and Guillermo, accompanied by his wife Lupé. First, we gave them the tour to show them what we'd done, which included the painted and furnished terrace. We wanted to make a good impression before making our requests. Everyone smiled and nodded, and we felt we'd established our credentials as desirable tenants.

Then we began the tour of inquiry, a sort of Spanish inquisition in reverse. During the inspection we learned that the dryer door could be closed by lifting it, and kept closed by placing a *bombona* against it. We were shown which washing machine drawer was for detergent, which for bleach, and so forth. We were told that the dishwasher didn't work, which we didn't care about anyway; there were only two of us. Then we showed her the stovetop.

"*Es muy antiqua,*" she said, and shook her head. "*Una antigualla.*"

All the Spanish speakers laughed. We looked at Guillermo.

"She says it's an antique, a museum piece."

Well, it wasn't that old. The two burners that worked did so reasonably well. It just needed knobs. She said that she would have her brother, who was an electrician, look at it.

"When?" we asked Guillermo.

"This is Spain," he replied. "It might not be soon."

Everyone shook hands, kissed cheeks, and they left. Kay and I felt that we'd made a good impression and were hopeful that the stove would be repaired soon.

A Village in the City

Learning the Neighborhood, Meeting New Friends

Although September was hot, it was not as hot as August had been. This made the terrace even more attractive and we spent more and more time there. Otherwise, our days were not much different than they had been before the move. Determined not to let the hill be a deterrent to our daily walks, we continued to do most of our business off the hill, and we walked down almost every day to the computer center, the post office, the Tienda de Oro, or to the Mercado Agustin, the central market, where we'd always bought olives and olive oil from the friendly young couple who had a small stall there. We bought much of our food at Mercadona, a large *supermercado* down the hill. We were sleeping in the Albaicín; we were hanging out in the Albaicín; but we hadn't made it our neighborhood.

Kay and I decided that we ought to do more of our business on the hill. A little exploration showed us that the Albaicín *alto* had more to offer than we'd thought. In addition to a medium-size *supermercado* down the street, there were three small family-run *mercados*, each with its own meat counter and butcher. There were also two butcher shops, two fish markets, a "destination" pastry shop, two bakeries, a candy store, and the morning produce market in Plaza Larga. We would not, we discovered, go hungry in the Albaicín. There was also a small hardware store, a video rental, a pharmacy, two banks, a florist, a barber shop, a hair salon, a newsstand, two *liberias* (magazines, books, stationery, newspapers, film, etc.), three Moroccan bazaars, a handful of realtors, and two *tiendas*, one specializing in housewares, the other in small appliances. These businesses were, with few exceptions, very small, often no larger than a room.

If you wanted to buy a couch, a bolt of cloth, a television, a suit, or any other item sold by stores that a population of only a few thousand couldn't support, you had to go down the hill. Living in the Albaicín *alto,* we discovered, was like living in a village, except this particular village wasn't in the countryside, it was in the city. We later learned that people living on the hill spoke of going down the hill as "going down to Granada."

We checked out the local markets to see which one we liked the best. Kay, who'd been buying plants at Plaza Larga's Saturday market, began buying produce at the plaza's daily market. Kay found the quality of the produce at the *Gitana* lady's stand to be very good and her pricing interesting. After weighing and bagging the produce, she announced the price along with a shrug and a smile, as if to say: *Does this seem okay?* Regardless of how much Kay bought, the number was always nice and even: one euro, one-fifty, two euros, and always considerably less than Kay expected. Although we often went to the larger market down the street—they didn't close for siesta—we made an effort to shop at the small market run by Luis and his family. I had my hair cut around the corner, Kay at the salon downstairs. We opened an account at the video rental.

In September we attended our first bullfight since moving to Granada. We've both seen bullfights before, but we wanted to see one in Granada's handsome and historic ring. I would never attempt to justify bullfighting. I do know that what happens to the bull during the fifteen minute fight is no more horrible than what happens to many of the animals we eat everyday without seeing their deaths. And, unlike some sport hunting, the meat is eaten.

The posters publicizing the event had horses on them, but how were we to know that a *Corrida de Rejones* meant that all the fights would take place from horseback? Horse lovers, rest easy. These magnificent animals were in no danger from the heavy, clumsy bulls. Instructed only by the rider's voice and legs, the horses charged the bulls, literally spinning away at the last moment, then danced sideways as the bull pursued, the horns actually touching the horse's flanks without making a scratch. During this death-defying maneuver, the rider leaned over and rested his hand between the bull's horns. It was breathtaking to watch, at least for me, as Kay's eyes were closed as much as they were open. There were three *rejoneadors* and each fought two bulls. Three horses were used for each fight, so the horse was always fresh.

One day while walking down toward Plaza Larga we saw a young woman putting up a flyer. The flyer, which was in English, encouraged Americans to vote in the presidential election of November 2004 and contained instructions as to how to register abroad. Surely this meant—clever Sherlocks that we were—that the young woman was an American. She was. She was also pregnant. She lived with her husband Manuel no more than a hundred yards from our house, perhaps a three hundred yard walk, there being no straight lines in the Albaicín. We chatted and promised to get together. A few weeks later we met for dinner, when we learned that both Alex, who'd lived in Granada for thirteen years, and Manuel worked as translators. The baby, their first, was due in early November.

Suddenly, our circle of friends had doubled. Anne and Steve lived a five-minute walk in one direction, Alex and Manuel five minutes in the other. Soon it would grow again.

One afternoon while shopping at Luis', we noticed a towheaded boy of about seven putting down some dance steps in the store's narrow aisles.

"Calm down," said the unmistakable voice of an English mother, "before you knock something over."

"You've got some real fancy moves there," I said to him.

"Oh, hello," said the mother, stepping around the corner. "He's a bit out of control right now."

We chatted for a few minutes. The dancer's name was Oscar. There was also a younger tow-headed brother, William. They'd just moved to Granada from the coast, which they hadn't cared for because it hardly seemed like Spain at all. Her husband Tammo, who was half Spanish and half Dutch, was out of town working as a member of a camera crew shooting a commercial. Caroline, Tammo, and their blond duo lived in a spacious apartment just off the plaza.

Luis' store is only a few doors down the street from Plaza Larga, where we'd met Anne and Steve. We'd met Alex a few doors up another street off the plaza. And now we'd met Caroline at Luis'. Plaza Larga seemed to be our lucky place for meeting English speakers.

A few days later we found a flyer and a note stuck in our door. *Thought you might be interested,* Alex's note said. The presidential debates were being taped and would be shown at an Irish pub. The contact names on the flyer were undoubtedly Americans. Suddenly Americans were coming out of the woodwork. Where had they been hiding? What an opportunity! No doubt every American in Granada would be there and we could meet then all.

The Case of the Missing Americans

Filled with anticipation, we made our way down the hill to Hannigan's for the first debate. The place was packed with Americans. We met Lucy and Pam, who had organized the event, and Lucy's husband Steve. Lucy and Steve, fellow Californians, had moved to Granada with their four-year-old daughter, and Pam had been living in Granada for years. We also met Celeste, a native Floridian and retired teacher, who'd been living in Spain for six years. As for the other sixty or so, the average age was twenty, all students. Was it possible that these four people, plus Anne, Steve, and Alex, made up the entire American adult community of Granada? To look on the bright side, the number of English speakers we knew had, in only a few weeks, quadrupled, from two to eight.

The evening was both comforting and strange, comforting in that we were, for the first time in over a year, spending an evening with a group of Americans and sharing a very American experience. But it did seem a bit strange to be sipping a scotch in an Irish pub in the heart of Granada while watching American television.

For the showing of the second debate, we took Steve along with us, and he brought along Richard, a young Englishman living with his wife and son in the apartment above Steve's. Meeting Richard proved to be very fortuitous, particularly during the upcoming Christmas holidays.

We attended all three debates, but we didn't meet any more English speakers. The events themselves were a success; the second was completely packed and the third required a repeat showing.

In late September, Conchita came by to collect for the utility bills. Both the electricity and water accounts were in her name and she dropped by every other month with the bills to collect. This sounded easy enough: she showed us the bill, we gave her the money. It was not, however, that simple. There were things that she wanted to explain to us. There were things that we wanted to ask her. It proved impossible on all accounts.

"*¿No entiendes?*" she asked after failing to communicate.

"*No entendemos,*" we answered. We understood how to say we didn't understand.

Conchita shrugged and smiled. She had expressive eyes and a broad smile. She was very sweet and seemed delighted that we enjoyed her former home so much. We couldn't communicate worth a damn, but we took good care of the place, and from a landlady's point of view, that was more important.

We asked about the stove again.

"*Si, si,*" she said. "*Es muy antiqua.*" She smiled. She shrugged. She left.

In mid-October, we joined our friends Anne and Chuck in Ronda, one of the famous *pueblos blancos* of Andalucía. They were touring Spain and asked us to join them there for a night, after which we'd drive back with them to Granada. We hadn't seen Ronda and were excited to see it. Considered as the birthplace of bullfighting, the town is divided, save for a narrow, spectacular bridge, by a hundred-meter deep gorge.

The three-hour train trip to Ronda was accomplished without mishap. We were in the right seat on the right train on the right day and headed in the right direction. How pleasant taking the train can be when everything goes as planned. Upon our return, we celebrated the first anniversary of our moving to Spain.

It had been an amazingly busy three months since our return from the States. We'd moved up the hill, acquired five new friends, discovered our neighborhood, and hosted visitors. Our next visitors weren't scheduled to arrive till spring, and our calendar was looking blank. Fortunately, Penny and Bob, who'd visited us in April, were spending November in Orvieto, Italy, where they'd taken a house with a guest bedroom. They invited us. We accepted. We were off to Italy.

Travel Woes Redux

Penny and Bob called a few days prior to our departure with detailed instructions on how to get to Orvieto. It could be a little tricky, as the last train to Orvieto left Rome at 10:40. But unless our flight was extremely late, we should be okay. The train wouldn't reach Orvieto until midnight, and neither the *funicolare*, the cable car, nor the bus, which climbed the steep winding road, would be running. Walking was not possible, she explained, as Orvieto sits high on the hill above steep cliffs, so they had arranged for a taxi to meet us at the station.

On the other hand, we could rent a car in Rome. Almost all our friends rent cars when traveling in Europe. The advantages are many, they told us. Luggage, for instance, was no problem: no matter how many bags you had, you simply loaded and unloaded at the hotel. You could set your own schedule, no getting up at six-thirty to catch the train. And best of all, you could tour the countryside, visiting picturesque villages and staying at country inns accessible only by car. It sounded great.

However. Our friends then proceeded to relate their tales of misadventure, of getting so lost they didn't reach their destination until early morning, of having the car broken into, of dealing with a fender bender in a foreign language, of having a breakdown in a small village miles and miles away from the nearest rental-car agent, and of mornings lost in search of a parking place. One friend described spending hours navigating medieval streets in search of their hotel before finally giving up and driving on to another town.

That's why we preferred trains and buses, we told them. It is less stressful and part of the European experience. We bought our tickets in advance, and we traveled light, a roller and a smaller, attached bag at most, so luggage was not a problem. Instead of poring over a map, we poured a glass of wine in our train compartment. If our hotel was close to the station, we walked; traffic, one-way, or construction-blocked streets were not problems. When walking wasn't practical, we took a taxi. What could be easier?

However. We then recited our travel stories of woe and absurdity, like the time in Paris when we took the wrong train to Chartres, were put off and sent back to the station, only to board the wrong train again with the same eye-rolling conductor. Or the trip to Venice; we arrived in Mestre on the mainland at 4:00 a.m., and, not knowing that it was necessary to change trains, watched our fellow passengers race to another train, after which we spent three hours on a hard bench in the cold November dawn waiting for the next train. Our most bizarre misadventure was a train trip from Milan to Switzerland. At least that was our intended destination—when I saw the Mediterranean on our right and a sign announcing Genoa, I knew that somehow something had gone terribly wrong. And, of course, there had been the botched ticket exchange for our trip to Madrid just two months earlier.

The trip to Orvieto began well enough. Our flight arrived on time, and we arrived at the train terminal well ahead of schedule. The train was late departing Rome, however, and it was after midnight when we approached Orvieto. We took our bags and headed for the door as the train slowed. No one else in our car seemed to be getting off, so we stood by the door alone. The train stopped by a large sign: Orvieto. Kay pushed the door. It wouldn't open. She tried again. No luck. After no more than half a minute, the train began to slowly move. Maybe we weren't in the station yet, I suggested. The train picked up speed. I stepped back out into the passageway. "Orvieto?" I asked. A man pointed back to the station, which was rapidly receding in the distance.

I returned to Kay.

"We are," I said, "in a difficult situation." I think I may have used a stronger adjective. How could this have happened? It was then, as we stared at the door, that we noticed, taped near the top of the door, far, far above the handle, a small handwritten note. Door broken, it said, in four languages. We returned to the passageway, where we saw the conductor. The door, we pantomimed, is broken. Yes, he nodded his head in agreement. Broken. The next stop was Chiusi, twenty-five minutes north.

We got off the train at Chiusi. It was 12:45 a.m., and, other than two bench sleepers in the station, there was no sign of life. None.

There were no taxis and the only hotel in sight was closed and dark. We found a phone booth and called Bob and Penny. We described our plight and informed them that the next train back to Orvieto was at four. The buses and *funicolare* up into the town didn't begin running till seven, they told us. They didn't know if a taxi would be available at four thirty. Our faithful and patient friends said they would wait up for further news. Outside the phone booth we saw a sign with a taxi number. Kay called. We heard the phone ringing only yards away in the empty taxi stand.

We staggered back into the station and slumped on a bench. With elbows on knees and head in hands, we watched the station clock tick off the minutes. Sixteen down, one hundred sixty-four to go. Then Kay heard a car outside and turned to look. It was a taxi looking for a last fare. We raced outside, hailed him, and began our inquiries, not so easy when you speak no Italian and the driver no English. But Kay, not easily deterred by small hurdles, pressed on, and she managed to negotiate a €70 fare to Orvieto. Expensive taxi rides were becoming an all too regular expense.

We arrived a little after two to find Bob and Penny waiting. We'd added still another chapter to our tale of travel woes.

The Streets of Granada 6: Fund Solicitations

Service Rendered, Wanted or Not, With a Smile

Granada, like every city, has its share of panhandlers. Actually, the term panhandling is too narrow, as its definition is to beg. Let's describe this activity as "the solicitation of funds from strangers for personal use." In Granada, fund solicitors apparently believed that their best strategy was to offer some small "service," no matter how unnecessary, no matter how unasked for. Simple begging was rarely encountered.

The most common unasked for service offered was, of course, some form of entertainment: singers, guitarists, jugglers, clowns, balloon twisters, and human statues. (How does one inform his mother that he makes his living as a human statue?) You could also have your portrait drawn or your name written in Arabic. When you think about it, even being a statue requires, if not talent, at least a bit of imagination. What opportunities were available to those with neither talent nor imagination?

One service requiring no talent or imagination, one offered at supermarkets around town, was that of door opener. In our Albaicín neighborhood, there was a man who stationed himself at the entrance of the *supermercado* down the street. Perhaps forty, he was tall and lean, with a beard and ponytail, a deeply lined face, and a sleepy smile. His wrinkled clothes looked like they'd been slept in, probably because they'd been slept in. The entrance to the market was two steps up from the street, and there, in the small foyer just outside the heavy glass doors, he stood from morning till afternoon. As we entered, he opened the door and greeted us a smiling *buenos*. On our way out, he opened the door and offered a smiling *gracia*, whether we gave him anything or not. A small contribution, say twenty *céntimos*, seemed quite satisfactory. During Christmas, he powdered his beard and wore a Santa hat. He was well known in the neighborhood and from his door-side station chatted with the store's checkers and passersby. Sometimes we found ourselves in line with him as he spent his "tips" to buy beer and snacks.

Parking assistance was another unrequested service. Parking assistants pointed out available parking places and provided parking directions. The first service could be useful when the open space was located out of sight on a side street. The second service was less so. Parking assistants, almost always men, stood in the street near recently vacated parking spaces, waving their arms and pointing to an empty space as if they'd just discovered a body or a bag of gold. When a car stopped to take the place, one that the driver would have taken whether the assistant was there or not, the assistant, with wildly exaggerated gestures, directed the driver into the place. Sometimes their directions were followed, sometimes not. Sometimes the driver, seemingly torn between his or her own parking techniques and the highly animated directions of the assistant, botched the job completely. The assistant shrugged a what-can-I-do-with-these-people shrug and began again. Once we watched as an increasingly flustered driver failed two parking attempts before angrily driving away. The assistant shook his head at such shocking ineptitude.

Once the car was parked, the assistant stood by its side beaming at a job well done. More often than not, the assistant received a coin or two; sometimes he was ignored. Rewarded or not, as soon as the driver walked away, the assistant rushed back out into the street in search of another available parking space "to sell."

There never seemed to be any consequences for failing to compensate door openers and parking assistants. We never heard a harsh word or saw a dirty look. Intimidation was not a factor.

Gallantry Lives On

One fine day while walking through Plaza Bib-Rambla, we paused to take in the setting. Ringed with café tables and flower stalls, the cathedral tower soaring high above one corner, it is Granada's finest, and certainly most historic, plaza. In the center there is a huge fountain surrounded by rose beds and protected by a wrought-iron fence. Standing near the fountain in the sun, we watched an older man, probably closer to eighty than seventy, as he reached through the fence with his cane, pulled a rose to him, and broke it off. What a rascal, we thought. Rose in hand, he looked around, saw us, and approached. With shaking hands, he pushed the rose through a buttonhole in Kay's jacket, then, with a flourish and a deep bow, stepped back to admire his handiwork. "*Muy guapa*," he exclaimed, indicating both Kay and the rose. Very beautiful. The rose, like our elderly gallant, was no longer in full bloom, but we pretended that it was as beautiful as he seemed to think it was. "*Sí*," we said, "*muy guapa*." Then, with a sweet, endearing smile, he held out his hand. As I gave him a euro, I wondered if I'd be arrested for buying stolen city property. A day or so later we saw him in another plaza, rose in hand, looking for a willing, *muy guapa* recipient.

The most irritating scam was perpetrated by the *Gitana* women who positioned themselves near the cathedral and along the route up to the Alhambra. As a passersby approached, he or she was "offered" a sprig of rosemary, which is supposed to bring good luck. The best response, we'd read and been told, was to ignore them, as they can be very persistent. There were very few takers, as the ruse seems so obvious. Yet inevitably, there were those who misread this form of extortion as a quaint *Granadino* custom and accepted the rosemary. The demand for money quickly followed. We heard women demanding as much as five euros for a sprig. Returning this dubious gift was not easy, as the women refused to take it back. They sometimes tried to block the way of the "recipients," haranguing them and shouting and looking furiously insulted, as if they'd been robbed, which, of course, was exactly what they were trying to do. Tourists sometimes gave them a euro or two just to escape. Being outrageously annoying, then being bought off, was probably their basic strategy.

The questions raised by this scam were not: *How did they get away with such a shameless charade,* but, rather, *Where did they come by this apparently endless supply of rosemary? And how could I get some?* I needed it for the white wine, vinegar, and rosemary chicken cacciatore that had become my signature dish, which is to say the tastiest of the three dishes I cooked. We often saw rosemary growing in the courtyards and gardens of the *carmens,* but gates and tall walls protected these Moorish-style homes. There were no unprotected yards from which to pinch a bit of ground-cover rosemary, as I had done in California, and fresh rosemary was rarely found in the markets. We finally discovered their source while on a long walk into the countryside that began up the hill from the Alhambra, just beyond where the *Gitana* women stand. A forest of rosemary covered the hillside. The obvious solution was to simply harvest a few sprigs on our next walk, which is exactly what we did.

As I said before, there were very few beggars. From time to time we saw a woman (only once a man) kneeling alongside a pedestrian way, head bowed, and holding a simple handwritten sign that inevitably gave the number of children she had to feed. They did not appear lame or ill. They did not move or look up. Their eyes were closed, as if they were in prayer or deep meditation. Few paid them any notice. We didn't know what to make of it. Spain is a modern European country with, at that time, a socialist government, and I found it hard to believe that children were allowed to starve.

Occasionally we encountered *Gitana* beggars, always women, usually with children. We saw them in Córdoba, Málaga, and Madrid as well as Granada. Sometimes they sent their toddlers to pull on your trousers as they held out their hands. Fortunately, this happened very infrequently.

And there were street people, hippies or whatever you want to call them. Although most were Spanish, we heard German, Scandinavian, French, and a good deal of British English. We never encountered any American street people. On a few occasions, they heard us talking and asked us for money in heavily accented English. Can multi-lingual begging be considered a skill? Body piercing was popular among the young Spaniards, but these people took it to such an extreme some looked like mobile jewelry shops. Being heavily tattooed was another tribal badge. Many were astoundingly dirty. They usually hung out in small groups, often outnumbered by their dogs. They leaned back against the walls of the houses along the narrow streets, inevitably sharing a liter of Alhambra beer and smoking, their dogs panting in the shade, an empty cap lying in the middle of the lane for "contributions." Rarely hostile or threatening, they were generally ignored. The cap collected very few coins.

Calle Elvira was a gathering place for these sad creatures. We didn't see much of them in the upper Albaicín, perhaps because there weren't many tourists and the locals had little sympathy for them. They were far more pitiful than annoying.

Singers, door openers, human statues, parking assistants, panhandling hippies, even the rosemary ladies were all part of Granada's always interesting street life.

Adventures in Cookie Diplomacy

Becoming Goodwill Ambassadors to Spain

We returned to Granada from Italy with two objectives. The first, and most important, was renewing our resident permits. We'd begun last year in mid-October and hadn't actually received our permits, which were valid only till November 19, until mid-January. It was time to get cracking. The day after our return we headed to the all-too-familiar police station. Fortunately, the smiling lady was at the window. This was lucky because we began with a communication problem. We kept asking for *aplicacións*, when what we needed, she said, were *solicitudes* (after consulting the dictionary, I still don't understand the difference). The kind, patient lady gave us two *solicitudes*, and on the back she wrote a list of what we'd need for a renewal.

We no longer had to establish our mental or physical health, our lack of criminal activity, or the validity of our marriage. I assumed that the breaking of Spanish laws or abuse of the Spanish medical system would be a matter of record and would disqualify us. All that was required for renewal was proof of continued income and health insurance. There were, of course, copies to make: our passports, current resident permits, and more photos. This was going to be a much simpler process than last year's.

We returned the following week with the same forms we'd used the year before to document our income and insurance coverage, plus the required copies. The clerk looked them over, accepted them, and told us we'd receive a letter in approximately fifteen days. I was a little nervous about using recycled forms that were dated seventeen months earlier, but Pollyanna assured me that everything would be fine, and I decided to believe her. There was nothing we could do but wait, so why worry.

The second objective was the baking of cookies. Like most rentals in Granada, our first apartment on Calle Elvira didn't have an oven. We had a microwave, but there are things you can do with a microwave and things you can't, like bake cookies. We'd roasted a chicken, which was okay, but not worth repeating, especially after we discovered takeaway *pollo asado.*

When Guillermo had shown us what would become our house, and Kay had discovered that there was an oven, she was beside herself with glee. "At last!" she proclaimed. "Cookies." Guillermo, who learned his English in London, did not know cookies.

"*Galletas,*" she'd said, remembering that the English called cookies *biscuits.*

"You'll have to make me some," he'd said. And Kay had promised that she would.

The last time we'd seen Guillermo was when he'd brought Conchita to the house in early September so that she could explain how the appliances worked.

"Where are my cookies?" Guillermo had asked.

"It's too hot to bake," Kay had told him. "Wait until it gets cooler."

Kay planned to make oatmeal cookies, one of her specialties. She had enough oatmeal, which we'd bought in Germany, to make one large batch. At that time we'd been unable to find oatmeal in Granada. Later we found that oatmeal was located in the health food section, not with the cereals.

Baking day finally came on a cool day in mid-November. Kay was used to a food processor, so getting the consistency of the dough just right was going to be difficult. That the oven settings were in Celsius wasn't a problem; we'd figured that out, but there was no way to know if the settings were accurate. There was nothing to do except start cooking and judge the results. The oven ran a bit hot and the first batch came out a little crisp. After that, she produced sheet after sheet of oatmeal cookies, cookies filled with butter, brown sugar, coconut, raisins, and crushed walnuts. They were, according to my unbiased opinion, superb.

"You know," Kay said, "I think I'll take some down to Javier." Javier was the young Argentinean who worked the afternoon and evening shift at the café downstairs. He'd made it a point to be friendly and, when he wasn't too busy, leaned out the window to say hello when we walked by.

"That would be nice."

"And that girl at the telephone shop just off Calle Elvira who's always so helpful." This friendly young woman spoke a little English and had helped us on a number of occasions.

"And how about the couple in the central market where we buy our olives?" The couple (they were probably in their late twenties) ran a small food store that sold cold cuts, olive oil, wine, canned goods, juices, and, to our taste, the best olives in town. The young woman was always warm and friendly to us, smiling and laughing and chatting away as she offered us samples. She always seemed happy to see us.

Kay was on a roll now.

"And Luis, who runs the little market a couple of blocks away." A genial, affable grandfather, Luis offered a fond greeting and a big smile for all his customers and pieces of candy for the children. He often showed us photographs of his grandchildren and corrected our Spanish. Although Anna, our Spanish teacher of the previous January, had told us that we could call bananas either *los plátanos* or *las bananas,* Luis would have none of it.

"No, no banana." He shook his head. "*Los plátanos.*"

He waited for Kay to ask for *los plátanos.*

"*Quatro platanos, por favor,*" Kay said.

"*Plátanos,*" he repeated. The accent was on the first syllable.

"*Plátanos,*" Kay said.

"*Bueno.*" Luis gave her his biggest smile. "*Quatro plátanos.*" He weighed them and put them in a bag along with the rest of our produce, which we'd properly pronounced and given its correct masculine or feminine article: *un pimiento, un tomate, un calabacín y una lechuga*—a pepper, a tomato, a zucchini, and a lettuce.

I agreed that Luis certainly deserved some cookies, but where was this going? Where it was going was to the lady who, along with her husband, ran the Tienda de Oro, the small store where we'd outfitted our first apartment..

We considered taking some to the guys at Navegaweb, the Internet center where we got our e-mail, but decided against it. There are three very helpful young men and three or four indifferent ones, and we couldn't figure out how to designate who would get cookies and who wouldn't.

We also crossed Antonio, our English-speaking Argentine dentist, off the list. His office was on the other side of town, and besides, he'd cleaned my teeth only twice and Kay's once, so we didn't know him all that well. We'd been given Antonio's name and phone number by the Englishman who ran one of the used bookstores.

"How about that nice lady at the post office?"

It was time to draw the line. "You can't give gifts to government employees." I shook my head at the audacity of it. "Who next? Juan Carlos?" Kay was, and still is, a big fan of the king.

"I don't see why not," Kay said.

Riding Shotgun with the Cookie Fairy

On delivery day we set out with the small bags, tied with ribbons and filled with *galletas typicas de americano*. Kay had packed a dozen for Guillermo so he could share with his office staff, and a half dozen each for the telephone lady, the olive lady, the *tienda* lady, and a giant gingerbread man for Javier. "And what," I asked her, "are you going to tell them? That you're the cookie fairy?"

"What I'm going to tell them," Kay said, having added the necessary words to her Spanish, "is that my new house has an oven and I'd made cookies and that I want to give you some because you are always so friendly. *Siempre eres muy simpatico.*" Putting aside my Scrooge persona and donning my very best American smile, I decided to join in the spirit of the expedition. Standing in the path of goodness is never a good idea.

Our first stop was downstairs at the café. Kay knocked on the window to get Javier's attention. She held out the bag.

"*Galletas typicas de Americano*," she said.

"*¿Para mi?*" Javier asked.

"*Si. Siempre eres muy simpatico.*"

195

"*¿Para mi?*" Javier seemed to be having a hard time getting the concept. Perhaps, I thought, the Spanish don't go around giving people they barely know bags of cookies. In fact, all the cookie recipients were a little bewildered when Kay first handed them the bag and gave her little speech. It took a second telling for them to take the bag and look inside. Their smiles were worth the effort.

Javier became a regular recipient of Kay's largesse. She took him lasagna, lemon meringue pie, a gingerbread man still hot from the oven, and a slice of apple crisp. In return, Javier had become somewhat smitten with Kay, gave her cheek kisses whenever possible, and once called her *mi reina*, my queen. We learned later that this was an expression often used by *Granadinos,* information that did not diminish Kay's pleasure at all.

I couldn't help but wonder if, from this time on, Kay would be forever known as the Cookie Lady.

A week or so later we went down the hill to drop off some film at the little shop we'd been going to since coming to Granada. It was well out of our way, but the man who ran the shop was always so friendly. He knew our names and filled out the order envelope as soon as we entered the shop. That day, for some reason, he'd closed early for siesta. The open sign was gone and the door locked. But we could see him inside. When he saw us, he unlocked the door, stuck his hand through and took the film.

"*¿Mañana por la mañana?*" we asked. Tomorrow morning?

"*Si,*" he said through the cracked door. "*Mañana por la mañana.*"

"I forgot the photo man!" Kay exclaimed after he'd closed the door and we'd walked away. "How could I have forgotten the photo man?"

He would have to wait till Christmas for his cookies.

Although we now had an oven and English speaking friends, we didn't have the will to put together a Thanksgiving feast. Last year's effort had been more for Flannery than ourselves and neither of us felt up to it. What we did feel like was having Alex, Manuel, and the newborn Pablo for lunch the day before Thanksgiving. We made a delicious but very un-Thanksgiving-like meal, but we did honor the spirit of the holiday by counting our blessings. Manuel and Alex offered a toast to "our good fortune to be living in Granada." Kay and I raised our glasses high in full agreement.

Letting the Holiday Happen

Santa Comes to the Albaicín

The Christmas season began the day when the yeller, who up till the first days of December had been only a yeller, became a mobile one-man Christmas concert. Now, in addition to shouting, he carried a suitcase-size boom box that played the same Flamenco-pop Christmas CD over and over and over at full volume. Even worse, when he went into the café downstairs or the one across the street, he left his box on the sidewalk, frequently directly beneath my balcony, where the volume literally rattled the windows. Just when I was ready to drop a flowerpot on the box, he would emerge and the music would fade away as he continued his route.

"I'm sure it's just for the Christmas season," Kay reassured me as I stormed up and down the hallway between the study and the living room. "It'll stop when the season ends."

Although the holiday season in Spain did not began until December, it continued till Three King's Day on January 6. I wasn't sure how long I could take the half-dozen or more daily aural assaults. Apparently, I wasn't the only one being driven out of their holiday gourd, for shortly after Christmas Day he began turning the volume down every time he entered the cafés. I could still hear it, but it was tolerable. He still played the box at full volume while walking the streets, but the sound came and went.

In early December we received the long awaited letter informing us that our visas had been renewed. We were to pay the tax at the bank and come to the police station fifteen days after receiving the letter (not from the date on the letter, as we'd learned the year before). The letter contained more great news: our resident permits would be valid for two years instead of one. Was this the result of cookie diplomacy? Later we found that our friend Alex's permit had also been renewed for two years, after twelve years of annual renewals, so it probably wasn't the cookies.

Last year we'd tried to recreate what we could of our traditional Christmas: Christmas Eve walk and buffet, decorations, stockings, gift exchange, even ham biscuits and mimosas for breakfast. We had Flannery with us, but everything else, family, friends, decorations, dinnerware, and music, were back in the States. It had been enjoyable, but there was an undercurrent, particularly for Kay, of what it hadn't been.

We couldn't decide how to approach the holiday. We considered taking a trip or spending a few days in some small coastal town. In other words, not doing much of anything. Finally we decided not to decide, but rather to let the holiday be what it *would be* and not attempt to force it to be what it *had been*. At least this year we knew some people, so who knew what might happen if we just relaxed and took it day by day? There would be no stockings, we agreed, and just a few small gifts. We had a fixed-line phone installed and declared it our gift to each other, certainly a gift that would keep on giving. There would be no more noisy street-side calls. Using a phone card, we could call family from the comfort of our couch for only a few cents a minute. And, even better, with Tammo's assistance, we were now online, so walking downhill to Navegaweb was no longer necessary.

Anne took the annual Christmas photo. We posed, Kay in her red Spanish shawl, by our front door just beneath one of the balconies. We bought Christmas cards, inserted the photo and a season's greeting, and mailed them. Beyond that, nothing was planned.

The season slowly unfolded. Back in October while watching the presidential debates, we'd met Richard, an Englishman living in Granada for six months with his family while his wife, Belinda, studied

Spanish. Not long after, Richard had come by our house with Belinda and four-year-old Ryan, and we'd taken an instant liking to them all. Kay, who really missed having kids in her life, had invited Ryan to come over and make gingerbread cookies. Ryan was thrilled.

Now, one can hardly decorate cookies in an undecorated house, so Kay bought a two-foot spruce, as she'd done the year before, and decorated it with the tiny lights and balls and a garland. She and Flannery had made wreaths the previous Christmas, and we attached them, along with strings of lights, to the balconies. And we bought two more Christmas CDs, so now we had four. We weren't flinging ourselves into the holiday, but neither were we muttering humbug.

On cookie-making day, Ryan arrived with his five-year-old cousin, who was visiting from England. We'd never found cookie cutters in the stores, so we created cardboard templates. The boys rolled out the dough and used cheese spreaders to cut out the gingerbread people, then decorated them with raisins and tiny candies. They loved it.

And there was music. We'd seen a poster announcing a Christmas concert in an historic church halfway down the hill, and we decided to go. The church wasn't very large, with only three small chapels on each side, and sat perhaps a hundred. Churches that old don't have central heating, so small *bombona*-fueled heaters were placed around to knock the chill off, though only those sitting within a few feet of a heater removed their coats. The rest of the church was definitely cold. How old was the church? The bell tower had originally been the minaret of a mosque, and the Moslems had been driven from Granada more than five hundred years ago. The music, performed a *cappella* by a choir of around twenty-five singers, reverberated through the old building, sounding, I imagined, just as it had hundreds of years ago.

We decided to entertain. After all, we now had friends and an oven. But the stovetop still hadn't been repaired despite efforts by our new friend Celeste, who we'd met at the debates. In late November we had invited Celeste over for dinner. Shortly before she arrived, Conchita dropped by. We asked her about the stove. She tried to explain the light bill. We were having our usual communication difficulties. Suddenly it occurred to us that Celeste, a fluent Spanish speaker, would be arriving any minute. What excellent timing. We asked Conchita to come back in fifteen minutes and she agreed. Celeste arrived a few minutes later, and then Conchita returned. We talked. No, they talked and Celeste translated.

Conchita explained that this month's electric bill was an estimate because the meter hadn't been read. Celeste explained to Conchita that we were serious cooks and that we needed a proper stove. But it is old, Conchita replied. And the city was requiring that the gutters be repaired. But it's Christmas, Celeste said. How are they going to cook Christmas dinner? Conchita's expression changed immediately. Ah, Christmas dinner. Now that was different. She promised to have something done before Christmas. The gutters were never mentioned again.

Ring, Ring, Ring Went the Doorbell

A week later the doorbell rang. It was Conchita and her brother, who also spoke no English. They had not called. He looked at the stovetop. They promised to return.

A few days later the doorbell rang again. It was Conchita and her brother. We had no idea that they were coming. He had a new knob, hoping somehow to install it on the damaged stem. It didn't work. They promised to return.

A few days later the doorbell rang. It was Conchita's brother, this time accompanied by her son, who spoke some English. They arrived, as always, unannounced, continuing what appeared to be a definite pattern. They had come to take measurements for a new stovetop, which they did, promising to return Saturday morning with a new stovetop. The day, *Sábado*, Saturday, was confirmed in both Spanish and English.

At last we had a prearranged visit. Except that on Saturday morning, the day they'd promised to come, the doorbell did not ring. It did not ring that afternoon. Nobody arrived, announced or unannounced. That evening at the local supermarket I saw the brother by the meat counter. We communicated. The son didn't call you? No. Sorry. We will be there Monday or Tuesday. This was confirmed in both English and Spanish.

We waited all day Monday and Tuesday. No doorbell. No phone call. Wednesday through Friday one of us stayed at home all day. We waited all day Saturday, December 18. Nothing. We didn't know what to do. We didn't know the son's phone number. We didn't even know his name. It was Christmas week and we weren't waiting at home any longer. Anne and Steve were coming over on Sunday for what we'd hoped to be a wonderful, though challenging, multi-course holiday meal using our oven and four burners. It would be even more challenging using only two. We resigned ourselves to a two-burner life.

The following evening we cooked a holiday meal of roast chicken with the works. The meal required a good deal of stovetop rotation, but Kay pulled it off beautifully.

Monday, fifteen days after receiving our letter, we went to the police station, where we turned in our tax form and additional photos. We were fingerprinted and signed the form. Our resident permits would be ready in forty-five days.

During the week we walked down the hill to see the lights and mingle with the shoppers and strollers. The nights were cold and clear. Lighted Christmas decorations hung across almost every street, and the pedestrian shopping areas were thronged with people.

On Thursday, Christmas Eve eve, we made our second cookie-delivery rounds, this time icing-topped Christmas cookies. We gave cookies to the entire staff of the downstairs café, our photo man, Luis and his family and staff, Guillermo, and the olive couple at the central market. Kay had also made apple-raisin chutney to give to friends, packaged in jars she'd saved for that purpose.

That evening Richard was throwing Belinda a surprise birthday party at six o'clock. Just as we were leaving, the doorbell rang. It was Conchita's brother and son. They had not, of course, called, but they did have the stovetop with them. Both wore wide grins.

"*Feliz Navidad,*" they exclaimed.

I took a deep breath. If the more than three weeks of impatience and irritation showed on my face, they didn't acknowledge it. It was Christmas, I told myself. This was Spain. We had a new stovetop. That we had waited and waited suddenly didn't seem all that important.

"*Feliz Navidad,*" I shouted. As we climbed the stairs, I dubbed the son Santa Claus and the brother San Nicolás. They laughed and nodded enthusiastically.

We explained that we were going to a party and would be back in an hour. No problem, they told us. We'll have the stove in before you get back and we'll close the door when we leave. We left for the party.

We'd stayed at the party for only an hour because we'd invited Caroline, Tammo, and the boys over for seven thirty. Kay thought the boys would enjoy the tree and lights on the balconies, and she had little gifts for them under the tree. We returned to our house at seven anxious to see the new stove. During the walk back, we prepared ourselves for all eventualities: the stove didn't fit, the stove didn't work, the house had burned down. The stove was fabulous. It was, like the old one, ceramic-topped and electric, and Kay said that it was by far the most efficient and quickly responsive electric stove she'd ever cooked on.

We had a lovely evening with Carolina, Tammo, and the boys. Kay mentioned having made cookies with Ryan, and, now bubbling over with holiday spirit, invited Oscar and William over the following week for a cookie-making workshop.

Because Ryan and his family were coming over on Christmas Eve, we did our traditional walk that afternoon, walking the road that winds along Rio Darro through the Sacromonte, once the heart of the Gitano community. On one side of the road, the cave houses and Flamenco clubs climbed up the hill; on the other side, far below, there was the river and beyond that a steep, bare hillside.

Move Over Father Christmas, Santa's Here

Kay decided to make Ryan a stocking using the one she'd made for Flannery the Christmas before. She'd sewn his name on it and filled it with stuffers, candy, games, paints, and modeling clay. He would, of course, be waiting for Father Christmas to fill his stocking on Christmas morning, but Kay told him that she was putting in a special request for Santa to fill an American stocking for an English boy. It was possible that, because of the time difference, Santa might be able to make it before he flew to America. She called Ryan on Christmas Eve around six thirty with the news.

"Santa has come!" she told him. "Can you come over right away?" He came, along with his parents, who were in on the ruse, along with his grandparents and aunt, who were visiting.

Christmas morning held more than a few pleasures. Flannery had sent stocking stuffers and wonderfully thoughtful gifts. As planned, Kay and I had toned it down, so scarves and knitted hats were the order of the day. With an oven, Kay was able to make biscuits, so we had our traditional ham biscuits and mimosas.

That afternoon we visited Alex, Manuel, Pablo, who was now seven weeks old, and Alex's mother, who was visiting. Kay volunteered to babysit as soon as Pablo was ready.

Two days after Christmas it snowed, an unusual occurrence for Granada. The previous winter it hadn't snowed at all. There wasn't much snow, just enough to cover everything. I woke Kay and off we went through deserted streets to Mirador San Nicolás from where we looked through the falling snow to the Alhambra and the rooftops down the hill. We were the only people there. It was very quiet and very beautiful.

The next day Oscar and William came over to make cookies. They are both quite talented and made their own templates. The results were moon cookies, rocket cookies, and one enormous cookie that looked like a jack-o-lantern.

Observing our traditional New Year's Eve was easy. The previous year had been unusual, with Flannery and her friend Martin being with us, and we'd gone down to City Hall to join the throng in eating grapes and drinking champagne in the square. Now we lived on the hill and were not particularly eager to climb it at one o'clock in the morning. So we returned to the tried and true: good dinner, champagne, and a video in the comfort and safety of home. At midnight, for the second time, we toasted the New Year in, and reflected on our year in Granada.

The holiday season ended on January 6, when we joined Tammo and his family and his parents and watched the Three Kings parade along Grand Via de Colón. It was a Christmas parade and it wasn't. Instead of reindeer there were camels, instead of a sled an elephant. There was also a touch of Mardi Gras, as thousands of small candies were flung into the crowd.

The next day it was over. The decorations came down and, even more important, the yeller's holiday concerts stopped, and there was only the shouting again. It had been an excellent Christmas, far busier and more enjoyable than we had hoped for. There had even been an unexpected bonus: kids. We hadn't made it happen; we'd simply let it unfold day by day.

Señora Albaicinera y Señor Albaicinero

At Home in the Heart of Granada

In late January, a polar front moved down across Europe, bringing with it freezing cold and heavy snow. Granadinos told us that they'd never been this cold, and that Granada had experienced only one freeze like it in one hundred years. On January 27, the temperature in Granada fell to −8 °C, about 18 ° F, and for several days never exceeded the low thirties. In Munich, those temperatures would be considered mild, but not in Granada, where very few homes have central heating. All over Granada, water pipes, which are often attached to the outside the city's old pre-plumbing buildings, burst. We walked downhill that first morning after the freeze to the sound of running water; some of the steeper lanes resembled spring creeks. Rooftop terraces and courtyards, once filled with unprotected plants, were wiped out, and dead plants hung from the balconies and down garden walls. Granada's ubiquitous bougainvillea did not survive, a loss that wouldn't be completely appreciated until spring. Fifteen of our nineteen outside plants were lost. We could have brought many of the smaller ones in but we had no idea the freeze was coming. Not being able to read the newspaper or understand TV news can have unexpected consequences.

What an incredible contrast to the week before when we'd picnicked in the hills above the Alhambra. Now we were desperately trying to stay warm. Cancel that. "Stay warm" implies that we'd been warm and were trying to stay that way. What we were doing was trying to *get* warm, and doing so in a house without central heat, and with uncovered tile floors and thin wooden shutters wasn't easy.

Our house came equipped with two electric oil-filled radiators on wheels and a *brazero*. A *brazero*, Guillermo informed us when we'd discovered it during our initial tour of the house, is very Spanish. The traditional *brazero* looks something like a shallow round Weber grill. Filled with hot coals, this metal disk is placed under the dining table. According to Guillermo, Spanish families spent winter evenings sitting around the table in the salon, a heavy tablecloth pulled out over their laps to keep the heat under, usually watching television. Our *brazero*, about sixteen inches wide and four inches thin, sat in a two-foot-wide wooden frame and was, like most modern *brazeros*, electric.

We tried it. Although we were reasonably warm, at least from the waist down, sitting at the table for the evening was uncomfortable. And it didn't heat the room. We found reading, watching videos, or listening to music more comfortable stretched out on the couch under a blanket.

Under normal winter conditions, when lows were in the thirties and the highs in the fifties, the house was cool but not uncomfortable. All three balconies faced south, so the sun streamed in through the windows all day, warming the house so we didn't need the radiators except in the morning and evening. The hallway, the back bedroom, and bathroom got no sun and remained pretty nippy.

During the freeze, however, these meager heat sources did not work. One morning I found ice inside the window in the salon. It took both radiators and an additional small heater we'd bought to warm the room. We adopted the Spanish manner of winter living: we retreated to the salon. The kitchen, at least when cooking, was comfortable enough. In the unheated areas of the house we could see our breath.

Fortunately, there was plenty of very hot water for showers. Unfortunately, eventually you had to get out. Stepping out of the shower was what I imagine diving into San Francisco Bay on New Year's Day was like. The shock was immediate. It wasn't necessary to rub the towel against my body to dry off; all I had to do was hold the towel still as my body shook against it. The same technique worked well when brushing my teeth. But being dry brought little relief, as I then stood naked in a room where the temperature was perhaps forty. My clothes felt as if they'd been stored in the fridge. And as for the toilet seat, although I never actually stuck, my efforts not to scream when I sat did not always succeed.

The back bedroom where we slept was the coldest room in the house. We couldn't take a radiator back because we needed it in the salon. Getting out of bed in the morning became a test of character. Going to bed, however, was not quite so painful, at least for the person getting into bed last. The trick was to avoid being first. The waiting game began each night a little before eleven.

"You look sleepy. Why don't you go on back?" I'd say. "I'll be along as soon as I finish reading this article." I'd just begun a sixteen-page *New Yorker* profile of the inventor of the cocktail shaker.

"Just as soon as I finish my wine," Kay would reply, taking a tiny, tiny, tiny mouse sip.

We watched each other from the corner of our eyes. Kay always gave up first and with a sigh, threw off the blanket and headed back. I heard her run down the hall, and then the sound of whimpering as she climbed into bed. I waited long enough for her to warm the bed before heading back. Now was time for my sacrifice. Because I didn't want to wake her in the morning fumbling around in the dark putting on my clothes, I undressed in the front bedroom, then raced down the dark hall and slipped under the covers. This I considered an act of true love.

In the morning the process was reversed. I got up first, streaked on tiptoes back up the hall to my clothes, and turned on the heaters. It took Kay a while to get up, as she pulled layer after layer of clothing, which she'd placed by the bed, under the covers to warm them before dressing. When finally dressed, she rolled from the bed and waddled to the kitchen to make tea.

The freeze lasted less than a week, but the weather remained colder than normal. We survived by reminding each other that those sun-drenched Andalucían days would soon return.

Our Last Visit to the Police Station

On February 4, exactly forty-five days after being fingerprinted, we went to the police station hoping that our permits would be ready. When we reached the window, Kay remembered to tell the clerk that we are getting *segundo Permiso de Residencia*, and the clerk went straight to the right box. He returned and requested our *primero permisos*, which, fortunately, Kay had with her. We exchanged old for new and left the station. It was a bit unsettling to have things go so smoothly.

How strange. No more trips to the police station for two years. The realization that there was nothing left to be done slowly sank in. Renewing our resident permits seemed particularly significant. Getting our first had merely marked the beginning of our life in Granada. Now we could say: We'd done it. We'd made a life here in Granada, Spain. The realization seemed momentous and matter of fact at the same time. We weren't sure what to do with ourselves. It was far too early for champagne, too early for lunch, too early, even, for *tapas*. We stood outside the police station for a moment and thought about it. Although the freeze was over, the day was cool. We decided to walk down to the river and simply savor the moment. The celebration could wait until later. Perhaps we'd invite someone over.

As we walked we laughed at the memory of how hard getting our first permits had been compared to our second, which led to comparing other aspects of our life sixteen months ago to the life we were living now.

For starters, during our first months on Calle Elvira, we knew no one except Enrique, our upstairs neighbor. Our little community now included Steve and Anne; Celeste; Alex, Manuel, and Pablo; and Caroline, Tammo, and the boys—all of whom we'd had over for dinner.

We remembered wondering if our friends back in the States would come to see us. They had. We'd had visitors all through the spring and the calendar for the coming summer was almost filled.

I'd been concerned, in those early weeks, if being together so much would strain the relationship. I was accustomed to having the house to myself for days at a time. If anything, we'd grown closer. We'd enjoyed being together day after day more than either of us had expected.

There'd never been a letdown when visitors departed, as we'd looked forward to there being just the two of us again.

We decided to detour through Puerta Real before heading down the promenade to the river. We walked past the vendors roasting chestnuts on their charcoal-filled drums, past the accordion player and the sidewalk tarp shops selling sweaters and wool caps. As we walked we compared our thoughts on our life in Granada.

"What surprised you most?" I asked her. "Good and bad."

She thought for a moment. "I love stepping out the door and being right in the middle of it," Kay said. "I love it that almost everything we need is right in the neighborhood, usually just a few steps from our front door."

She also loved our routine. Two or three times as week she walked down to Plaza Larga to buy the *International Herald Tribune*. She usually arrived just as the newsstand was opening. When the owner saw her, he dug down into the pile, pulled out the paper, and handed it to her with a smiling *"Buenos."*

Every Friday we walked down the street to the ATM machine to withdraw our weekly allowance. Once a month we went inside the same bank and deposited our rent directly into our landlady's account. Every other month we paid the telephone bill in the same bank. Twice a week we rented a movie at the video rental across from the bank.

I loved the fact that she loved her mornings, while I was at my desk writing the blogs that became this book.

For me, the terrace had been both an unexpected treat. For twenty-five years we'd had a yard, porches, a covered patio, and a garden. Now we had a terrace—which neither of us had thought about, much less planned on—a space that offered the pleasures of a yard, sitting in the sun, potting and watering plants, grilling dinner, without having to cut the grass or rake the leaves.

Finding three bookstores that sold used English-language books had been another surprise. Because the choice of books was limited, we found ourselves reading authors we might not have otherwise read, like Joanna Trollop and Maeve Binchy; both seemed to be great favorites of English travelers. There were also plenty of English classics available, especially, for some reason, George Eliot. I don't think I ever went into any of the bookstores, even the one in Nerja, the English enclave on the coast, without seeing a copy of *Mill on the Floss*. Kay said that she'd never enjoyed reading more.

When we reached the river it was still a bit early to stop; the cafés were just getting set up, so we decided to walk along the *paseo*, the park-like strip of trees, pathways, and gardens that runs alongside the Rio Genil. In the distance we could see the snow-covered Sierra Nevada.

There had also been a few unpleasant surprises, like the declining value of the dollar. Our cost of living had increased by more than $200 a month since our arrival sixteen months before, but we were still on budget, still living the quality of life we wanted. We went to the symphony, the opera, the jazz festival, and even the bullfights. We ate lunch out often, though dinners at fancy restaurants were few. Spain, we agreed, had clearly been a wise choice. We could only hope that the dollar would regain its strength.

I confessed to being disappointed in the minimal progress I'd made learning Spanish, though Kay felt satisfied in her ability to communicate. We hadn't worked at it as much as we should have; we were busy enjoying the city, traveling, and hosting visitors. We'd had fewer opportunities to use it conversationally than we thought we would, so once we were able to have our needs met, we got a little lazy. But each month found us a little further along.

"This Christmas turned out well," Kay said. "Don't you think?"

I agreed. Our second Christmas here in Granada had been more enjoyable than either of us had anticipated. We'd learned a lesson: excessive expectations often lead to disappointment. Relax and let it happen.

As we walked, Kay teased me about my dreams of the perfect European apartment. I'd wanted a massive wood door with a big knob in the center, claw-foot bathtub, parquet floors, and at least one balcony with a view of an outdoor café or a plaza. And I'd wanted to hear church bells. I remind her that our tub, although not a claw-foot, was certainly large enough. And as for the parquet floors, I felt that having *three* balconies and beautiful etched-glass doors more than made up for it.

But best of all, we agreed, at least as important as the house, was the neighborhood. Living in the Albaicín was something that neither of us could have imagined. What had we imagined? I don't remember. But I don't think we'd envisioned ourselves being greeted with a smiling

"*Hola!*" as we walked through the neighborhood, "*Holas*" from Javier, downstairs at the café, from Luis at the market, from Manuel and Encarni at the florist, Juan at the video rental, Isa, who ran the hair salon downstairs, and the waiters, especially the one at Café Ladrillo, who always waved and shouted, "*¿Que tal?*" as we passed by.

After walking to the end of the *paseo*, we turned back toward one of our favorite cafés, one that served fabulous *tapas*. The tables were out and we sat and ordered two beers. As we waited for the plate of ham and pork on sliced bread, fried potatoes, and grilled peppers and tomatoes that we knew were coming, I complimented Kay on her hair. She'd had it cut the day before by Isa and she looked terrific.

"Did I tell you?" Kay asked me. "After she finished, I looked in the mirror and proclaimed myself *una Granadina*. But Isa shook her head no and said, '*Una Albaicínera.*'"

I guess that makes me *un Albaicínero. Señora Albaicínera y Señor Albaicínero*, at home, high in the Albaicín, in the heart of Granada, in the south of Spain.

The *tapas* and beers arrived. We sat in the warm February sun and continued to reminisce. We examined our new two-year resident permits again. Our greatest challenges were now behind us. Life, we felt sure, could only get better.

Epilogue

What we didn't know that February day, sitting there in the café by the river reminiscing about our sometimes frustrating, always exciting first sixteen months, was that we were halfway through our Granada adventure. We'd had a stay of three years or so in mind; we lived in Granada for thirty-two months.

There were times when life was so good that we couldn't imagine leaving, and we entertained the idea of staying forever, or at least until some event or circumstances dictated our return. We considered keeping our flat and living six months in California and six months in Granada. I ran the financial numbers, and it was doable. But, as they say, the devil is in the details, and there were a good many details. It is exceedingly difficult to live in California—San Francisco being the only exception—without an automobile. It didn't seem practical to maintain and insure an automobile for six months a year. We did not want to spend our summers in Granada, but if we lived in Granada from fall till spring, we'd miss both Thanksgiving and Christmas with our family. We wondered about future travels, of seeing the rest of the world. Would we want to spend three weeks in Thailand or Turkey if we were going to be "at home," whether Granada or California, for only six months?

An enormous issue, as important as any other, was health care. Our health care provider in California did not know we were living in Spain, as we showed up every year for our checkups. We couldn't get away with this forever. We'd been very, very fortunate in that neither of us had needed medical care or ongoing prescriptions. Our good fortune wouldn't last forever. Our friend Alex had bought into the Spanish health care system. Would it be possible for us to buy in for six months a year?

As we contemplated our decision, two things became increasingly clear. First, the call of family was strong; not only did we miss them, but our being part of their lives, especially our grandson Gray's, would be difficult on a part-time basis. Second, the complications of splitting the year, though not insurmountable, would definitely violate our Less-Stress guidelines. By the time we celebrated our second year in Granada, we'd made our decision. We spent our last eight months in Granada knowing that we would be returning to California when our lease ended.

That decision intensified the experience. As the months went by and the number of future trips down the hill diminished, each walk down became more precious. Every experience—attending a concert, walking by the river, buying vegetables in Plaza Larga—was imbued with a sweet poignancy, and I found myself acutely aware of details, as if committing every day to memory. Even today I can close my eyes and picture every step of our seven walking routes down the hill, every plaza and every café, the view of San Miguel Alto from our terrace, the dazzling panorama of the Alhambra from Mirador San Nicolás. I can almost taste the *boquerones*, the fried anchovies that I loved so much.

Knowing that we were leaving refocused our attention on the trips we'd planned to take while in Spain and how little time we had to take them. Over the course of our last year, we made a third visit to our family in the United States and took two extended train excursions, one to northwestern Spain and another to Seville, Gibraltar, and the hill towns of southeastern Andalucía. In April of our last spring, we spent two weeks in Greece.

Our second eleven-month lease ended May 31, which was perfect in that we wouldn't have to endure another Andalucían summer. Preparations for our leaving began in the early spring. We sold a few things to our friends: television, desk, bookcase and books; the rest we gave away. Steve and Lucy, who we'd met during the presidential debates, were returning to California at the same time, and they invited us to piggyback our two large boxes with their shipment.

Kay and I returned to California near the end of May 2006. We left with a week left on our lease because Flannery was receiving her master's degree and was being hooded, a special ceremony we didn't want to miss. While we were in Spain, Baxter and his family had moved to Petaluma, in Sonoma County, thirty-five miles north of San Francisco. We'd stayed with them there during our last two visits and fell in love with this historic river town. Renée found us a bungalow only minutes from their house, and on June 1, we became residents of Petaluma, California.

Every once in a while Kay and I look at each other and shake our heads. We know what the other is thinking: We did it. We dreamed it. We made it happen. We lived in Granada for more than two and a half years. Sometimes it seems like yesterday, at other times, long, long ago.

Do I miss Granada? Yes, I do. I miss its "foreignness." I miss the slower pace and that so much of life is lived outdoors. I miss living in a culture that places such high value on enjoying life.

But as much as I miss Granada itself, I miss how I felt while living there. Every time I walked out the front door, I entered a world that required my complete attention. I couldn't switch on automatic pilot; I didn't have an autopilot for Granada. Every misadventure, every mission accomplished, every mundane chore demanded a certain level of awareness. I felt wholly alive and in the moment.

We've not regretted, not once, returning to California. For us, the world of family and friends (plus living life in our native tongue) turned out to be stronger than the world of challenge and wonder. Although Granada did not become our permanent home, our adventure there had exceeded our every expectation and dream. Granada would forever be in our hearts and our memories, a major chapter in our lives.

Acknowledgments

I found the following books to be both informative and enjoyable:

The Story of Spain by Mark Williams
Granada, City of My Dreams by Lorenzo Bohme
The New Spaniards by John Hooper
The Spanish Temper, Travels in Spain by V.S. Pritchett

I am grateful to Karen Lowe, Gary Lowe, and Sudie Sides for reading my book and for their most helpful suggestions.